IDEAS is a new Blackwell series whicn makes available in paperback some of the most adventurous writing in the social and humane sciences in recent years, extending the frontiers of research, crossing disciplinary borders and setting new intellectual standards in international scholarship. Published and forthcoming titles include:

John Baechler, John A. Hall and Michael Mann, *Europe and the Rise of Capitalism*

Colin Campbell, *The Romantic Ethic and the Spirit of Modern Consumerism*

William Connolly, *Political Theory and Modernity*

John A. Hall (ed.), *States in History*

Alan Macfarlane, *The Culture of Capitalism*

Derek Sayer, *The Violence of Abstraction*

Michael Peter Smith and Joe R. Feagin, *The Capitalist City*

To the memory of
Florence Violet Stirling Rhodes James
1896–1986

The Culture of Capitalism

ALAN MACFARLANE

Basil Blackwell

First published 1987
Reprinted and first published in paperback 1989

Basil Blackwell Ltd
108 Cowley Road, Oxford, OX4 1JF, UK

Basil Blackwell Inc.
3 Cambridge Centre
Cambridge, MA 02142, USA

British Library Cataloguing in Publication Data

A CIP catalogue record for this book is available from the British Library.

Library of Congress Cataloging in Publication Data

Macfarlane, Alan
    The culture of capitalism

    Bibliography: p.
    Includes index.
    1. England—Social conditions.   2. Capitalism—
England.   3. Peasantry—England.   4. National
characteristics, English.   5. England—Civilization.
I. Title.
HN398.E5M28   1987   306′.0942   87–8028
ISBN 0–631–13626–6
      0–631–165576 (pbk)

Typeset in 11 on 13 pt Ehrhardt
by Opus, Oxford

Contents

Preface

I T IS now almost exactly nine years from the day when I sat down to
write a short article on peasants in sixteenth- and seventeenth-
century England. Instead of being able quickly to pass on to the work
I intended to write during the sabbatical leave, on kinship and
marriage, the essay exploded in my mind to alter my whole concept of
the English past. I became possessed by a theme and suffered a
mental change which seemed to overturn much of what I had until
then accepted as true. The outcome was *The Origins of English
Individualism*, written in 1977, and published in 1978. I described the
main aim of the book to be to answer the four following questions.
'Why did the industrial revolution occur first in England? When did
England start to be different from other parts of Europe? In what,
principally, did that difference consist? How far is the history of the
English transformation a useful analogy for contemporary Third
World societies?'[1] My answers to these questions were not as I
expected. During my education as a historian at Oxford, both as an
undergraduate and during my D.Phil. on witchcraft, I had gradually
absorbed, without really being aware of it, a 'revolutionary' view of
English history. This had been reinforced by my subsequent reading
of the works of sociologists and anthropologists during my years as a
Master's and Doctoral student in anthropology at London University.

Over these years, between 1960 and 1975, I had accepted a picture
of the past which could roughly be summarized as follows. Up to
about 1450 England was a 'traditional', 'peasant', 'feudal' society.
Then, through a series of revolutionary and connected changes which

[1] Macfarlane, *Individualism*, 8.

altered simultaneously the legal, political, religious, cultural, economic, demographic and social system roughly during the sixteenth to
eighteenth centuries, England became the antithesis of all these
things. After about 1800 it was fully established as 'modern',
'individualist', 'capitalist'. The 'watershed', to use Tawney's metaphor, was the sixteenth century. From then the rivers of change
flowed in a different direction. This major transformation started and
was completed several centuries earlier than in most of the rest of
Europe and this provided the basis for a new industrial and urban
civilization. To change the metaphor, England was several rungs
ahead of its competitors, with the exception of Holland, and hence
was the first to reach the 'modern world'. Having started from
roughly the same position, it somehow overtook its competitors and
won the race. Now it may have been naive of me to have come to
believe this on the basis of the work of historians and sociologists
whom I read and admired, people like R. H. Tawney, Christopher
Hill, R. H. Hilton, G. C. Homans, Lawrence Stone, Max Weber and
others, but I cannot deny that I certainly did absorb such a message.

It is difficult to say what undermined this view, apparently
supported by the latest research and based on the majestic shoulders
of Marx and Weber. Yet there can be no doubt that during those
months of 1977 the whole structure fell away. The central theme of
Individualism was that there was much more continuity between the
medieval and early modern period than I had come to believe and that
England's peculiarities were not a product of revolutionary changes
between the sixteenth and eighteenth centuries. Historians of science
and philosophy would look for both very general and specific reasons
for such a dramatic shift in interpretation. There were probably very
broad general changes as a background; the later 1970s were a time
for questioning revolutionary theories, for revisionism, for a stress on
continuity, which some might link to economic recession and a
looming conservative reaction. There may have been national
influences, a reaction against growing pressures to make the English
feel a part of Europe. This was suggested in a letter to me by Dr
Colin Matthew, a school friend, who saw the book as 'quite clearly the
product of (a) a general movement of search for identity in the
post-imperial period; (b) anti-EEC-ism as well as the result of trends
within the profession'. Put rather more brusquely by Lawrence Stone
in Princeton, the book is saying something 'comforting to the natives

(i.e. English) in their time of troubles: namely that the English have *always* been different from everybody else'.[2] It would be foolish to deny these invisible pressures which work on a historian.

The pressures of which I was more fully aware were the personal intellectual difficulties of reconciling a theory of revolutionary change with the detailed findings which were emerging from my research. These growing anomalies between prediction and data, which Kuhn has pointed out are the usual way in which paradigm shifts are manifested,[3] are partially explored in the Introduction to *Individualism*.[4] I was aware that a number of the central theories concerning the family, marriage, demographic structure, geographical mobility and social stratification were being challenged by Peter Laslett and his associates, who now stressed continuity rather than revolution.[5] What I have subsequently realized is that similar anomalies were being felt by a number of younger political historians; thus Conrad Russell, Anthony Fletcher and John Morrill, among others, were questioning the whole thesis of the political revolution of the seventeenth century.[6]

In my own case, the real problem was that the overall theory of a massive and revolutionary change, the birth of a new social world, did not seem to fit the very detailed evidence from the archives. Nor did the revolutionary view seem to reflect the views of those living in the period of supposed revolution, who did not seem to be aware that such a dramatic break was occurring. A general theory that does not help one to make sense of the scraps of evidence is not worth supporting. Yet it is not always easy to find an alternative.

Here, however, I was fortunate. I found that a scheme of continuous change and elaboration had already been developed and satisfactorily used in the fields of constitutional history, legal history, and, to a certain extent, economic history, by historians working in the later nineteenth and early twentieth centuries. The discovery of this lost framework was accidental. The great works of the later Victorian historians like Stubbs, Maitland, Green, Freeman, Thorold Rogers, Bury and others were no longer on recommended reading

[2] Lawrence Stone in *New York Review of Books*, 19 April 1979.
[3] Kuhn, *Structure*.
[4] Macfarlane, *Individualism*, 2–5.   [5] Especially Laslett, *Lost World*.
[6] For instance, Russell, *Parliaments;* Fletcher, *Civil War;* Morrill, *Britain*, and a full summary of their views in Clark, *Revolution*.

lists when I read history, nor were they usually on the open shelves of libraries or in first-hand bookshops. We may not destroy books intentionally in some Orwellian manner as intellectual views change, yet fashions change and we bury past interpretations very rapidly through neglect. Because I was, without really knowing it, searching for some alternative theory at the same time as spending some of my time on my chief hobby, searching the top shelves of second-hand bookshops, I picked up these dusty classics with amazement and pleasure. In their pages I found, in elegant prose, the framework which helped me to understand the original records of the period with which I was dealing. Above all, they made me realize that what I had unthinkingly assumed to be the only interpretation of English history, was in fact only a relatively very recent development. I was too young to be able to know when the change had occurred from my own experience, but what was only a hunch when I wrote *Individualism* was confirmed in a curious way.

After the book was published I received many interesting and enthusiastic letters. One came from the master who had taught me history during my last two years before going to university. He explained a puzzle he had found when he read my book.

To put it crudely, I ask myself why it was necessary to write the book at all! . . . I was brought up in the early 40s at school by a man who was a brilliant teacher with a deep sense of English and European history, but who was not a historian. Still, even from him I got a deep sense of the individuality of English history stemming from pre-Reformation times. In the late 40s I studied at Queen's [Oxford] under John Prestwich, from whose tutorials and recommended reading lists I came away with certain very clear notions: there never was a 'peasantry' in England; the medieval economy had plenty of wage-paid labour; it was not a subsistence economy; pre-industrial capitalism was strongly evidenced in medieval England; primogeniture and alienability of land were of prime importance in pin-pointing English uniqueness. Now you mention many other facets and characteristics of a classical 'peasant' society which I had no cognizance of, but my list above is a fairly formidable statement of areas where I might be tempted to say: 'why is he putting up these Aunt Sallies when we already know them to be fictions?'

This provides a very good summary of the argument of my book. It appeared that all that I had rediscovered was the conventional wisdom of the 1950s. My former teacher's later career took him further away from recent scholarship and he had not realized that the historical world view had changed and that we now had a newly established view of the past. He continues by trying to explain what seemed to have happened. He speculates that

It seems to me that something has gone awry between 1950 and 1970 and I haven't been aware of it until I look at the dates of publication of most of the works whose views you (rightly) dispute. It seems that in the 50s and 60s the field has been captured (a) by Marxists and (b) by 'peasant-model-minded' scholars who, as you point out, have so often ignored the conclusions of their own findings and forced them into a preconceived pattern.

Thus he concedes that I did need to write the book, not for him, but for present-day students.

This brief history may help to explain two things about the book and the reaction to it. The work itself has something of the breathless vehemence and possible overstatement of a conversion experience about it. This added to its impact, both positive and negative. While I received many enthusiastic letters and reviews from people who had been reassured or liberated from what they considered an unsatisfactory but hitherto unassailable framework, a certain number of reviewers reacted in a very negative way. Most of those who reacted angrily were medievalists. The reaction of certain reviewers was particularly violent because they found themselves caught in the central ambivalence which the letter I have quoted exposed. This was nicely summarized by Professor Elton in a review; the thesis of the non-existence of peasants 'has already caused much anger and anguish, especially among medievalists who are busy maintaining the difficult position that on the one hand the thesis only spells out what they have always said while on the other it is not true'.[7] One can see the difficulty. It is indeed correct that, in essence, my views in *Individualism* are not fundamentally new. They share the vision of the past of men like Maitland and Stubbs. There is therefore a good deal of latent sympathy among many reviewers. On the other hand I appeared to be quoting a number of authorities who took a view diametrically opposed to that of the continuity school. As Stone interpreted the book, it challenges 'the whole corpus of conventional wisdom about the

[7] In the *Times Literary Supplement*, 23 Nov. 1979, 27.

evolution of the modern world', it 'sets out to show that not just one but a whole pride of emperors have no clothes'. As he lists them, these include Marx, Weber, Tocqueville, Durkheim, Tonnies, and 'almost every scholar who has ever attempted a general interpretation of the English transition from traditionalism to modernity. Tawney, Postan, Hilton, Hill, Homans, C. B. Macpherson, C. H. Wilson, this reviewer . . .'[8] It is not really surprising that there should be a desire to cut such an arrogant enterprise down to size. No one likes to have even partial nakedness exposed or to be accused of having started to write myth rather than history.

The fact that my views may indicate some deep shifts in historical understanding, what some might call, after Kuhn, a paradigm shift, is indicated by the totally divergent reactions of reviewers. These varied from the highly impressed, to the scandalized. A few examples of each will suffice here.[9] Alan Ryan, Reader in Politics at Oxford, declared it to be 'an altogether admirable piece of work. It is that most attractive of intellectual achievements, the short book that makes a lot of difference to a large subject'. Ernest Gellner, then Professor of Philosophy at London, described it as 'an outstanding book in virtue of the daring and importance of the ideas it puts forward, and the range and thoroughness of the scholarship with which they are sustained'. Peter Laslett, Reader in Politics and the History of Social Structure at Cambridge thought it 'a very important book . . . If he does win the controversy which this book seems likely to arouse, our view of social history as a whole, but especially of English social history, will have to change, fundamentally'. Equally distinguished were those who dismissed it; for instance David Herlihy, Professor of History at Harvard, thought it 'a silly book, founded on faulty method and propounding a preposterous thesis'. Lawrence Stone, Dodge Professor of History at Princeton, found that it put forward 'an implausible hypothesis based on a far-fetched connection with one still unproven fact of limited general significance'. If I was only saying what was obvious in the 1950s, why the fierce reaction? And, more importantly, who won the controversy which the book has opened up?

The book itself was only 206 pages long. The printed reviews of it which I have seen come to more than 160 printed pages. The

---

[8] Stone, ibid.

[9] Full references to the reviews from which these quotations are taken are given at the end of the Bibliography, pp. 240–1.

audacity of the challenge as well as the vehemence of the reply provide an interesting cross-section of historical opinions and methods. They raise theoretical, methodological and ethical questions about the historian's craft which do seem worth pursuing, irrespective of whether this particular book is generally 'right' or 'wrong' in its conclusions. It is proper that there should be strong arguments in a living discipline like history and right that people should defend their life's work. It is revealing to see the ways in which people do support a paradigm. While Kuhn provides some outline of the surface reasons for paradigm shift and indicates that there are associated fierce controversies, he does not go into details about the ways in which people try to defend their world view against intellectual threats. This particular case provides for me a lesson in how people try to counter arguments which seem to undermine an orthodoxy. I have therefore decided to set out the more thoughtful counter-arguments to *Individualism* and to try to answer them in the Postscript to this book.

In the present selection of essays written over the last ten years I have tried to show how my thoughts have developed since starting *Individualism*. The usefulness of a thesis lies not so much in whether it is in abstract right or wrong, as in whether it leads to original and convincing insights into the past. Personally, I have found the revised framework which I began to work out in *Individualism* allows me a more flexible approach and enables me to understand some of the paradoxes and puzzles which still face historians. I have continued to try to answer questions about the nature and origins of the first fully industrial and capitalist society and the present essays indicate a few of the results of this endeavour.

For those who missed *Individualism*, or wish to be reminded of how the thesis began to be developed, the first essay, 'Peasants', is a plain statement of the central thesis of that book, namely that there was not a peasant society, in the strict sense, in seventeenth-century England and perhaps long before. The essay was written in July 1977 and thus started the whole search for a new framework for analysis. It is also included because it alone deals with the social and economic features of English society. In January 1978, I wrote and delivered the second essay, 'Population', as the Malinowski Memorial Lecture at the London School of Economics. It explores the *Individualism* thesis in relation to demography. Some of the political and legal dimensions of the argument were set out in *The Justice and the Mare's Ale: Law and*

Disorder in Seventeenth-century England, written in collaboration with
Sarah Harrison and published in 1981. The conclusions from that
work are included in the third essay, 'Violence'.

During the year 1982 I revised an account of how the
administrative and legal system in England worked from the
thirteenth to nineteenth centuries to produce the records which I
had studied for the history of English villages. This was published in
1983 as *A Guide to English Historical Records.* What the book showed
was the unbroken continuity of the great legal courts and institutions
of the land which had so impressed earlier constitutional and legal
historians. The results of this work form an implicit background to a
number of the essays in this volume.

Several critics of *Individualism* felt that I should explore the thesis
in relation to mentality, morality and sentiment. I had indeed
promised to do this in the postscript to *Individualism,* and my
anthropological training made me interested in the cultural dimensions of the social, economic, demographic and legal features which
had preoccupied my work between 1977 and 1982. In 1983 I wrote
a review of Keith Thomas's *Man and the Natural World* and this is
the basis of the fourth chapter here, 'Nature'. Later in 1983 I was
asked to write on the theme of 'Evil' for an anthropological
collection of essays; the resulting piece is included here as the fifth
chapter. In 1984 I decided to make one last effort to pull together
some of my disparate thoughts on marriage, kinship, sex, the family
and other matters which I had been working on since the late 1960s.
The result was *Marriage and Love in England: Modes of Reproduction
1300–1840.* Some of the findings of that book have been included in
a new essay, 'Love', which also draws on other thoughts over the
years and a little from an essay entitled 'Death and the Demographic Transition'.[10] We thus have social, economic, political, legal,
moral, mental, and sentimental approaches represented here, if only
in a light and tentative way. Each essay stands on its own, but since
they are also arranged in date order, and move from the 'firmest'
(economics) to the 'flimsiest' of topics (love), they also constitute a
whole which I hope is more than a sum of its parts. Although one's
caveats are not always heeded, I would like to stress again that I
realize that there are many other topics I have not covered, that

[10] In Humphreys and King, *Mortality.*

there are many books and authorities which I am aware of but have not cited, and that inevitably I will have oversimplified some complex matters.

In this collection I did not wish merely to present examples of the approach I have adopted since *Individualism*. I thought it would be of interest to include a second, shorter, part on the methods and assumptions of my approach, and on some of the deeper causes of the peculiarities I have tried to explore in the first part of the book. The essay 'Revolutions' was written in the autumn of 1984. Its rather heavy emphasis on marriage reflects the fact that I was asked to write about the demographic and familial aspects of revolutions for a collection of essays. A year later, in autumn 1985, I wrote the essay 'Capitalism'. This is a digest of four lectures which I had given in 1983 and 1984 to anthropology undergraduates at Cambridge. The final essay, 'Individualism', a reflection on the whole enterprise and particularly a reaction to the critics of *Individualism*, was written for this collection in July 1986.

I have decided to leave several of the published essays as they were written, except for some footnotes to indicate any serious criticisms that have been made and minor corrections of grammar etc. They retain more of their original flavour if left untampered with, even if I would write parts of them differently now. The exceptions to this rule are the following. I have cut the essay 'Violence' out of a whole book; it is therefore truncated and I have had to add in a few connecting passages, and take a little from the first chapter of the book to put with the section included. The essay 'Nature', originally rather short and entirely devoted to reviewing one book, has been broadened in scope and lengthened. I have added a section on witchcraft to the article 'Evil'. The essay 'Revolutions' has some slight rephrasing in the conclusions.

The title needs a little explanation. It was suggested to me by my publisher, John Davey, and I like its ambiguity. 'Capitalism' is a word with a very wide range of connotations. In order to explain very simply what I take it to mean, I have tried to tie it down in an appendix. 'Culture' also has an intriguing double meaning; I take it in both senses. On the one hand it has an anthropological meaning. One famous definition of this will suffice. Boas wrote that 'Culture may be defined as the totality of the mental and physical reactions and activities that characterize the behaviour of the individuals composing a social group collectively and individually in relation to their natural environment, to other groups, to members of the group itself and of each individual to himself. It also includes the products of these activities and their role in the life of the groups'.[11] In this sense this volume analyses the cultural system of capitalism, its mentality, morality and emotional structure.

The second meaning of 'culture' is the almost exclusive sense given to the word in the *Oxford English Dictionary*. Here it means to grow, cultivate, make to flourish and develop, as in a phrase such as 'the culture of mushrooms'. The book is about this as well, for I am particularly interested in the way in which capitalism was 'cultivated', that is, sheltered, grown, nourished and developed on this island over long centuries. It flourished and sprouted and many of its seeds were to spread all over the world so that it is now part of the air we breathe. So wide has been its influence that formal distinctions between 'capitalist' and 'socialist' countries have broken down. Much of the 'culture of capitalism' is now to be found in Moscow, Havana or Beijing, as well as in Los Angeles, Paris or London. Yet at its heart this culture still carries those paradoxes and contradictions which I have tried to analyse in relation to attitudes to nature, evil, love and other basic features. The phenomenon is worth our understanding, prisoners as we are in this world culture, yet partly liberated by knowing something of the roots and growth of the tree high up in whose branches we nervously rest.

A.M.

---

[11] Boas, *Primitive Man*, 159.

Acknowledgements

THE RESEARCH on the parishes used as a background for chapter 1 was funded by the Economic and Social Research Council and King's College, Cambridge, to whom I am most grateful. Much of the work was carried out by Sarah Harrison. I would also like to thank Cherry Bryant, Charles Jardine, Jessica King, Tim King and Iris Macfarlane for their help with this. The chapter is reproduced from David Green et al. (eds), *Social Organisation and Settlement*, British Archaeological Reports, International Series (Supplementary), 47(ii), 1978.

Chapter 2, 'Population', was first published in the *Journal of Development Studies*, vol. 14, no. 4 (July 1978), and in a special volume of that journal entitled *Population and Development* edited by Geoffrey Hawthorn (1978). I am grateful to Frank Cass & Co. Ltd for permission to use this and to Geoffrey Hawthorn for his early comments on drafts of this article, which was originally delivered as the Malinowski Lecture at the London School of Economics in 1978.

Chapter 3, 'Violence', is abstracted from *The Justice and the Mare's Ale* (Blackwell, 1981). I am grateful to my collaborative author, Sarah Harrison, for permission to use this material.

Chapter 4, 'Nature', appeared originally in a shorter form as a review of Keith Thomas, *Man and the Natural World* in the *London Review of Books*, vol. 5, no. 9 (May 1983). I am grateful to the *London Review of Books* for permission to use this material.

Chapter 5, 'Evil', appeared in an earlier version in David Parkin (ed.), *The Anthropology of Evil* (Blackwell, 1985). I am grateful to David Parkin and other contributors to the volume, particularly Lionel Caplan, for their comments on an early draft.

Chapter 6, 'Love', will be appearing shortly in *Cambridge Anthropology*. The editors have kindly given me permission to use that article here.

Chapter 7, 'Revolution', first appeared in Roy Porter and Mikulas Teich (eds), *Revolution in History* (1986). I am grateful to Cambridge University Press for permission to use this and to the editors for their helpful comments on the article. Geoffrey Elton also kindly read the article and made a number of helpful suggestions for improvement.

Chapter 8, 'Capitalism' appears as 'The Cradle of Capitalism: the Case of England' in Jean Baechler, John A. Hall and Michael Mann (eds), *Europe and the Rise of Capitalism* (Blackwell, 1987). I am grateful to John Hall for his suggestions for improvements in the draft of this article.

As well as specific help and permissions as listed above, and permission from Basil Blackwell to use the material in chapters 3, 5 and 8, there are more general thanks to be given. John Davey of Basil Blackwell was, as usual, a constant support, and suggested the title. He also put me in touch with an anonymous reader who gave much good and helpful advice. I thank her or him very much. Robert Rowland, Julian Jacobs and Sarah Harrison all read the whole book and made many wise and useful suggestions for ways in which it could be improved. I am very grateful to them all.

NOTE ON REFERENCES

The footnotes give an abbreviated title and page number. The usual form is author, short title, page number. The full title of the work referred to is given in the bibliography at the end of the book.

1
Peasants

The Peasantry in England before the Industrial Revolution – a Mythical Model?

I T IS generally agreed by historians and sociologists alike that England was a 'peasant' nation between the eleventh and eighteenth centuries. In this respect it is broadly comparable to other 'peasant' civilizations both in the past and in the present. Thus geographers, anthropologists, archaeologists or historians examining England during any part of this period will bring to their analysis implicit or explicit analogies to other 'peasant' societies, whether in the Mediterranean, China, India, Russia or Latin America. Furthermore, those interested in contemporary change in the Third World will look to England as perhaps the best documented case study of a progression from a 'peasant' to an industrial society.[1] It will be argued here that this is a powerful, yet incorrect and hence mythical, charter of social development, which distorts the analysis undertaken in the disciplines listed above.

Among historians of both the medieval and early modern period there is a consensus of opinion that we are dealing with a 'peasant' society. One or two books or articles may be cited as examples of the view, but since it is invidious to mention names, it should be said that almost every historical work on the period assumes the presence of peasantry. Furthermore, it is a view which I myself have accepted for a number of years. For the medieval period, we may note that the major works by Postan do not question the 'peasantness' of English

[1] Dalton, 'Peasantries', 385.

society. Thus in *The Medieval Economy and Society*, as both index and
text show, 'peasant' is used interchangeably with other terms for
ordinary villagers and smallholders. Or again, a recent article by
Britton nowhere questions Homans's implicit assumption that a
medieval peasantry existed.[2] The furthest medievalists go is to ask
whether any lessons can be learnt from 'Medieval Peasants'.[3] We
might have expected historians to have become uneasy about the
concept by the time we reach the seventeenth century, for there had
been a very considerable increase in international trade, markets, the
use of money, geographical mobility and literacy. Yet those who are
most knowledgeable about rural dwellers continue to believe that they
are dealing with 'peasantry'. They title their books *The Midland
Peasant* (Hoskins, 1957) or *English Peasant Farming* (Thirsk, 1957).
They continue to assume, along with Tawney, that countrymen were
'peasants'.[4] Few would disagree with Thirsk's generalization that
'English society until the mid-eighteenth century was a predominantly rural and a peasant society'.[5]

   If the experts are agreed, it is not surprising that national historians
like Laslett or sociologists who rely on their works should be equally
unanimous.[6] Cast into a receptive frame of mind by the well-
documented studies of French peasants or east European peasantries,
comparative sociologists readily believe in the English peasantry.[7]
Moore assumes the presence of an English peasantry, as do Redfield
and Dalton, who lumps together the whole of 'Europe', including
England, as a 'peasant' society up to the nineteenth century.[8] The
map of 'the major peasant regions of the world' in Wolf's authoritative
textbook shows England as 'peasant' and Thorner includes the
feudal monarchies of thirteenth-century Europe as 'peasant'.[9] Shanin
avoids any direct comment on the English situation, but accepts the
general developmental model which states that 'small producers'
society falls historically in the intermediate period between tribal-
nomadic and industrializing societies'.[10] This would encompass
England between the Anglo-Saxons and the eighteenth century and

[2] Britton, 'Peasant'; Homans, *Villagers*.   [3] Hilton, 'Medieval Research'.
[4] Tawney, *Agrarian Problem*.
[5] Thirsk, *Peasant Farming*, 1.   [6] Laslett, *Lost World*, 12–13.
[7] Le Roy Ladurie, *Peasants;* Thomas and Znaniecki, *Polish Peasant.*
[8] Moore, *Social Origins*, 20–9; Redfield, *Peasant Society*, 66–7; Dalton, 'Peasantries'.
[9] Wolf, *Peasants*, 2: in Shanin, *Peasants*, 204, 217.   [10] Shanin, *Peasants*, 247.

mean that the 'pattern-transformation of the peasantry' which is 'clearly seen in most parts of North-Western Europe' also occurred in England.[11]

It has become increasingly clear over the last 15 years that England and parts of north-western Europe exhibited certain features in the sixteenth century which set this area off from the other 'classical' peasantries of which we know. Among these features were a 'non-crisis' demographic pattern,[12] a curiously late age at marriage and high proportion of never-married persons,[13] very small and simple households[14] and high geographical mobility.[15] It is therefore time to reassess the conventional wisdom within the framework of recent analytic discussions of peasantry and its characteristics.

One major difficulty in this task lies in the continued dispute over the definition and meaning of 'peasant'. It is probable that a number of those who employ the term merely use it in the common-sense or dictionary meaning of 'countryman, rustic, worker on the land'.[16] Used in this way, the term is practically synonymous with 'non-industrialist'; hence the great contrast is between 'industrial' and 'peasant' nations. This dichotomy can be elaborated and quantified. Thorner suggests that two of the five criteria which a society must fulfil to be called 'peasant' are that 'half the population must be agricultural' and 'more than half of the working population must be engaged in agriculture'.[17] By these criteria, England was clearly a 'peasant' society until the middle of the nineteenth century. It fits well into the definition of peasantry given by Firth: 'by a peasant economy one means a system of small-scale producers, with a simple technology and equipment often relying primarily for their subsistence on what they themselves produce. The primary means of livelihood of the peasant is cultivation of the soil'.[18] But anthropologists, who have to differentiate their objects of study not only from industrial nations, but also from societies at the other end of the continuum of complexity, cannot be satisfied with such a

---

[11] Ibid., 250. [12] Wrigley, *Population*, ch. 3; Macfarlane, *Resources*, ch. 16.
[13] Hajnal, 'European Marriage'.
[14] Laslett, *Household*, ch. 4.
[15] Rich, 'Population'; Laslett and Harrison, 'Clayworth'.
[16] *Concise Oxford Dictionary*. [17] In Shanin, *Peasants*, 203.
[18] Firth, quoted in Dalton, 'Peasantries', 386.

crude dichotomy which would, as Dalton states, encompass New Guinea, Africa, India, Latin America, as well as pre-industrial England.

In order to separate off what are often lumped as 'tribal' societies, a new set of criteria were added to the old ones, principally by Kroeber and Redfield. They stated that peasants formed a 'part society': 'the culture of a peasant community, on the other hand, is not autonomous, it is an aspect or dimension of the civilization of which it is a part. As the peasant society is a half-society, so the peasant culture is a half-culture'.[19] This is elaborated by Thorner in the form of two further criteria. One is that a peasantry can only exist where there is a state, in other words a ruling hierarchy, an external political power sovereign over the particular community of 'peasants'. The second is that there are almost inevitably towns with markets, the culture of which is substantially different from that of the countryside.[20] Wolf summarizes the position when he states that 'the State is the decisive criterion of civilization . . . which marks the threshold of transition between food gatherers in general and peasants'.[21] Yet here again, even taking these more precise definitions, it would seem that England would fall into the category 'peasant' from the twelfth century onwards, for it was noted for its powerful centralized state and the growth of important towns.

Building on earlier work, economists and sociologists have recently tried to provide a sharper definition of peasantry. While accepting the preceding criteria as necessary prerequisites for the presence of a peasant society, a number of writers argue that they are not sufficient in themselves. One added criterion makes it possible to distinguish between rural nation-states which before would all have had to be lumped together as 'peasantry' but which clearly exhibit very divergent demographic, economic and social patterns. This criterion has been elaborated by Chayanov and those influenced by him, among them Shanin, Thorner and Sahlins. The feature is described by Thorner as follows:

Our fifth and final criterion, the most fundamental, is that of the unit of production. In our concept of peasant economy the typical and most

19 Kroeber, *Anthropology*, 284; Redfield, *Peasant Society*, 40.
20 In Shanin, *Peasants*, 203–4.
21 Wolf, *Peasants*, 11.

representative units of production are the peasant family households. We define a peasant family household as a socio-economic unit which grows crops primarily by the physical efforts of the members of the family. The principal activity of the peasant households is the cultivation of their own lands, strips or allotments . . . In a peasant economy half or more of all crops grown will be produced by such peasant households, relying mainly on their own family labour.[22]

Above all, the stress is on the nature of the particular unit of consumption, production and ownership: 'The family farm is the basic unit of peasant ownership, production, consumption and social life. The individual, the family and the farm, appear as an indivisible whole . . . The profit and accumulation motives rarely appear in their pure and simple form . . . '. Among the consequences of this situation is the fact that 'the head of the family appears as the manager rather than proprietor of family land', that marriage of children is essential to increase labour power, that peasant villages or communities are usually more or less self-sufficient.[23] These writers are developing and expanding Chayanov's earlier discussions where, for example, as quoted by Wolf, he states that

The first fundamental characteristic of the farm economy of the peasant is that it is a family economy. Its whole organization is determined by the size and composition of the peasant family and by the coordination of its consumptive demands with the number of its working hands. This explains why the conception of profit in peasant economy differs from that in capitalist economy and why the capitalist conception of profit cannot be applied to peasant economy . . .[24]

This central feature, namely that we are not just talking about rural 'part-societies', but those which have a specific basic unit of production and consumption, has earned the category the title of the 'Domestic Mode of Production'.[25] This prompts a further question as to whether there is a type of society which we can negatively define as non-tribal, non-peasant and non-industrial? To my knowledge, no very convincing examples of this anomalous class have yet been

[22] In Shanin, *Peasants*, 205.   [23] Shanin, *Peasants*, 241, 242–4.
[24] Wolf, *Peasants*, 14.
[25] Sahlins, *Stone Age*, chs 2, 3.

Peasants

Table 1   Features usually associated with peasantry

Variable	Situation in 'model' peasant society	England 16th–17th centuries
Basic unit of production	extended household	manor, estate
Basic unit of consumption	extended household	man, wife and small children
Link between land and family	very strong indeed	weak (except gentry)
Village self-sufficiency	almost entirely	far from
Production mainly for	immediate use	exchange
Ownership of resources	by village household	by individual
Degree of market rationality	little	great
Individual inheritance of land	no	yes
Children remain at home	in most cases	most children leave home
General household structure	ideal of multi-generation household	ideal of nuclear household
Fertility rate	high	controlled
Social mobility pattern	'cyclical'	spiralling, families split
Long-term economic differentiation	little	a great deal
Female age at first marriage	soon after puberty	delayed for ten or more years
Mortality pattern	periodic 'crises'	relative absence of 'crises'
Growth rate of population	rapid, then crash	moderate or no growth
Children regarded as economic asset	yes	no
Adoption widely favoured	yes	no

Table 1 (Continued)

Degree of geo- graphical mobility	little	great
Strength of 'community' bonds	great	little
Method of tracing descent	unilineal	cognatic
Kinship terminology	does not separate off nuclear family	separates off individual and nuclear family
Marriages	arranged by kin	individual choice
Patriarchal authority	great	little

documented. We may therefore turn to the English evidence to see whether in the sixteenth and seventeenth centuries England fits into a previous category, or belongs to this newly isolated type.

It is impossible here to give more than a preliminary answer to the questions that have been raised. If we are attempting to discover whether England can be lumped with traditional China, India, eastern and southern Europe, and Latin America, two main strategies are open to us. One is to examine the situation in England in the sixteenth and seventeenth centuries at a very general level. Peasant civilizations tend to have associated with them a set of features which appear to be intimately linked to their particular social structure. These may be summarized in Table 1. We may then observe whether, generalizing from the data, and speaking mainly of the sixteenth and seventeenth centuries, England manifested these symptoms of 'peasantness'. If it did not do so, we have a prima-facie case for delving deeper. These 'pattern variables' have been elaborated from general works already cited, as well as from monographs primarily concerned with India. For the present, the generalizations will have to remain unsubstantiated.

Further variables in the realm of culture, thought and religion could be elaborated. But there is probably enough here to enable us to decide whether England was similar to a model 'peasant' society, without pointing out differences in the attitudes towards ancestors, towards the ritualization of religion and social life, towards time and accumulation and many other topics. It would also be foolish to

continue since there is probably enough in the table to rouse many
people's ire. Demands for proof of some of the characterizations are
inevitable, since some do not conform to the generally accepted
wisdom. For example, some may still believe in the strong
'communities' of pre-industrial England, though I have elsewhere
tried to show that these are also a myth.[26] Others may still subscribe
to the idea that this was a 'patriarchal' society,[27] a view which it would
take a separate article to refute. But even if some of the assessments
listed in the table are challenged and turn out to be mistaken, we do
know that enough of them are right to give us grounds for believing
that England was already far from being a model 'peasant' society.
The only way in which the case will be proved, however, is to
undertake detailed studies of particular areas of the country, to see
whether the extensive documents support the model of peasantry.

   We may look at the situation in two very different parishes, that of
Earls Colne, near Colchester, in Essex, and the parish of Kirkby
Lonsdale in Cumbria. From the very earliest times it is known that
England showed enormous regional variations in agriculture and
social structure, reflecting its history and settlement, as well as
physical differences. It is therefore necessary to pick two areas which
are as different as possible. In this article we will describe the parish
of Earls Colne, with a population of about a thousand persons in the
middle of the seventeenth century, a parish that was relatively near to
London, in the economically precocious and religiously radical area
of East Anglia. Enclosed before the period with which we are
concerned, it seems to have combined arable corn production of hops
and fruit. In every respect it can be contrasted with the upland parish
of Kirkby Lonsdale on the edge of the Yorkshire moors which will be
examined in a companion essay to this one.[28] The two parishes were
originally chosen not only for the contrast, but because they are each
covered by at least one particularly useful and unusual historical
source. In the case of Earls Colne, this is the recently published diary
of one of the villagers, the farmer and vicar Ralph Josselin.[29] This
allows us to see into the mind of one of the inhabitants over a period
of 40 years in a way that is unique in England. From his diary and the

---

[26] Macfarlane, 'History'.   [27] Laslett, *Lost World*, 3, 4, 17–19 and passim.
[28] In Smith, *Land*, ch. 10.
[29] Macfarlane, *Ralph Josselin*.

very rich set of manorial documents, we may see whether this area exhibits 'peasant' characteristics in any sense. Kirkby Lonsdale, a parish with over twice the population, was chosen because a listing of the inhabitants in 1695 has recently been discovered.

It is difficult to envisage anyone further from the ideal-type 'peasant' than Ralph Josselin. On almost every one of the criteria listed in table 1 he departed from the normal peasant. Only in the fact that he was engaged in agriculture to a considerable extent, and hence subject to the uncertainties of weather and prices, does he come near to the stereotype. His extremely detailed diary makes it clear that the basic unit of production in his case was not the extended family; he did not cooperate in economic affairs with his parents, and his siblings and children did not work the farm with him. It was Josselin, his wife, servants and labourers who constituted the unit of production. Nor was the basic unit of consumption the household. His children left home in their early teens and henceforward fended for themselves, eating and earning elsewhere.[30] Nor was the link between his family and a particular landholding strong. His paternal grandfather was a wealthy yeoman who farmed in Roxwell, but Josselin's father sold off the patrimony in 1618 and went to farm in Bishop's Stortford, where he lost most of his estate. Josselin then settled in Earls Colne and built up a farm there. As for the purpose of Josselin's farming, it appears to have been mainly in order to sell produce for cash, rather than for use and home consumption. Other parts of his estate he let out for rent. Thus he estimated that in the years 1659–83 his landholdings brought in a total of approximately £80 p.a. Given the cost of foodstuffs in the period, less than one quarter of this could have been consumed directly as food.

Turning to the crucial question of who 'owned' the land in Josselin's family, the diary leaves no doubt whatsoever that this was a situation of complete, absolute, and exclusive private ownership. Josselin was not, as he would have been in a traditional peasant society, merely the head of a small corporate group who jointly owned the land. The land held in his name in deeds and court rolls was not family land, but his land. It seems unlikely that he would have been able to comprehend, and certainly would not have agreed with, the idea central to Russian peasantry, that lands 'are regarded as the property not of the person

---

[30] Macfarlane, *Family Life*, App. B and chs 3, 4.

legally registered as the proprietor, but of all the members of the family, the heads of the household being only the household representative'.[31] The difference can best be illustrated by taking the two extreme situations which can occur. In Russia the head of a household could be removed from his headship for mismanagement or misbehaviour.[32] In Josselin's case, on the contrary, he threatened on several occasions to disinherit his only surviving son. He was finally driven to such distraction that he wrote: 'John declared for his disobedience no son; I should allow him nothing except he tooke himselfe to bee a servant, yet if he would depart and live in service orderly I would allow him 10 li. yearly: if he so walkt as to become gods son. I should yett own him for mine'.[33]

In a peasant society, birth or adoption, plus participation in the basic tasks of production, give people an inalienable right to belong to the small property-owning corporation. Disinheritance for misbehaviour is inconceivable. In Josselin's case, his children's rights in his property were non-existent. Since this is such a crucial matter, and it might be thought that Josselin was exceptional, we will return to it when considering the pattern of landholding in the parish as a whole. We will also expand on the question of inheritance, closely linked to ownership. We are told that in Russia, 'inheritance, as defined in the Civil Code, was unknown in peasant customary law, which knew only the partitioning of family property among newly emerging households'.[34] There were no written wills, since it was clear that all males should receive an equal share of what was in nature theirs. It was a matter of splitting up temporarily a communal asset, the shares returning to the common pool when the demographic situation had changed. In contrast, Josselin's own will and the provision for his children recorded in the diary and court rolls show that we have a fully developed system of post-mortem and pre-mortem inheritance, in which each child was given a part largely at the discretion of the parents.[35] Again, as we shall see, Josselin was by no means exceptional in this respect.

It would be possible to continue in this fashion through all the major indices of peasantry; noting that Josselin's economic behaviour

---

[31] Shanin, *Awkward Class*, 220, quoting the Court of Appeal.
[32] Shanin, *Awkward Class*, 221.
[33] Macfarlane, *Ralph Josselin*, 582.   [34] Shanin, *Awkward Class*, 222.
[35] Macfarlane, *Family Life*, 64–7.

was highly 'rational' and market-orientated, that he did not suffer from the 'Image of Limited Good', at least in relation to his neighbours,[36] that his own marriage and those of his children were not arranged by kin, that his family life was far from the patriarchal stereotype both in relation to his wife and his children, and that his children were not an economic asset to him. For those who seek proof, it would be instructive to read some of the classic accounts of peasantry cited above, and then to read Josselin's own diary. Yet even if we accepted unequivocally that Josselin was not a 'peasant', though he farmed, it would be possible to dismiss him as exceptional on several grounds. First, he kept a diary, which suggests that he was an unusual man. Secondly, he was university educated and hence moved in a broader intellectual world than most of his neighbours. Thirdly, he was a devout Puritan and a vicar. He thus belonged to the 'intelligentsia' rather than to the 'peasantry' if there was one. Some counter-arguments can be brought forward from the diary. Although it shows strong divisions between the wealthy and the poor, it nowhere gives an impression nearly as strong as that obtained in India or Russia of a great split between the 'Great' and 'Little' traditions, between the 'intelligentsia' and the 'mere peasants'. Secondly, it is clear that Josselin's horizons and mentality were very different from the ideal-type peasantry long *before* he had been to university or thought of being a minister. One early account of his youthful musings describes a mind that hardly fits the peasant stereotype, although he was at that time merely the son of a failing Essex farmer.

I made it my aime to learne and lent my minde continually to reade historyes: and to shew my spirit lett mee remember with griefe that which I yett feele: when I was exceeding yong would I project the conquering of kingdoms and write historyes of such exploits. I was much delighted with Cosmography taking it from my Father. I would project wayes of receiving vast est(ates) and then lay it out in stately building, castles. Libraryes: colledges and such like.[37]

He wrote this describing the time when he was aged 12. Yet, even with these counter-arguments, the case cannot be proved from the life of a single individual. The records describing Josselin's neighbours and parishioners help to fill this gap.

[36] Foster, 'Peasant Society'.   [37] Macfarlane, *Ralph Josselin*, 2.

We may select four of the central characteristics of peasantry in order to test them against the evidence for Earls Colne; the patterns of land ownership, transmission of wealth, geographical mobility and social mobility. We have seen that peasantry is basically an economic and social order founded on household and for village ownership. Thorner states that, as a result,

In a peasant economy half or more of all crops grown will be produced by such peasant households, relying mainly on their own family labour. Alongside of the peasant producers there may exist larger units: the landlord's demesne or home farm tilled by labour extracted from the peasants, the *hacienda* or estate on which the peasants may be employed for part of the year, the capitalist farm in which the bulk of the work is done by free hired labourers. But if any of these is the characteristic economic unit dominating the countryside, and accounting for the greater share of the crop output, then we are not dealing with a peasant economy.[38]

If we look at Earls Colne at any point from the time the records start, in 1400, onwards, it was not a peasant economy. It was dominated by large landlords, in the early period by the Priory and the Earl of Oxford, later by the Harlakendens. In 1598 a detailed set of maps and a survey were made of the parish, showing the ownership of land.[39] From these the area of demesne land farmed and owned directly by the lord of the manor can be estimated and it is evident that approximately two-thirds of the parish was held by one person. Most of the rest was copyhold land which, in practice, was held by about 20 individuals. In effect this means that about three-quarters of the people in the parish held nothing beyond a house and garden. By the definition quoted above, this was clearly far from a peasant economy, not composed of self-sufficient small farming households. The fact that the large manorial estate was a rational, modern, capitalist enterprise, run for economic profit, is shown by the detailed account books of the family which survive for the late sixteenth and early seventeenth centuries.[40] A certain number of the landless were employed as casual labour on others' land, but numerous documents show that there was a very great deal

[38] In Shanin, *Peasants*, 205.
[39] Essex Record Office (ERO), Chelmsford: D/DSm/P1; Temp. Acc. 897.
[40] ERO Temp. Acc. 897/8.

of non-agricultural activity in the town. As well as baking, brewing, butchering and tailoring, there was considerable employment in the East Anglian cloth industry.

The lord's account book and Josselin's diary both show that the bulk of the food production, particularly the growing of fruit and hops, was not for local consumption, but for cash sale in nearby markets at Colchester and Braintree, from where it found its way to London and other parts of the country. This is not an area of subsistence agriculture, but cash cropping. Thus what at a preliminary glance looks like a rural village filled with small yeomen families, turns out on closer inspection to be one dominated by a few large landowners, with a multitude of small producers, agricultural and otherwise. The parish was fully involved in a capitalist and cash marketing system and differed as much from a traditional peasant society as do modern Kent, Somerset or Essex.

One central feature of peasantry is the absence of absolute ownership of land, vested in a specific individual. The property-holding unit is a 'corporation', to use Maine's term, which never dies. Into this an individual is born or adopted, and to it he gives his labour. In such a situation, as described, for example, for Russia,[41] women have no individual and exclusive property rights and individuals cannot sell off their share of the family property. It would be unthinkable that a man should sell off land if he had sons, except in dire necessity and by common consent. There is unlikely to be a highly developed land market. As we have already seen in the case of Josselin's threatened disinheritance of his only son, the inhabitants of Earls Colne lived in a different world. The transfers in the manor court rolls, the deeds concerning freehold property, the lengthy cases from the village in the Chancery court, and all other sources bearing on economic life in the parish suggest that by the later sixteenth century ownership was highly individualized. Land was held in their own right by women, men appearing to do suit of court 'in the right of their wife'. Land was bought and sold without consideration for any wider group than husband and wife. It was, in fact, treated as a commodity which belonged to individuals and not to the household. There is no hint, for example, in the statements concerning transfers in the court rolls, that a plot was passed to a family rather than an individual. Examination of

[41] Shanin, *Awkward Class.*

the manor court rolls back to their origin in 1400 does not suggest that family or household ownership had ever been practised from that date. Since this appears to be the crucial foundation of the difference between a peasant and non-peasant social and economic structure it is worth digressing briefly to consider whether the situation in Earls Colne was abnormal.

In discussing the question of family and individual ownership in this period three distinctions need to be made: between 'chattels' and 'real estate', between freehold tenure and other kinds of tenure, and between the rights of wives and the rights of children. The legal and practical situation concerning goods or chattels was very different from that concerning real estate. By common law, the wife had rights to one-third of her husband's estate, including goods, but the children had no rights in their parents' goods.[42] By ecclesiastical law, during the sixteenth and seventeenth centuries 'by a Custom observed, not only throughout the Province of York, but in many other Places besides', if there was only a wife, the husband could only dispose of one-half of his goods by will, if there were children, only one third.[43] Thus, assuming that he had not sold his goods and bought land, or given the goods away during his lifetime, within certain parts of England up to the repeal of the custom by an Act of 1692, wives and children had a certain stake in the man's goods. The heart of the matter lies in the question of real estate, principally land, for it is here that we will see whether the family and the landholding were identified.

A simplified summary of the position of women in relation to real estate shows that unlike the situation in peasant societies, women could be true landholders. In the case of freehold land, a woman could hold and own such property. During her marriage or 'couverture', the husband 'gains a title to the rents and profits', but he may not sell or alienate it.[44] If the man holds the title and marries, the woman has an inalienable right to at least one-third of his estate for her life by common law. She had a right to this 'dower' even if she remarried or the couple were divorced (*a mensa et thoro*) for

---

[42] Pollock and Maitland, *English Law*, II, 348–55.
[43] Swinburne, *Last Wills*, 204–5.
[44] Blackstone, *Commentaries*, II, 433.

adultery.[45] There was no way of excluding a woman from her common-law dower, though it might be increased, or the particular share of the estate specified, by a 'jointure' which set up formally a joint estate for husband and wife for life. The situation with regard to non-freehold land, and particularly copyhold land, was very different. Except when an heir was under 14 years of age, and only until he or she reached that age, a married woman did not automatically obtain any rights over the real estate of her husband.[46] Copyhold estates were not liable to 'freebench' as it was known, unless by the special customs of the manor it was stated to exist.[47] Although it would appear that most manors in England did have such a custom up to the eighteenth century, as Thompson has pointed out,[48] there were a minority of cases where no freebench was allowed. Earls Colne was one of these, for in the court roll for June 1595 it was stated:

At this court the steward of the manor by virtue of his office commanded an inquisition to be made whether women are indowerable of the third part of the customary lands of their husbands at any time during the marriage between them. And now the homage present that they have not known in their memory nor by the search of the rolls that women ought to have any dowry in the customary tenement of their husbands but they say that in times past diverse women have pretended their dowries but have always been denied and therefore they think there is no such custom.[49]

In such a situation, a woman could be made a joint owner with her husband by a surrender to their joint use in the manor court, or the estate could be bequeathed to her by will. Both these devices were used. In other areas of England her position was much stronger; by the custom of 'tenant right' or 'border tenure' which encompassed our other parish of Kirkby Lonsdale, a widow had the whole estate for her widowhood.[50] But here, as elsewhere, the right was far less than that in freedhold estates, for the widow usually lost her freebench if she remarried or 'miscarried', in other words had sexual intercourse. Women could also hold copyhold property in their own person, either

---

[45] Blackstone, *Commentaries*, II, 130; Pollock and Maitland, *English Law*, II, 419.
[46] Order, *Court Leet*, 36.
[47] Blackstone, *Commentaries*, II, 132.   [48] In Goody, *Family*, 354.
[49] ERO D/DPr/76.
[50] Bagot, 'Manorial Customs', 238.

by gift, purchase, or through inheritance, for example when there were no male heirs. To a very limited extent, therefore, we can view husband and wife as a small co-owning group. We may wonder whether we can add any further members of the family to this corporation.

The situation with regard to freehold property seems abundantly clear. Maitland stated that, 'in the thirteenth century the tenant in fee simple has a perfect right to disappoint his expectant heirs by conveying away the whole of his land by act *inter vivos*. Our law is grasping the maxim *Nemo est heres viventis*'.[51] Although Glanvill produced some rather vague safeguards for the heir, Bracton in the thirteenth century omitted these and the King's Courts did not support a child's claim to any part of his parent's estates. The only major change between the thirteenth and sixteenth centuries was that by the Statute of Wills in 1540 a parent could totally disinherit his heirs not only by sale or gift during his lifetime, but also by leaving a will devising the two-thirds of his freehold estate which did not go to his widow.[52] Swinburne, a leading authority on testamentary law, nowhere mentions the children's right to any part of the real estate of their parents. This had been formalized in the Statute *Quia Emptores* of 1290, which stated that 'from henceforth it shall be lawful for every freeman to sell at his own pleasure his land and tenements, or part of them . . .', with the exception of sales to the church or other perpetual foundations.[53] In this crucial respect, English common law took a totally different direction from continental law. As Maitland put it,

Free alienation without the heir's consent will come in the wake of primogeniture. These two characteristics which distinguish our English law from her nearest of kin, the French customs, are closely connected . . . Abroad, as a general rule, the right of the expectant heir gradually assumed the shape of the **restrait lignager**. A landowner must not alienate his land without the consent of his expectant heirs unless it be a case of necessity, and even in a case of necessity the heirs must have an opportunity of purchasing.[54]

Thus children have no birthright from the thirteenth century onwards, they can be left penniless. Strictly speaking it is not even a

[51] Pollock and Maitland, *English Law*, II, 308.   [52] Swinburne, *Last Wills*, 119.
[53] Simpson, *Land Law*, 51.   [54] Pollock and Maitland, *English Law*, II, 309, 313.

matter of 'disinheritance'; a living man has no heirs, he has complete seisin of property. As Bracton put it, 'the heir acquires nothing from the gift made to his ancestor because he was not enfeoffed with the donee', in effect he has no rights while his father lives, they are not co-owners in any sense.[55] This is illustrated by the fact that in the thirteenth century, and to a certain extent later, the heir has no automatic 'seisin' in his dead ancestor's property. We are told that

If a stranger 'abates' or 'intrudes' upon land whose owner has just died seised, he has committed no disseisin. The lawful heir cannot say that he was disseised unless he had in fact been previously seised. In other words, the heir does not inherit his ancestors's seisin. Like everyone else, an heir cannot acquire the privileges of seisin unless he enters, stays in, and conducts himself like the peaceful holder of a free tenement.[56]

Again there was nothing comparable to the French custom, equivalent to the principle of *le roi est mort: vive le roi*, whereby *le mort saisit le vif*.[57] In the case of freehold real estate from the thirteenth century, the children had no automatic rights. The custom of primogeniture might give the eldest child greater rights, where the estate was not disposed of, than other children. But ultimately even the eldest son had nothing except at the wish of his father or mother, except where the inheritance had been formally specified by the artificial device of an entail. Even such entails could be broken. As a result, as Chamberlayne put it in the seventeenth century, 'Fathers may give all their Estates un-intailed from their own children, and to any one child'.[58]

Children had no stronger rights in the non-freehold property of their parents. Originally most of this land was held 'at the will of the lord', which meant that at a person's death his heirs had no security. But gradually over time in many areas of England copyhold estates became hereditable. In practice, as we see in Earls Colne by the later sixteenth century, a copyholder could sell or grant away his land, or he could surrender it to the lord 'to the use of his will'. In this will he could specify his heirs. Thus up to the sixteenth century a man could alienate his land from his children while alive. After the Statute of Wills of 1540, all socage tenures, including copyhold, became freely devisable

---

55 Simpson, *Land Law*, 49.
56 Plucknett, *Common Law*, 722–3; Pollock and Maitland, *English Law*, II, 59–61.
57 Plucknett, *Common Law*, 723. 58 Chamberlayne, *Present State*, 337.

by will.[59] We have seen that a widow might have a free-bench, but children had no inalienable rights, no birthrights. Children had no legal claim against a person to whom their parent's land had been granted or given. In sum, neither in the case of freehold nor non-freehold, except where an entail was drawn up, did a child have any rights. Even entails were contrary to the idea of 'family estates', since they could take the land away from children, as easily as ensuring them a portion.

It has been necessary to spend some time on this topic in order to show that what we find in Josselin's diary and in Earls Colne was only a particular instance of a central characteristic of English law and society. The family as the basic resource-owning unit which characterizes peasant societies does not seem, in law at least, to have existed in England from about 1200 onwards. England was here not only very different from the Third World societies where the introduction of English common law in the nineteenth and twentieth centuries caused such dislocation,[60] but also from Europe at that time. If the essence of peasantry is the identification of the family with the ownership of the means of production, it is difficult to see how England can have been a peasant society in the sixteenth century, or long before. The consequences of this situation are apparent in the records for Earls Colne.

From 1540 to 1750 there survive over three hundred written wills for inhabitants in Earls Colne, indicating a fully developed system of individual inheritance. They included land, houses and goods. This is in direct contrast to the situation in a traditional peasant society, where the agricultural assets are not being bequeathed, but partitioned, usually before death, and where, consequently, a will would be a violation of children's rights. For example, in relation to Russian peasantry we are told that 'inheritance by will did not exist as far as land and agricultural equipment were concerned, and, in other cases, was extremely limited and open to challenge as unjust before the peasant courts'.[61] Furthermore, if we look at the principal land registration record, the manor court roll, we find a fully developed land market with the sale and mortgaging of land to non-kin. At least

[59] Swinburne, *Last Wills*, 119.
[60] Boserup, *Agricultural Growth*, 90; Myrdal, *Asian Drama*, II, 1036–7.
[61] Shanin, *Awkward Class*, 223.

half of the transfers of land registered during the sixteenth and seventeenth centuries were between non-kin. For example, during the five-year period 1589–93 on the manor of Earls Colne, 51 parcels of copyhold land were transferred. At least 21 of these were sales of copyhold land to non-kin for cash, while a number of others were surrenders at the end of mortgages or leases. Just under half the transfers were by 'inheritance' between kin.[62] Detailed examination of this period shows that this cannot be explained by suggesting that the vendors were heirless individuals, or very poor individuals 'falling off' the bottom of the economic ladder. What we are witnessing is a continual process of amalgamation, exchange and accumulation, in which estates were constantly changing shape, ownership and value. They were not tied to specific families.

Although a man could give away, sell or devise any or all of his real estate, excepting the widow's share, either in his life or by will, if he did not do so, then the estate could by custom descend to a particular child. In Earls Colne, as in most of England, the first-born male would inherit the estate by law. Although no written statement to this effect has been discovered for Earls Colne, detailed study of wills and court rolls shows this to be the case. It also shows that the severity of male primogeniture was modified by the giving of 'portions' to younger sons and to the daughters. In general, however, from the start of the court rolls in 1400, the major share of the landholding went to one child. Maine has pointed out that this 'Feudal Law of land practically disinherited all the children in favour of one'.[63] In essence, primogeniture and a peasant joint ownership unit are diametrically opposed. The family is not attached to the land, one favoured individual is chosen at the whim of the parent, or by the custom of the manor. It has already been suggested that primogeniture and complete individual property in real estate are intimately interlinked, both apparently firmly established in England by the thirteenth century.[64] If peasantry and primogeniture are in principle opposed, we would expect the rule to be limited to parts of western Europe. This seems to have been the case. Lowie long ago noted that 'the widespread European dominance of primogeniture' marked it off from Africa and Asia, and a recent sweeping survey of property rights

[62] ERO D/DPr/76. [63] Maine, *Ancient Law*, 225.
[64] Pollock and Maitland, *English Law*, II, 274.

states that primogeniture among the upper classes 'has been a great rarity in the world'.[65] Yet even within Europe, England seems to have been by far the most extreme in its application of this principle, as contemporary commentators quoted by Thirsk show.[66] Indeed, while primogeniture among the gentry and aristocracy was fairly widespread in Europe, further research may show that England was the only nation where primogeniture was widespread among those at the lower levels in society; in other words, amongst those who might have constituted a 'peasantry'. Although there were considerable regions where partible inheritance was common, and younger children could be provided with cash or goods, it is clear that a custom such as this would have profound consequences.

One of these consequences was that England during the sixteenth and seventeenth centuries witnessed very high rates of geographical mobility. Taking Earls Colne, this would mean that the families present in, for example, 1560, were different from those present in the same parish in 1700. Even in a peasant society with little disruption by war or famine, there is likely to be considerable change in families as they die out in the male line. But the situation is more dramatic in Earls Colne. For example, of 274 pieces of property listed in a rental for the two Earls Colne manors in 1677, only 23 had been held by the same family, even if we include links through females, some two generations earlier in 1598. A massive shift can be seen in even shorter periods. Comparing two sixteenth-century rentals for Earls Colne manor we find that of 111 pieces listed in 1549, only 31 were owned by the same family some 40 years later in a rental of 1589, again including the links through women.[67] The result is that individuals appear, build up a holding, and then the family disappears, all in a generation or two. It also seems to have been the case that most people, especially younger sons, and daughters, would end up in a parish other than the one in which they were born. A parish or village, far from being a bounded community which contained people from birth to death, was a geographical area through which very large numbers of people flowed, staying a few years, or a lifetime, but not settling with their families for generations.

[65] Lowie, *Social Organization*, 150; Kiernan in Goody, *Family*, 376.
[66] In Goody, *Family*, 185.
[67] ERO D/DPr/99, 110.

Another effect of the particular landholding situation was on social mobility. It has been demonstrated by Shanin that the Russian peasantry were characterized by two major features in their system of mobility. At the level of the individual peasant family, the family as a whole underwent what he calls 'cyclical mobility', a pattern which he portrays as an undulating wave-like motion over time.[68] There were certain negative and positive feedback mechanisms which kept it oscillating about a mean. For example, as it gets richer, the number of children increases and the estate has to be partitioned among more households, so that each is individually poorer, while poorer households amalgamate their holdings and so become richer. One corollary of this is that over long periods no permanent 'classes' appear; the 'middling' peasants predominate, and there is no spiralling accumulation whereby the rich continue to get richer and the poor to get poorer. The contrast between the two systems and the reasons for the two patterns have been discussed at some length with an independent, but curiously parallel model to that of Shanin, where it was suggested that Tudor and Stuart England was already witnessing a different phenomenon, with spiralling accumulation.[69] The records from Earls Colne and elsewhere suggest that certain individuals rose, and then one of their children likewise did so. Families did not move in a block, but shed some of their younger or less talented children. As a result, after several generations, as for example noted by Spufford,[70] grandchildren of the same person could be at extreme ends of the hierarchy of wealth. One long-term effect of this pattern is the well-known general phenomenon by which England is characterized between the fifteenth and eighteenth centuries, a growing split between a wealthy minority of landowners and an impoverished labouring force. One of the central themes of much of the social history written since Tawney has been the way in which absolute divisions grew, so that by the eighteenth century it is possible to speak of 'classes' rather than estates. The process of differentiation which failed to materialize in Russia in the first years of this century had occurred. In Earls Colne, comparisons of the distribution of land at the start of the sixteenth and end of the eighteenth century support this idea of increasing differentiation.

[68] Shanin, *Awkward Class*, 118.   [69] Macfarlane, *Resources*, 191–200.
[70] In a talk given at King's College Social History Seminar, February 1974.

This contrasts with the situation in parts of Asia, where temporary increases in production are invested in demographic or social expansion, rather than being accumulated and hoarded by one heir. It seems abundantly plain that we are not dealing with a 'peasant' village in Earls Colne in the sixteenth to eighteenth centuries. Comparison with the records of other Essex villages, particularly the neighbouring parish of Great Tey and those of Hatfield Pevel, Boreham and Little Baddow, suggests that Earls Colne was not exceptional within Essex. Yet it could be argued that Essex was exceptionally advanced. We may briefly look at some published studies of other parishes in ecologically different areas in England.

The open-field parish of Wigston Magna in Leicestershire has been described by Hoskins. Although the turnover of family names was not quite as great as that in Earls Colne, of 82 family names in 1670, 44 per cent had been present a hundred years before, 20 per cent two hundred years before; in other respects the pattern of social mobility and the land market seem to have been of the same order as in Essex. We are told that there 'always had been, as far back as the records go, a good deal of buying and selling of land between the peasant-farmers of Wigston', but by the later seventeenth century 'the fines, conveyances, mortgages, leases and marriage settlements alone for this period, in such an incessantly active land-market as Wigston, are bewildering'.[71] It is also clear from the inventories that the farmers were producing for the market. The pattern of social mobility was one which led to the opposite situation to that described for Russia. There was a growing cleavage between rich and poor. Wigston witnessed, as did the whole of the Midlands, the emergence of a group of farmers in the late fifteenth century who were above the average in wealth, as can be seen in the Lay Subsidy of 1524.[72] During the later sixteenth century and seventeenth century there was a growing problem of poverty, while a few families accumulated almost all the land in the village. By the time of a survey of 1766 the village had become completely polarized between a rich few and numerous landless labourers.[73] The cyclical mobility of the Russian peasantry had not been present.

The same splitting apart of the village combined with an active land market is documented for the Cambridgeshire village of Chippenham

[71] Hoskins, *Midland Peasant*, 196, 115, 194–5.   [72] Ibid., 141–3.
[73] Ibid., 217–19.

studied by Spufford. This parish in the sheep and corn area of Cambridgeshire witnessed a build-up of larger than average holdings even in the fourteenth and fifteenth centuries.[74] But the author argues that the crucial period in which the small farmers were pushed out was 1560–1636. Economic polarization meant that a roughly egalitarian distribution of 1544, as shown in a survey of that year, was replaced by one where absentee large landowners held almost all the land in the map of 1712.[75] During the crucial period of division, over half the transactions in the manor court were sales of property – presumably to non-kin. The author also believed that there was a good deal of emigration, which helped to keep the population from growing during most of the period.[76]

A more extensive survey of village monographs would show that there were some areas where geographical and social mobility were less pronounced in the seventeenth century or earlier.[77] Yet in no study of Tudor and Stuart England have I come across the traces of anything approaching a real 'peasantry'. The area where one would most expect to find one would be the 'upland' area on the northern and western fringes. It is generally accepted by those familiar with such regions that kinship and family were more important there than elsewhere and that there, if anywhere, we will be dealing with a domestic economy, based on family labour. Of all the areas within this general regional type, the archetypal family farm appears to be in the hills of southern Cumbria, where it is known that a special form of social structure, based on small family 'estates', was present, where manorialism was weak, and where, we are often told, the economically backward and socially closed communities of the northern hills were inhabited by a real peasantry. I have examined this claim in relation to the parish of Kirkby Lonsdale in a complementary paper to this one, and it appears to be as mythical as the claim for peasantry in Essex.[78] The highly individualized, geographically and socially mobile, situation we found in Essex meets us in the Lune valley also. Property is held by individuals, children leave home at an early age, the basic unit of production, consumption and ownership is not the family. We still await an example of a peasant community.

[74] Spufford, *Contrasting Communities*, 65.   [75] Ibid., 67, 71.   [76] Ibid., 90.
[77] Hey, *Myddle;* Howell in Goody, *Family.*
[78] In Smith, *Land,* ch. 10.

The discovery that England was not, in the terms of the more precise definition advanced at the start of this chapter, a peasant society in the sixteenth to eighteenth centuries raises as many questions as it solves. A minor one is terminological; we do not have a word to characterize this social structure, except negatively or in relation to earlier or later 'states'. Thus to call it 'non-peasant', 'post-feudal', 'early modern' and so on is hardly satisfactory. Another problem is the extent to which England was different from other areas of Europe in that period: were there any other non-peasant rural societies? We also need to know more about when the pattern emerged. If there was no peasantry in sixteenth-century England, when had it disappeared? One recent suggestion is that while there was clearly a peasant social structure in the later fourteenth century, as argued by Hilton, there is evidence to suggest that it disappeared by the middle of the fifteenth century.[79] Since there was no obvious and traumatic break between 1380 and 1450, this leaves Blanchard and us puzzled. It is clearly time that someone considered the proposition that there never had been a peasantry in England.

Finally, we return to the question of how to characterize this highly idiosyncratic society; rural and agrarian, yet different in almost every respect from the other large agricultural civilizations which we know of through anthropological, archaeological or historical investigation. This essay has been devoted to suggesting that England cannot be described as 'peasant'. Upon this demolished site it is necessary to erect an alternative model of the society. If it was not peasant, or industrial or feudal, what was it?

---

[79] Hilton, *English Peasantry;* Blanchard, 'Review'.

2
Population

Modes of Reproduction

T HE CONTINUED rapid growth of population in many parts of the
world and the failure of most family planning campaigns makes
the topic of the value and desirability of children into more than a
purely academic one. If some general theory could be devised which
would account for the very different fertility rates and attitudes to
fertility in different societies, this would be of practical as well as
theoretical importance. Despite intensive research and a vast
expenditure of time and money we still do not know how to influence
reproduction, largely because we do not yet know *why* children are
highly valued. Yet the importance of the topic justifies what is bound
to be an over-ambitious solution to the puzzle. Firstly we may briefly
look at some previous theories which provide hints of a solution, but
which in their crude form have not been accepted. The question we
are seeking to answer is this: what accounts for the very large
differences in attitudes towards having children in various societies?[1]

One suggestion is a demographic answer which has already
become part of the conventional wisdom. It is the argument that high

---

[1] Some useful criticisms of the earlier, demographic part of this essay are contained
in Simons and Dyson, 'Comments'. Among the points they rightly make are the
following: that to describe family planning campaigns by the blanket term 'failure' is
too strong; that certain hunter–gatherer groups neither control their fertility nor
have conspicuously low fertility; that Thai and Burmese fertility levels are relatively
high; that the individualistic mode does not necessarily lead to low fertility, as in the
case of the high fertility in England in the nineteenth century; that it is difficult in
practice to classify societies as purely 'individualistic' or purely 'peasant'. Further
suggestive refinements and comments are contained in Smith, 'Nuclear Family'. A
fuller and less dichotomized statement of the thesis in this chapter is contained in
Macfarlane, *Marriage*, chs 1–6, 14.

fertility and desire for children is the 'result' of high infant mortality. It is pointed out that in many societies, in order to ensure living heirs, parents needed to stockpile children, as, for example, argued by Gould.[2] The practical consequence is that family planning will not work until death control is introduced. There is an element of truth in this, but as a general theory to account for all differences over time and space it is far too simple. It is not difficult to find instances where, as in Taiwan in the late 1960s, people living in areas of high infant mortality show more enthusiasm for birth control than those where infant mortality is much lower.[3] Historical data from England in the seventeenth century also shows that family planning can be combined with very high mortality rates.[4] One reason for the absence of a direct connection is the fact that perceptions and attitudes are involved. Mortality rates may decline, but individuals may still operate *as if* they were high. There is no direct link between reproductive behaviour and contemporary events. This is well shown in a study of an Eskimo community by Masnick and Katz which shows that women's fertility does not reflect their *present* economic circumstances, but those in which they began their reproduction.[5] It could also be shown that fertility has been encouraged and children highly desired even where mortality rates were low and many children survived. A simple demographic explanation only gets us a little way. As Mamdani states: 'an overwhelming majority of the people . . . have a large number of children not because they overestimate their infant mortality rates, but because they want *larger* families'.[6]

Others see the explanation lying in what may broadly be termed 'technology' and non-human resources. This is roughly where Malthus stands. He noted that pastoral and arable parts of Switzerland varied greatly in their population growth rates; population was stationary in pastoral regions, whereas it grew rapidly in arable areas. He generalized even further when stating that corn countries are more populous than pasture countries, and rice countries more populous than corn countries.[7] He also noted that population where

[2] In Marshall and Polgar, *Culture*, 188–91.
[3] Kantner and McCaffrey, *Population*, 273.
[4] Wrigley, 'Family Limitation'.   [5] In Kaplan, *Human Fertility*, 37–58.
[6] Mamdani, *Myth*, 43.
[7] Malthus, *Population*, I, 314.

potatoes were grown was denser than in areas where wheat was grown.[8] He did not consider the alternative explanation of the correlation put forward by Boserup that population density altered the agricultural technology.[9] For Malthus it was the nature of the means of subsistence which 'allowed' births to exceed deaths. A more careful reading of Malthus suggests that he did not predict that every increase in food would *necessarily* lead to increased population, but that in the absence of preventive and other checks it would do so. The sequence, oversimplified, was firstly the discovery of a new technique, or an accidental 'windfall' in the shape of a new food source appearing, then increased food which *allowed* the natural pressure towards higher fertility. Recently an alternative and attractive form of technological determinism has emerged in the work of several anthropologists. It is the view that the tools/crops and 'means of production' generally will determine the value of labour, and that the value of labour will determine the attitude towards having children. We may look at three rather different applications of the argument.

Nag in a recent survey has tried to take account of the fact that even in densely populated countries such as India, parents who are poor seem to want *more* children, even though it would appear to planners to be against their self-interest. Nag's argument is that this is rational behaviour. Making a broad dichotomy between industrial and agricultural societies, he brings forward some statistics to show that, in the absence of machinery, the scarce factor in production, at least in terms of power, is human labour.[10] This is the development of an argument put forward long ago by Kingsley Davis.[11] It is one of the essential components of 'Demographic Transition Theory', which argued that fertility was bound to fall rapidly as heavy industry made human labour redundant. The explanation has been most powerfully put forward by Mamdani as the major explanation of the desire for children in a Punjab village, which undermined an intensive family planning project in the area. People *need* extra labour: 'Given a very small income, to have to hire even one farm hand can mean disaster. If such a farmer is merely to survive, he must rely on his family for the necessary labour power'.[12] 'Labour is the most important factor [in

[8] Ibid., II, 73.   [9] Boserup, *Agricultural Growth*.
[10] In Marshall and Polgar, *Culture*, 3–23.
[11] Davis, 'Institutional Patterns', 37.   [12] Mamdani, *Myth*, 76.

production]. For them, family planning means voluntarily reducing the family labour force'.[13] All but the very young and the very old make some productive contribution to the economy of the household.[14] With intensive agriculture, and a very marked seasonal demand for labour, children are economically valuable. But with the introduction of other forms of power, he argues, the desire for children may decline; the introduction of tractors among the upper level Jats may already be having this effect. 'It is therefore true that the newly married sons of the mechanized farmers are the Jat group most favourable to the idea of family planning through the use of modern contraception'.[15] This type of argument is given an added dimension by contrasts between 'hoe' cultures of Africa, where female labour is often more valuable than male, and the 'plough' cultures of Asia and Europe, where the demand for male labour means that there is a male-specific desire for children.[16] In both areas human labour is the source of wealth and prestige, and children, who become net producers in their early teens, are greatly desired. There is much to attract us in this theory, since it strikes one as plausible and explains a good deal. Yet it is again too simple. We know that the attitude towards having children and fertility rates varies enormously between societies with the same agricultural technology; for instance, that Japan and China in the early twentieth century had contrasted fertility patterns, though both were wet-rice cultivating countries or that northern Thailand and India are contrasted. Furthermore, we know that many of the simplest societies, where human labour is even *more* basic in production and even animal power is absent, namely hunters and gatherers, usually have little stress on fertility.

The reason for the inadequacy of the theory seems to lie in the fact that the objective value, from an economist's point of view, of the child's labour both as an adolescent and later as an adult is not the issue. It is the value to its parents. The crucial factors concern the length and nature of the children's contribution to their parent's prestige and economy, how long they are expected to contribute to the family fund. This suggests that it is not in the *means of production*, but in the *relations of production*, in Marx's sense, that we are likely to find the solution to the desirability of children, and the reason why

---

[13] Ibid., 103.   [14] Ibid., 129.   [15] Ibid., 87.
[16] Boserup, *Women's Role*, 15–52; Goody, *Production*.

identical technologies produce entirely different fertility patterns. This was the heart of Marx's criticism of Malthus. We must look at the specific 'mode of production', which encompasses the family organization if we are to see what determines fertility patterns: 'In different modes of social production there are different laws of the increase of population and of over-population'.[17] The 'baboon' Malthus had oversimplified far too much in making a general law based on a 'false and childish' conception of a simple relationship between only two variables, reproduction and the means of subsistence. In fact we need to look at the 'very complicated and varying relations' within a 'specific historic development'.[18] We will do this shortly. But before doing so it is worth considering one further general hypothesis concerning the determinants of fertility which approaches closer to an analysis in terms of the relations of production than any other.

Two inextricably muddled but separate arguments have been put forward concerning the way in which social structure, as manifest in kinship, has influenced fertility. One is that there is a correlation between household structure and fertility, the other is that household structure is only one aspect of kinship in a society and that the important variable is the whole kinship system including the method of reckoning descent. Frank Lorimer long ago argued that fertility would be higher in societies with 'corporate' kinship groups, which usually means those where descent is exclusively traced through males or females. With bounded groups formed, children are especially valued as they expand a particular lineage.[19] Thus large-scale societies with unilineal kinship such as India or China had high fertility; bilateral societies in modern industrial settings, or even the small groups of hunters and gatherers who usually have cognatic descent, have a low emphasis on fertility. There appears to be a certain plausibility in this argument, but it became discredited largely because it became muddled with another concerning the nature of the household. Unilineal systems often, though not invariably, produce households where, for a time, married brothers live together with their parents. It was suggested that there were several reasons why the combination of permanent groups and large, complex households, should encourage fertility. These were summarized by Kingsley Davis:

[17] Marx, *Grundrisse*, 604. [18] Ibid., 605–6. [19] Lorimer, *Culture*, 200, 247.

1 The economic cost of rearing children does not impinge directly on the parents to the same extent as in a 'nuclear' family system.

2 The inconvenience and effort of child care do not fall so heavily on the parents alone.

3 The age at marriage can be quite young, because under joint household conditions there is no necessity for the husband to be able to support his wife and their family independently immediately at marriage – a woman and her children are absorbed by a larger group.[20]

Although attractive, both parts of the argument came under attack. As regards household composition, there is considerable evidence, for instance from India, that fertility in households with a 'nuclear' structure is often higher than that in 'joint' households.[21] A recent study by Ryder tests the hypothesis in Yucatan and supports the growing number of studies which have failed to show any simple correlation between household structure and fertility.[22] Defined in terms of residence, recent work from south India by Montgomery also finds no correlation.[23] The difficulty here is that the counter-evidence comes mainly from census-type data. If the hypothesis were more carefully formulated to contrast not residence, but *operation*, it might have more chance of survival. An Indian village may be filled with groups of brothers and their parents who live apart but who operate social and economic units larger than the nuclear family. In such a situation there may well be a different attitude to fertility than in a system, such as that of the modern west, or small bands of hunters, where the effective unit is husband and wife who are cut off from their kin. The second major attack has been made on the negative side of the argument. It is predicted that, all else being equal, fertility in non-unilineal systems will be lower. Put in this simple form, it is easy to find counter-examples and Nag cites two American tribal groups which he studied with high fertility and in which 'no corporate unilineal descent groups were present'.[24] Yet he admits that 'the traditional ideal in both the tribes is an extended family system based upon patrilocal residence', even though most households at present are

[20] Davis, 'Institutional Patterns', 34–5.
[21] Myrdal, *Asian Drama*, II, 1515; Freedman, 'Human Fertility', 50.
[22] In Kaplan, *Human Fertility*, 93–7.   [23] In Marshall and Polgar, *Culture*, 50–6.
[24] Nag, *Human Fertility*, 69.

nuclear units (as they often are in unilineal systems), and that there are 'bilateral kin groups'. Much of the criticism against Lorimer is now irrelevant in view of the emergence during the 1950s and 1960s of a new contrast which makes a distinction not between unilineal and non-unilineal but between those societies, whether cognatic, agnatic or uterine, where the formation of groups is possible through an ancestor-focused descent system, and those where there are no groups because descent is reckoned from the *ego*.[25] Using this new distinction, the thesis could be reformulated to state that where there are *groups* formed, by whatever principle, fertility will be favoured, whereas where *individuals* are the centre of a web of relations, as in the simplest hunting and gathering bands or the most complex of modern cities, there will be a de-emphasis on fertility. But such a thesis is only one step in the direction of suggesting a new interpretation. We need to complement kinship with economics, particularly ownership of property. In order to do this we must approach the puzzle from a different direction.

On the basis of recent work in historical and comparative demography it is possible to suggest that three models describe the population patterns of most historically recorded societies. These have been analysed in my work on the Gurungs of Nepal.[26] The 'pre-transition phase 1' model postulates perennial and uncontrolled fertility controlled by perennial high mortality, which cancel each other out and keep the population steady. Few societies have conformed to such a model for long periods. More frequently they have fitted into a 'crisis' model, where perennial high and uncontrolled fertility is not counterbalanced by annual high mortality, but periodic crises – war, epidemics, famine – topple the population, which then mounts again. This is characteristic of China, traditional India and much of Europe. The third, 'homeostatic', model is one where fertility is controlled, even in the presence of abundant resources, by social and economic controls, and mortality is not the main factor in preventing population growth. This fits certain animal and human populations and parts of western Europe in the seventeenth to twentieth centuries. When discussing fertility, the first of these models can be amalgamated to form the 'uncontrolled' situation, the third being 'controlled'. For certain purposes, as Matras

[25] Fox, *Kinship*, chs 1, 6.   [26] Macfarlane, *Resources*, 303–10.

has argued,[27] it is useful to break each of these in half in terms of age at marriage, thus:

| | | *Fertility* | |
		Uncontrolled	Controlled
	Early	A	B
Marriage			
	Late	C	D

This makes it possible to compare societies which move from A to C or from A to D. But for the purpose of the present argument, just two models will suffice: the 'uncontrolled' and the 'controlled', whether the means is contraception, abortion or late age at marriage, thus amalgamating Malthus's prudential checks (celibacy, late marriage) and 'vice' (contraception, abortion). In summarizing these models, apart from noting their approximate location and some instances, no attempt was made to explain *why* they occurred in various societies, to what social, economic or ideological facts they were related. In order to proceed with this much harder task we may first look at a few hints offered by others who have attempted to find a solution.

It will be remembered that the answer seems to lie not in the means of production, but in these combined with the relations of production – in other words, as Marx claims, in the whole assemblage of beliefs and practices he labelled 'mode of production'. This is indirectly alluded to by Mamdani, but never directly confronted. In explaining a possible growth of a desire to limit childbearing, he is not content to stop at tractors; something is also happening to the relations of production: a labourer is paid for the work he does, rather than being given a customary amount in bundles of wheat. 'In short, labour is becoming a commodity in Manupur. Feudal relations of work are giving way to capitalist relations of work'. This is an important clue. Another is his statement that the 'fact that the family is the basic unit of work has important social implications'.[28] It also has important demographic implications, but these are not explicitly pursued since it would only have been by comparing India with other countries that Mamdani would have seen that what he took to be the result of a certain type of

---

[27] Quoted in Zubrow, *Anthropology*, 211.   [28] Mamdani, *Myth*, 91, 132.

agriculture, is in fact the result of a certain social structure, or mode of production. This solution is indirectly implied by the common assumption that 'peasants', by whom are meant those who not only live in the country, but organize production in a certain way, have an almost universally pro-natalist attitude. Goode has assumed that fertility is a highly valued attribute in peasant societies;[29] Notestein stated 'peasant societies in Europe, and almost universally throughout the world, are organized in ways that bring strong pressures on their members to reproduce'.[30] Galeski noted that peasant families in Poland were distinguished by a higher birth rate than other groups.[31] At first sight this fits well. If we look at a map of areas of dense population on the earth and a map of the distribution of peasantries the two exactly overlap; India, China, Europe are both. Of course there is still a chicken and egg difficulty, and there may well be tautology, since the word 'peasant' may have built into part of its definition features which necessitate there being a dense population. Yet there is something intriguing and worth pursuing. To do this let us construct two further ideal-type 'modes of production' which seem to coincide quite well with the 'controlled' and 'uncontrolled' fertility models earlier alluded to.

The first can be termed 'peasant' or 'domestic' according to one's fancy. The central feature of this mode is that production and consumption are inextricably bound to the unit of reproduction or family; units of social and economic reproduction are identical. The farm and family are found together as the place where both wealth and children are produced. This central feature of peasantry is described by Thorner as follows:

> Our fifth and final criterion, the most fundamental, is that of the unit of production. In our concept of peasant economy the typical and most representative units of production are the peasant family households. We define a peasant family household as a socio-economic unit which grows crops primarily by the physical efforts of the members of the family.[32]

As Shanin puts it, 'the family is the basic unit of peasant ownership, production, consumption and social life. The individual, the family

---

[29] Goode, *World Revolution*, 111.   [30] Notestein, 'Economic Problems', 15.
[31] Galeski, *Basic Concepts*, 58.
[32] In Shanin, *Peasants*, 205.

and the farm, appear as an indivisible whole . . .'.[33] Or as Chayanov summarised the position: 'The first fundamental characteristic of the farm economy of the peasant is that it is a family economy. Its whole organization is determined by the size and composition of the peasant family and by the coordination of its consumptive demands with the number of its working hands'.[34]

This has nothing, as yet, to do with the nature of the residential household, nor even the kinship system. It is basically the assertion that in many agricultural societies the *basic* or smallest unit of production and consumption is not the individual, but the members of a family, which may merely consist of parents and children, or a larger group. All those born into this minimal group have an equal share and rights in the resources, labour is pooled in the group, the 'estate' is passed on undiminished from generation to generation. In this situation, each new child is an asset, giving his labour and drawing off the communal resource, contributing to the welfare of his parents as they pass their prime, increasing the prestige, political power, as well as the economic well-being of the group. It is this system which Mamdani found even after the introduction of individualistic western law had destroyed much of the original fabric. In this situation family planning appears to go right against the interests of both the group and the individual. The unit of production and the unit of reproduction coincide. To increase production, one increases reproduction; likewise in reverse, as Malthus would argue, if production increases, so will reproduction. As Ryder has perceptively remarked, 'it may be that fertility should be examined in relation to family structure only in so far as family structure is related to control over production and distribution of economic resources'.[35] Where the basic unit of production/consumption is the domestic group, whether co-residential or operationally united in work and consumption, there fertility will be highly valued. It may be against the interests of the state or of family planners, but each small group will try to maximize its size. Fertility will be valued and high, as in traditional China, India, eastern Europe. Until this is realized, attempts to bludgeon unwilling 'peasants' to give up what they perceive to be their economic livelihood are bound to fail. Economics,

---

[33] Shanin, *Peasants*, 241.   [34] Quoted in Wolf, *Peasants*, 14.
[35] In Kaplan, *Human Fertility*, 98.

social structure, politics, ideology and demography have become intertwined; to control fertility is to alter part of a delicate structure which also threatens many other areas.

This hypothetical model only gains significance when we contrast it with another. It might be objected that the argument above merely resuscitates the old contrast between non-industrial/industrial, 'group'/'individual', 'pre-transition'/'post-transition' which has continued over the years. This would be true if all non-industrial societies could be lumped together under the 'domestic' or 'peasant' mode. Fortunately, however, there is an alternative model which is the social and economic correlate of the 'controlled' pattern earlier described.

This alternative we will label as the 'individual' pattern. This model has been less extensively described. The central feature is that the lowest unit of production and consumption is not the family, but the *individual*. There is an enormous stress on the individual as opposed to the group in every respect; the kinship system (as in the 'Eskimo' terminology of many hunting–gathering groups or modern England and North America) is ego-centred; property is not communally owned – there is either no group property at all, as in the simplest hunting bands, or else there are extreme individual property rights; production is not based on the family but on non-familial lines (the capitalist market, feudal ties); the permanent unit of consumption is never larger than husband and wife.

The extreme and ultimate form of such 'possessive individualism' is set out bleakly among the starving Ik, who act as lonely individuals and forage for themselves, pushing their children away from their food, letting their old people die.[36] In a less desperate situation, we see such a society in parts of Europe and America today. Thus the pattern cuts across normal tribal/peasant/industrial boundaries. By focusing on the individual, rather than the family, many demographic features are changed. Instead of a population expanding in quantity, as Malthus had predicted, an increase in the means of subsistence is used to increase the quality of life for the individual. He or she does not see production and reproduction as inextricably connected; sex and childbearing are separate things; women's main role is no longer as a productive and reproductive machine; extra children do not increase the prestige and well-being of a group or even of their parents. In fact,

[36] Turnbull, *Mountain People.*

additional children become a threat to the happiness of their parents, to their mother's health, to their father's peace and pocket, a drain on the individual which is not recompensed by labour invested in a common resource which provides a store for the future. This pattern helps to explain why it is that only societies which have ego-centred systems, which also means, when put in kinship terms, cognatic descent, have taken to fertility control with enthusiasm. It has often been noted that hunting–gathering bands limited their fertility by numerous methods,[37] those societies with cognatic kinship in Asia, broadly in the Tibeto-Burman area, that is Thailand, Burma, Tibet and most conspicuously Japan, have all controlled fertility. China provides an interesting example of a case where, when the 'domestic mode' was abolished with the destruction of the traditional family, one of the most successful family planning campaigns in history may have occurred. One could push the argument further, noting that a tell-tale mark of such societies is the high respect for celibacy in the monastic institutions of Buddhism and Christianity in these two areas. But enough has probably been said to show the lines of the argument. The other major example, of course, is the modern European/North American family system, which is often combined with controlled fertility.

To summarize the argument: in a 'peasant' or 'domestic' mode, fertility increases the well-being of the smallest unit of the society, and particularly of those who will have to do the reproducing, namely the parents. As a Spanish farmer told the poet Laurie Lee: 'Buy land and breed sons and you can't go wrong. Come wars and thieves and ruined harvest – they don't signify at all ... If a man's got strong blood like me, and scatters his seed wide enough, that man must flourish'. Or as a Punjabi water carrier reprimanded Mamdani, mistaking him for the family planner who had visited him years before:

You were trying to convince me in 1960 that I shouldn't have any more sons. Now, you see, I have six sons and two daughters and I sit at home in leisure. They are grown up and they bring me money. One even works outside the village as a labourer. You told me I was a poor man and couldn't support a large family. Now you see, because of my large family, I am a rich man.[38]

[37] Douglas, 'Population Control'.   [38] Mamdani, *Myth*, 109.

To invest in reproduction is to increase production and consumption. The equation is frighteningly simple: peasant/domestic mode of production is connected to high fertility. In reverse, where society is so structured that what holds people together is not kinship but relations of power (feudalism), economics (market capitalism) or merely geographic proximity (hunter–gatherer bands), then children are as much a burden as an asset. The individual has to choose *between* children and other leisure goods, between a child and a mortgage, between a child and geographical mobility, perhaps a child and wealth. Acquisitive individualism, whether among the Ik or the inhabitants of modern western Europe seems intimately connected to the controlled fertility model.

The argument above has suggested as a hypothesis that peasantry =high fertility, individualism=controlled fertility. There are plenty of documented cases of the former, perhaps the best of them being India, on which there is now a very considerable literature. Nearer at hand, there is evidence of a considerable demand for children in much of pre-industrial western Europe. There is, however, a dearth of examples of one particular category of the 'individualist' pattern. The examples that have been examined are at the two extremes of the spectrum, either the very simplest of human groups, the Ik, Hadza, Kung, Netsilik Eskimos, or at the supposedly most complex, modern European, American and Japanese society. We may wonder whether there are middling societies, still predominantly agricultural yet with a state and towns which would make them comparable to the large agrarian civilizations of China and India. It is possible that parts of south-east Asia would fit within this category, but probably the best documented of all examples, which illustrates in practice the mechanisms we have described abstractly, is England between the thirteenth and eighteenth centuries.

THE CASE OF ENGLAND FROM 1200 TO 1750[39]

The majority of historians and sociologists would class England as a society moving from 'peasant' to proto-industrial during this period. For most of the period it is held to be socially a peasantry, similar to

---

[39] For the full documentation of this argument, with references to all the historical sources cited or quoted here, see Macfarlane, *Marriage*, chs 3–7.

other European nations in its structure. If this were true, we would expect, according to our hypothesis, that it should have a high fertility pattern. The features of such a system may be briefly summarized as follows. In our model peasant society the desire to maintain fertility, and hence production and consumption, as high as possible, is expressed in many ways. Marriage is regarded mainly as a way of producing children, rather than for companionship; if a woman is barren she is returned to her home. The woman's status is dependent on the number of children she produces, her main role is as a childbearer. Thus, typically, her sexual capabilities are carefully guarded before marriage and she is married off soon after puberty. In order to ensure the success of the marriage as a reproductive enterprise, however, there may be a period of licensed sexual testing or 'bundling', as it is known in western Europe. Premarital pregnancy is not regarded with horror, if it is by the future husband. All women who are physically capable of doing so, marry, and non-married persons are regarded as socially immature. If a couple do not manage to produce sufficient children of the right sex, they adopt sons and daughters. Sexual intercourse is undertaken largely for the purpose of procreation with one's wife, not for its intrinsic pleasure. Contraception is infrequently used and abortion, infanticide and child abandonment are only very occasionally resorted to. The fertility of the woman is encouraged by means of ritual and magic through puberty rituals, pregnancy rituals, fertility-inducing drugs and ceremonies. There is abundant evidence in people's statements that they want children. No single peasant society would exactly conform to all of this archetype, but most would have many of these features. We would expect England in the five hundred years up to the industrial revolution to exhibit most parts of the pattern if the two premises above are correct, namely that peasantry implies a high stress on fertility and England was 'peasant'.

A superficial reading of early modern sources could be made to yield evidence for the belief that marriage was mainly undertaken for procreation. For instance, the First and Second Prayer Books of Edward VI, still in use, reiterated the old church priorities concerning the 'causes for which Matrimony was ordained': 'one was the procreation of children . . . Secondly it was ordained for a remedy against sin . . . Thirdly, for the mutual society, help and comfort, that the one ought to have of the other.' Pamphleteers also provide some evidence that procreation of heirs was an important motive; those who wrote about women's menstrual disorders claimed that barrenness was 'the greatest misfortune' and churchmen argued that one of the aims of marriage is 'by children and succession, to have his family and name extended'. Osborne in his *Advice to his Son* speaks of those 'that Cry, Give me Children, or else my Name dies'. The astrologers were also frequently questioned about whether a person would have heirs. Yet if we search the most likely source, the rich autobiographical literature of the sixteenth to eighteenth centuries, it is impossible to sustain such an argument. When people wrote down why they decided to marry they gave a variety of reasons. Some did so for companionship and support. John Pym in 1613 'seeing so much wickedness in the world and so much casualty among men, thought good to choose out a companion for me in an honest course and took a wife'. John Milton argued that marriage should be a total relationship, whose main purpose was to control 'defects of loneliness'. It appears that it was emotional and physical attraction, the desire for comfort and companionship, the 'romantic love complex' which pushed most people into marriage in England in this period. This was not a situation where marriages, except among the higher nobility, were arranged between groups of kin in order to consolidate an estate or increase the political and economic power of a kinship group. Such a romantic love ideology is consistent with a view of marriage as a partnership and a pleasure, not with a view of it as mainly a mechanism to obtain legal offspring. There were also economic motives: as Tusser had put it, 'To thrive one must wive'. Yet the interesting point is that the 'thriving' was not thought to come from having children to increase one's labour power, but from the fact that the wife would by her housewifely activities save one from the expense and mischief of servants and lodging. Thus a rector in 1605 was accused of wheedling a betrothal out of a girl by saying that 'I am a sole man, I pay for my diet and lodging at Mistress Widdowson £10 by the year, which I am put to for want of a wife'. When the autobiographer Thomas Wright's first wife died he had a succession of servants: 'One was an incurable drunkard, and proved very expensive to me; the other, the greatest liar and the greatest thief that ever fell under my observation', so that 'I now plainly perceived that I must have a wife, or be ruined'. When a late-sixteenth-century clergyman's wife was in great pain and about to give birth, he listed the difficulties which would ensue if she died; most of these were social and economic, none were to do with reproduction.

First the fear of marrying again, dangerous as 2 marriages are. Want of it in the mean while. Forgoing so fit a companion for religion hoswifery, and other comforts. Loss and decay in substance. Care of household matters cast on me. Neglect of study. Care and looking after children. Forgoing our borders. Fear of losing friendship among her kindred. These are some.

It was recognized that it was the relationship between prospective husband and wife, of an economic, social and erotic nature, that was important and that this relationship would grow with time. This was encapsulated in Francis Bacon's aphorism that 'Wives are young men's mistresses; companions for middle age; and old men's nurses'. It is always impossible to document an *absence*, but in comparison to our ideal-type peasant society the lack of interest in marriage for propagation is very marked indeed. Our predictions do not appear to work.

An indirect indicator of whether marriages are largely undertaken to produce children is the attitude towards unions which lead to no children, to barrenness and infertility. This is taken as an index by demographic anthropologists and there is abundant evidence from many societies from traditional western Ireland, through Africa to New Guinea that childless women are looked on with intense dislike amounting almost to horror, the 'marriage' is dissolved and they are sent home to their family.[40] Usually the woman is blamed for the lack of children, as reported for the Punjab.[41] Childlessness is often a great personal tragedy and humiliation, 'a woman with a large family is highly honoured; a childless wife is an object of pity, often tempered with scorn'.[42] Again a superficial glance at the English evidence might give support for such a view. Astrologers were besieged by clients who wanted to know how to overcome childlessness. Various magical and other cures were advocated for its cure and it was even believed that God had a hand in helping, sending an angel to anoint the genitals of Strafford's father, for instance. Yet again, if we search more deeply, the evidence points in entirely the opposite direction to that for pro-natalist societies. Barrenness or infertility was not one of the recognized grounds at law for either the annulment of marriage (*a vinculo*) or the separation (*a mensa et thoro*) of married

---

[40] Nag, *Human Fertility*, 70.   [41] Mamdani, *Myth*, 140.
[42] Schapera, 'Population Growth', 25.

partners; 'impotence', or the inability by man or woman to perform the sexual act *was* such a ground. Sexual relations were necessary for a true marriage, but not procreation. A woman could not be sent away for this reason, barrenness was no justification for breaking off a marriage. Nor in all the voluminous court material dealing with sexual affairs and marriage in the church and other courts have I ever come across any attempts to separate or annul a marriage on these grounds. Nor is there any evidence that it was held to be shameful; while Elizabethan abusive vocabulary was extremely rich, among the 'whoremaster', 'bugger', 'lewd fellows', 'jackanapes', 'bastard', I have never come across barrenness in any form being used as a term of abuse, nor have I in the very considerable number of slander and libel cases in the ecclesiastical courts heard of people either making jokes, innuendoes, or spreading scandal concerning this topic. Witchcraft beliefs were widespread in this society, but whereas in Scotland and the Continent witches would make men and women sterile, in England this effect of their power is never brought in specific trials. It does not seem to have been something sufficiently serious and mysterious for a witch to have caused. Nor is there any evidence that childless women were particularly victimized or that their status increased with the number of children they had. If this had been deeply felt, we might have expected that a large proportion of the women contemplating suicide and visiting the astrologers would have had this as a reason. But neither in the casebooks, nor in the general discussions of why people attempted to take their own lives, is there any stress on barrenness as a motive. Furthermore, there seems to have been a general recognition that the cause of infertility might as well be in the man's physique as the woman's. There were folk and semi-medical methods of discovering whether a woman or man was the infertile one – a handful of barley in the respective urine was one suggested by Culpepper in the seventeenth century. Sometimes the cause lay in women: 'there are certain women who have the neck of the womb long and hardened . . . [which] . . . renders them incapable of conceiving'; menstruous blood could also be to blame, a woman could have been bled too early, before puberty or have had some accident. But it could also be the result of bad blood on the male's part, or defective genitals, or even because the couple were too similar, of 'one Complexion'. Ultimately, barrenness could be born patiently, for it was sent by God, though it might be caused by more humdrum actions such as over-frequent sexual intercourse, or over-eating. Again it is difficult to document something that is absent, but, with the possible exception of the higher gentry and nobility, it would appear that there was a singularly tolerant attitude towards infertility. As in England today, there were clearly people who were unhappy that they could not have children. But the disaster, shame and ridicule which breaks up marriages and demeans women seem to have been conspicuously absent. Again England fails to fulfil the prediction.

The dishonour of sterility, especially for women, is closely associated with the general role of women in society. In our archetypal peasant society they are, above all, producers of children; that is their major role, from which prestige for them and wealth for their kin flows. This is so widely documented in the anthropological literature that we need only refer to three examples: in traditional Ireland, we are told that their main function was to provide children and it was by this that they were judged; in nineteenth-century France they were regarded by many as 'une machine a enfantement'; in Africa they are often mainly looked on as reproductive assets.[43] They were not primarily valued for their intelligence, independence, physical attractiveness. Looked at from the legal and social angle, their status when regarded as baby-creating machines is often extremely low, their role limited. We might therefore expect to find women's roles defined in terms of childbearing and their status very low in pre-industrial England. Yet the expectation is again thwarted. Contemporaries were not wrong when they described England as a 'Paradise for married women'. As compared with other agrarian societies, their jural, economic and social position was amazingly high. And there is no evidence that any of this was related to their reproductive capacities. Their position before the law and economically was highest when they were unmarried and by definition had no children; their power within marriage did not increase in any obvious way with the birth of children. The marriage was not cemented by childbirth. Nowhere is there evidence that their status, prestige or power was enhanced by their reproductive performance. Again, a negative finding is impossible to prove. But nowhere in the very considerable literature and law of the period is there strong evidence

---

[43] Arensberg, *Irish Countryman*, 89; Shorter, *Modern Family*, 77; Lorimer, *Culture*, 370.

that a married woman with a large family was treated as superior to one with few or even no children. The idea present in some societies that a woman is incomplete until she has a child, sometimes expressed in the view that she is without a soul until she gives birth, is nowhere to be found. Women are full, complete persons without children and they seem, for many centuries to have had many roles and outlets – economic, social and religious – which were independent of their reproductive ability. The poetry addressed to them extolled their beauty, their wit, their elegance; it did not praise their childbearing hips, large suckling breasts or fertile womb. The plays of the seventeenth century saw women as dominant, scheming, independent – not as childbearing appendages of men, whose prestige increased with every child.

A further feature of the ideal pattern is the protection of women's 'honour' or virginity before marriage. Their wombs will be their husband's or husband's kin's joy, and therefore their sexuality should not be tampered with. This varies in emphasis and expression across societies. In traditional India it took the form that a Hindu father ought to marry off his daughter as soon as she menstruated; a nubile unmarried daughter was a threat and an invitation and her honour and that of the family should not be put in jeopardy. In the Mediterranean area it took the form of the 'honour and shame' complex where a girl was carefully watched by her family, where her brothers and kin would avenge any dishonour to their sister. The ultimate test of the virginity and wholeness of the bride, whose full potential childbearing ability was reserved for her husband, was the viewing of the blood-bespattered nuptial sheets which would show that the hymen had been broken for the first time. Among the Greek Sarakatsani shepherds, we are told, virginity almost provokes a sense of awe, there is a very heavy emphasis on the girl's virginity before marriage and in a Turkish village, a girl is inspected before marriage in order to see if her hymen is intact.[44] In Yorubaland, where fertility is very highly valued, there is also the custom of the virginity sheet.[45] We might expect some similar institution in England, especially as a work translated into the language in the early sixteenth century, and describing contemporary Germany, gives enormous praise to those

[44] Campbell, *Honour*, 100–1, 178, 278; Stirling, *Turkish Village*, 184.
[45] Marshall and Polgar, *Culture*, 130.

who retain their virginity and stresses the social pressure against those
who fail. Again there are a few preliminary hints of a mild interest in the
topic: there are lamentations over the untimely loss of virginity, people
went to astrologers to ask 'whether she has her maidenhead or no',
others dreamed that they were feeling women to see if they were still
virgins. Yet the weight of the evidence again forces us towards a
different conclusion. It seems certain that if the bridal sheet institution
had been present, some trace of it would have been left in
autobiography or literature. There is no such trace. I have nowhere
seen even an oblique reference to it. This appears to have been evident
to contemporaries. Mrs Sharp in her Midwives Book of the later
seventeenth century had heard about the showing of the bloody sheet
as a sign of virginity as a custom of certain African tribes described by
Leo Africanus. But she not only failed to link it to anything similar in
England, but doubted whether it was much of a test in any case: 'the
sign of bleeding perhaps is not so generally sure; it is not so much in
maids that are elderly, as when they are very young; bleeding is an
undoubted token of Virginity: But young Wenches (that are lascivious)
may lose this, by unchaste actions, though they never knew man'.

I have come across no reference in the ecclesiastical courts to a man
trying to break off a marriage or gain some kind of compensation
because his wife was not a virgin. There is little evidence, in fact, that
the family or kin were greatly interested in the subject. The detailed
analysis of pre-marital sexual behaviour which it is possible to make
from contemporary sources suggests that many parents shielded and
protected and supported their incontinent children and that it was the
church courts and village officers who tried to prevent the offence.
Nowhere have I come across a man being attacked physically for
deflowering a virgin or threatening the honour of her brothers and
parents. The chastity belt, of which drawings and examples from the
period can be seen, seems to have been something which prevailed in
Spain, Italy and Germany, but never to have been used in England.
There was freedom and unchaperoned contact between the sexes in
the long period between puberty and marriage and that does not fit well
with an 'honour and shame', high-fertility, structure.

Yet there is another institution which appears to be diametrically
opposed to the bridal sheet and chastity belt; that is the pre-marital
testing of the woman's fertility or custom of 'bundling'. In order to
ensure that the wife is fecund, there is in a number of societies an

institution whereby a couple who are known to have serious intentions of marriage are allowed, even put under pressure, to cohabit sexually. If the woman becomes pregnant, they marry, if the 'test' fails, they do not. This has been noted, for example, as an index of a high desire for children in Africa.[46] The custom seems to have been present in several parts of pre-industrial Europe, in fact, possibly in all those areas where its logical opposite, the virginity sheet, was absent. Thus we find it widely reported for parts of Scandinavia, for France, and in Scotland where, in the Outer Isles, for example, there was a trial 'marriage' for a year.[47] If no child was conceived, the relationship was broken off. If we turn to England, at first sight there appears to be an institution which fits well with this. In the period after a formal betrothal, popular opinion and even the authorities often allowed the couple to cohabit. There is very considerable evidence concerning this.[48] Yet on closer examination this institution was not a form of fertility testing, but the reverse. Once the young people were betrothed, and particularly if the betrothal was cemented by sexual intercourse, they were in the eyes of the church married: to break off a betrothal was as difficult as to terminate a marriage; it could only be done on a limited range of grounds. The young couple must marry, whether the wife became pregnant or not. Preferably this marriage should take place within a couple of months, when, in any case, it would be difficult to tell whether the wife was with child. Nowhere in the extensive descriptions of premarital intercourse or the cases brought by disappointed lovers whose betrothal had been broken off have I come across a single instance where the reason given for terminating the relationship was infertility. Betrothal was merely the first stage of a process which led to a full and indissoluble union. Another superficial argument might seem to support the 'fertility-testing' hypothesis. There was considerable sexual freedom allowed between the sexes throughout the period, including heavy petting. They were allowed to spend days and even nights kissing and cuddling. The descriptions of courtship in the diary of Roger Low and autobiography of Thomas Wright show young couples spending evenings and nights in long discussions and in physical contact. It is

[46] Southall, *Social Change*, 311.
[47] Shorter, *Modern Family*, 102–3; Goody, *Production*, 44.
[48] Laslett, *Lost World*, 138–54.

easy to mistake this for a form of institutionalized 'bundling', especially as the superficial descriptions look rather similar. Yet in England there is no evidence that what the young couple were trying to do was find out if the girl would be able to bear children. In fact, when she became pregnant, the man would often abscond. Nor is there any evidence that the parents were interested in finding out that the wife would be able to bear children. Those seventeenth-century historians who have considered the question most extensively from the local evidence are agreed that bundling was absent in England during this period.[49] Young men were never advised in the books of advice which were popular at the time, or in any other literature, to test their spouse's fertility. Nor did those like Stubbes who so fiercely anatomized the failings of their countrymen ever suggest that one of the reasons for the all-too-prevalent vice, the 'whordom' which had 'now become a play, a pastime, a sport' was even partly a desire to make sure that a marriage would not be barren. It seems to have been sexual gratification, companionship and 'romantic love' and other motives which impelled many people to live together or have sexual relations before marriage, not a desire to find out if the wife would be fertile.

Where the aim is to increase the store of children, an obvious strategy is to commence sexual relations as early as possible, particularly in the case of women. In most human populations with the 'uncontrolled' pattern, therefore, women have entered sexual union at, or soon after, puberty and started to produce children in their late teens as the effect of the 'reduced fertility' post-menarche period wears off. As female reproduction usually tails off in the late thirties, this gives them an effective reproduction span of some 20 years in which to produce up to ten offspring at two-yearly intervals. This is the pattern in most agricultural societies, notably much of traditional India and China and eastern Europe, as well as most of tribal Africa. If the aim had been to push fertility to its maximum, then we would have expected a similar pattern in England and Europe. During the last 15 years it has become increasingly obvious that this was not the case.

The work of Hajnal and others has shown that in parts of north-western Europe and particularly in England, from at least the early sixteenth century, girls did not have this 20-year span. The mean age of women at marriage and consequently first childbearing

[49] Laslett, *Family Life*, 110.

fluctuated in England at between 25 and 30 in many parts of the country from the sixteenth century to the mid-eighteenth century.[50] In effect this would cut the reproductive period by between one-third and two-thirds, which would have an enormous effect on completed fertility. Furthermore, long-term population growth would be slowed down very considerably since the average gap between one generation and the next would be lengthened from about 18 to 28 years. Although it would be facile to believe that people 'design' an institution like the age of marriage specifically to limit fertility, thus confusing its function with the ends of the actors involved, it is clear that where such an institution does exist it is difficult to see how a very obsessive desire for large families could co-exist. If girls can remain single and childless until their late twenties, it is difficult to believe that there were strong pressures towards high fertility.

Not only is it normal in human societies for women to be married soon after puberty, but maximum reproduction is encouraged by making sure that all women (and most men) who are not physically or mentally deformed in some way become married. This can be shown by statistical evidence from societies where 'universal' marriage is reported, and also from the attitude to those who do not marry in most non-western societies. Particularly for women, marriage is not a matter of choice, or chance, it is a life-cycle stage, as inevitable as puberty or death. When we turn to England and parts of north-western Europe, Hajnal has again shown that the high-fertility expectation does not work. There is now considerable evidence that in the period between the sixteenth and eighteenth centuries there were a large number of unmarried and never-married persons of both sexes. The demographer Petty noted that as a combination of the late age at marriage and high proportion never marrying, 'of 100 capable women only 32 are married, and these 32 brought 11 children p.a.' It is clear that the early-twentieth century proportion of 15 per cent of women single at the age of 45–9 was, if anything, exceeded in the sixteenth and seventeenth centuries. There were also very many elderly bachelors. This pattern was contrasted with that of neighbouring Celtic societies where marriage was almost universal, as Arthur Young noted in the eighteenth century. The statistical situation is correlated with a remarkable tolerance towards non-married persons. Unmarried

[50] Hajnal, 'European Marriage'.

women were of equal status and position in private law to men. There is no evidence that it was believed to be physically or mentally dangerous never to marry. There is very little evidence of unmarried persons being ridiculed or condemned in the diaries and letters of the time. It was marriage, not the single life, which was the subject of ridicule in the plays and poetry of the period.

Elsewhere I have presented evidence to show that on a number of other indices England clearly fails to fit the predictions we made for a 'peasant' society.[51] It is argued that there was a high valuation of celibacy and marriage was regarded as a sometimes inferior option. People were only put under mild pressure to marry. Furthermore, the whole sexual ethics of the period were conducive to controlled fertility. Sexual relations were considered as an end in themselves, not merely a means to childbearing. Women were not seen as passive sexual objects upon whom children were engendered, but as equal partners in a pleasurable activity. The treatment of women in pregnancy and after childbirth also suggests greater concern for sexual pleasure than procreation, indeed pregnancy was even looked on as almost an unfortunate disease. After childbirth there were no attempts to protect the young infant by taboos on intercourse. Another index of the desire for children, the adoption of children, also indicates a negative attitude. Indeed, adoption was legally impossible in England up to the nineteenth century and few cases of even quasi-adoption can be found. With this negative attitude, it is not surprising that recent historical demographic work should suggest that at least in the seventeenth century, in some parishes, some effective form of birth control was practised, and there is considerable evidence of abortion and infanticide.[52] All these findings suggest a marked lack of emphasis on having children; none of them fit the predictions of the peasant model. One final index may be examined briefly to establish the argument.

If there had been a pro-natalist attitude in the society, similar to that in many non-industrial societies, the great anxiety to increase the number of births should have been echoed in art and literature as well as in biographical and other sources. I have collected a very

[51] Macfarlane, *Marriage.*
[52] Wrigley, 'Family Limitation', though Wrigley is now less convinced that family limitation was practised.

considerable amount of information which again goes flatly against such an interpretation; from diaries, autobiographies and many other sources it becomes clear that people, on the whole, were quite happy to have one or two children, but after that they became a burden and a nuisance. Even their motives for those one or two are curious. If we bear in mind that such children are a social, economic and often ritual necessity in most agrarian societies, we may look at the reasons given by Culpepper in the middle of the seventeenth century to explain why 'all Men and Women desire Children'. The first reason is very abstract: 'they are blessings of God, and so saints desire them' but Culpepper then immediately admits that only 1/100 at the most are moved by this as an important cause. Secondly, 'because they are pretty things to play withall, like desiring to play with his like', in other words they are a source of emotional gratification, or, in the crude theory of modern demographic enquiry, a consumer good, to be compared in pleasure-giving to other goods, for example, pets. But Culpepper thinks that the main reason why people desire children is 'most probably, Lust [which] is the cause of begetting more Children' than the other reasons. Of course, looked at from this point of view, children are the *price* one pays for sex; sex is not to produce children, but for itself; pleasure always has its cost, and children are the by-product in this case. This view, so extraordinary for people in the many societies which see things the other way round, sex as the means, children the ends, is an essential prerequisite for widespread birth control. It is also curious to notice a complete absence of two strong motives which might have been mentioned by Culpepper. Parents do not desire children to increase or maintain their family line; nor do they desire them as an economic support, their labour for middle age and support in old age. In fact they were often looked at as an economic disaster. Francis Quarles wrote:

Seest thou the fruitful womb? how every year it moves the Cradle; to thy slender chear Invites another guest, and makes thee Father to a new son, who now, perchance, had'st rather bring up the old, esteeming propagation a thankless work of superrogation . . . Perchance thou grumblest, counting it a curse unto thy faint estate, which is not able to increase the bounty of thy slender table; poor miserable man what e'er thou be.

This is a view diametrically opposed to the quotations concerning the Punjabi peasants with whom we started, and there is plenty of evidence that it is not merely a view ascribed to the 'peasants' by an intellectual. It is an attitude which could easily lead to the condemnation of reproduction as wasteful, to the sarcasm of a late-seventeenth-century diarist who wrote that 'The Clergy . . . begin to look plump, and get children without mercy: as if they had nothing else to follow but the Catholic cause of generation'.

THE THESIS RE-EXAMINED

The preliminary equation of 'peasantry' with 'uncontrolled fertility' appears to be totally incorrect for England. Here is a society which historians and anthropologists are fully agreed was 'peasant' in every sense until the seventeenth century, yet which, on every index we use is, in terms of fertility, diametrically opposed to what we would expect. It is a classic 'controlled' fertility society, the best example we have for a 'middle-range society' lying between the two better-documented extremes of post-industrial or early hunter–gatherer societies. The hypothesis appears to be disproved. But before abandoning it, we may look briefly at the other end of the equation which has been left unexamined. Was England, as the conventional wisdom assumes, broadly a peasant society between the thirteenth and eighteenth centuries? Was it truly based on the 'domestic mode of production', on the identification of farm and family, similar in its structure to the peasantries of India, eastern Europe, traditional China? I have examined this question at some length elsewhere.[53] There I have maintained that England has never, at least from the time when detailed records begin in the mid-thirteenth century, been a 'peasant' society in the sense defined earlier in this essay. Its kinship system and property law, its basic social structure and ideology have always been much closer to an individualistic system. Why this should have been the case, we do not yet know. But this sets it off in many respects from other 'peasant' societies, whether in the Celtic fringe, continental Europe; eastern Europe or Asia and Africa. This difference was not a product of the spread of market capitalism or protestantism in sixteenth-century Europe; it is much older. If I am right in this argument it turns what looks like a complete refutation of the original hypothesis into one of the strongest confirmations of it. The singularly

[53] Macfarlane, *Individualism*.

controlled attitude towards fertility fits well with an economic and social system which is ultimately based on the individual and no larger group. Parents do not recoup what they invest in their children, nor is there any larger kinship 'line' or 'group' which is embellished by having children. When considering the 'cost' of rearing children, it is insufficient to look merely at what is spent. We have to look at what is returned by the children. It is here that we find that a combination of kinship and economics in pre-industrial England meant that parents could not hope to recoup *anything* from their children – not even much love and affection. The analogy for English children is the domestic pet, kept mainly because it is 'a pretty thing to play with', but not something which will last a lifetime or which will contribute its labour to the family enterprise or provide support in old age. Max Weber singled out as one of the two essential prerequisites of modern capitalism 'the separation of business from the household, which completely dominates modern economic life . . . our legal separation of corporate from personal property.'[54] This is also, it would seem, one of the prerequisites for the success of birth control; where ownership is in some form of corporation, a 'household' or a 'lineage' for example, it is in the interests of parents to increase reproduction and thereby production and consumption. Where the individual is alone and 'free', then children do not provide the means to affluence or social prestige, but must be chosen as one among a set of paths, others of which may be more efficient. The 'mortgage *or* the child' system is not the product of the rootlessness of post-industrial society. We can push it back well beyond that.

What we have tried to do is to show that there does seem to be a close association between reproduction and the mode of production, in Marx's sense. This does not have much to do with technology; English plough culture was not very different from that on the continent at the same time. Nor is it very subject to rapid changes. The basic non-peasant 'individualistic' social and economic system seems to be present the moment the documents for its observation emerge; in other words, in the thirteenth century, and it continues to this day. The Black Death, the Civil War and the Industrial Revolution have not shaken the patterns altogether. Of course, this hypothesis only suggests a host of other questions – where did the English pattern originate? why was

---

[54] Weber, *Protestant Ethic*, 21–2.

England so different? It should also be said that the final version of the thesis will need numerous qualifications: there were always sectors, groups, strata in a large and complex society such as England over five centuries which do not fit. The nobility and upper-middle class, for example, may have conformed to a different pattern. But before we descend to exceptions, it is helpful to have the rule. We will also need to explore the implications for current family planning programmes. It is clear that technology is not at the root of the matter, but kinship and social and economic relations. Those who wish birth control to work now know that it is not enough to provide techniques, there must be a strongly felt desire to limit a family. The thesis outlined above suggests that such a desire is unlikely unless the connection between reproduction and production is carefully disentangled. As long as reproduction is believed to increase production and consumption people will not willingly control their fertility.

3
Violence

Peasants and Bandits

H ISTORIANS ARE in some disagreement as to the levels and nature
of violence in England during the fifteenth to eighteenth
centuries. On the one hand there are those like Professor Beattie who
believe that the criminal system in England 'worked reasonably well
in the rural and small-scale communities in which most Englishmen
lived' up to the 1780s. As a result 'serious crime was rare, and
informal controls in conjunction with the threat of the royal courts
served sufficiently to restrain more minor offenders'.[1] Many historians of the subject do not see a dramatic or revolutionary break in the
amount, nature, or treatment of physical violence in England during
the sixteenth to eighteenth centuries. There is, however, another
powerful school of thought, which has grown since the 1930s, which
argues that the supposed transition from 'feudalism', or 'peasantry' to
'capitalism' or 'individualism' was reflected in massive changes in the
dimensions and nature of violence.

The survey of the works of some leading social historians showed
that a number of them believe that before the eighteenth century
England was inhabited by people who were intrinsically more brutal,
'savage', less controlled than we are.[2] We are presented with a picture
of the sixteenth and seventeenth centuries as a time of violent
upsurge, with high crime rates, physical brutality, a breakdown of law
and order. This is alleged by this school to be the by-product of two
features. First, there was the endemic brutality of a population
ground down by poverty, perennial sickness and high mortality. This
was exacerbated by the penetration of a new mode of production,

[1] Beattie, *Crime*, 624.   [2] See Macfarlane, *Justice*, ch. 1.

capitalism, which destroyed the old community controls and undermined the moral order of a pre-capitalist society. The model of a revolutionary transition from one mode of production to another has led a number of historians to expect heightened violence, and they have apparently found it. The purpose of this brief essay is to test this prediction.

In assessing the nature and dimensions of violence in England in the early modern period it is useful to make explicit the comparative framework. When one talks of a society as being 'violent' or 'non-violent', with what is it being compared? The procedure of some historians seems to be to compare it with their own, often unexamined, impression of their own society. It would seem important to supplement this by comparing a basically agrarian society such as England up to 1780 with other agrarian civilizations. The choice of comparative cases is not easy. There are thousands of nations and societies in the world and we could select almost any of them at almost any point in their history. For purposes of comparison I chose four areas of study. One was in late seventeenth-century China, analysed by Jonathan Spence; a second was eighteenth- and nineteenth-century France, described by Le Goff and Sutherland, Olwen Hufton and Eugene Weber; a third was nineteenth- and twentieth-century Sicily investigated by Anton Blok; and a fourth example is the general study of bandits by E.J. Hobsbawm.[3] A detailed survey of these accounts suggests some of the dimensions of violence to be found in societies that were either broadly 'peasant' or going through the transition from 'peasant' to 'modern'. While it would not be accurate or fair to leave the impression that 'pre-modern' societies are universally characterized by the often extreme violence documented in these studies, the accounts do suggest some of the features we might look out for in England in the sixteenth to eighteenth centuries. We might expect to find bandits, something akin to *mafiosi*, youth gangs, family feuds and vendettas, a high level of physical violence but low level of theft, wandering bands of vagrant beggars and a prevalent atmosphere of fear and distrust.

We may start by looking at some of the many sources for sixteenth- and seventeenth-century England in order to see how far they suggest

[3] Spence, *Woman Wang;* Le Goff and Sutherland, 'Britanny'; Hufton, 'Languedoc'; Weber, *Peasants;* Blok, *Mafia;* Hobsbawm, *Bandits.*

either the violence of certain 'peasant' societies, or that heightened
violence which occurs when such peasantries are being destroyed
and a modern capitalist society is emerging. One impression is given
by those who travelled through the country in the late sixteenth and
seventeenth centuries. The overwhelming impression from their
tours is of an orderly, controlled and non-violent society.[4] Even
those, like 'Drunken Barnabee', who specialized in frequenting the
most likely scenes of aggression – the pubs – noted scarcely any
physical or verbal violence.[5] They often travelled alone and over
long distances, sometimes through the supposedly wild north. Yet
they were curiously blind to the facts which some modern historians
have discovered about their society. Those who wrote autobiographies and diaries during the period also show an almost complete
ignorance of the violence that soaked their world, whether in the city
like Pepys, or in a country village like Josselin, whether at the level
of the gentry like Thomas Whythorne, or that of the apprentice like
Roger Lowe or the journeyman tailor Wheatcroft. The very strong
impression these autobiographical works give is of a society in which
people were not moved by irrational anger and fury, where people
did not live or travel in fear, where despite physical hardships there
was a great deal of tenderness and affection.[6]

   It might be argued that the picture of brutal and violent peasant
life up to the eighteenth century is not totally discredited by
evidence from travellers' and autobiographical accounts. It is just
conceivable that being educated, literate and of the high culture,
such writers omitted this dimension. To gather material more
strictly comparable to that of the French, Chinese and Sicilian
studies we need to use detailed village studies and legal records. We
may start by looking at the impression of pre-eighteenth-century life
from just such village studies.

   Old-style local histories of particular parishes or lordships tend to
portray sophisticated, highly regulated and property-conscious

---

[4] For example, Moryson, *Itinerary;* Machell, *Antiquary,* written mainly in 1692;
Morris, *Celia Fiennes,* compiled mainly in 1702.
[5] *Barnabee's Journal* (7th ed., 1818), originally published in the first half of the
seventeenth century, and probably written by the Kendal Justice of the Peace,
Richard Braithwait, who took the nickname 'Drunken Barnabee'.
[6] Latham and Matthews, *Diary;* Macfarlane, *Ralph Josselin;* Osborn, *Thomas
Wythorne;* Sachse, *Roger Lowe;* Kerry, 'Leonard Wheatcroft'.

societies with little violence.[7] Thus, writing of Hawkshead in north Lancashire, H. S. Cowper concluded that 'crime of any sort was rare, as it is now, through all the dales of Cumberland, Westmorland, and Furness ... Little acts of meanness and petty theft were hardly known'.[8] More recently, the new studies of the economy and society in particular parishes also give an impression of little physical violence.[9] Certainly the villages are described as going through great economic change, rising problems of poverty, and religious divisions. But while the poor are present, criminals, deviants, brigands and feuds are almost totally absent. This could be accounted for by the nature of the local documents used by these historians. Land records, wills, parish registers and other documents usually show a highly intricate, continuous and effective governmental machine and a great deal of control and organization. Thus, as one of the greatest local historians, J. Horsfall Turner, wrote after printing numerous records for the Halifax area, 'the reader may be struck with one thing, the glamour of romance and unreality has to give place to a matter-of-fact life very little different from that of the public life of to-day'.[10] In fact, we will only find the added dimension of violence if we use legal records, as a number of historians have recently done.

F. West studied the Lincolnshire village of Wrangle for the period 1603–37. He used the Quarter Sessions records, yet even so he came to the conclusion that 'a study of the cases at the sessions gives the impression that not only Wrangle, but Holland as a whole, was remarkably free of serious crime'.[11] What is even more surprising is the very small amount of petty crime that is presented, an absence which West puts down to the inefficiency of the petty constables. This 'dark figure' of real but undetected or unpresented crime is a perennial problem for the historian of violence, and it is one to which we shall return later. If we turn to other specific studies of crime and violence at the village level, they also fail to confirm the general expectations concerning a blood-spilling society. In a recent study of crime in Elizabethan Essex, J. Walker discovered that 'there were

---

[7] For examples of this genre, Millican, *History;* Rennell, *Valley.*
[8] Cowper, *Hawkshead,* 199, 224.
[9] Two notable examples of this approach are Hoskins, *Midland Peasant* and Spufford, *Contrasting Communities.*
[10] Horfall Turner, *History,* 238.   [11] West, *Wrangle,* 25.

only a handful of parishes which experience a felony as frequently as once a year, while there were more than 25 parishes with no record of felonies during the whole 45 years of Elizabeth's reign'.[12] In his study of the Essex parish of Kelvedon, J. A. Sharpe examined a population of roughly 500 persons over the period 1600–40. He found 24 cases of theft, burglary and breaking and entering, but in terms of violent physical assaults, there was only one case of manslaughter and two of infanticide (one of them by a girl in a neighbouring village).[13] A study of the parish of Earls Colne in Essex over the longer period 1560–1750, using all types of local and criminal records, gives some suggestion of the amount of violent assault within a population of very roughly 800 persons over nearly two centuries. One woman was hanged for killing her child in 1608, another woman was acquitted on the charge of poisoning her husband in 1626, a man was branded for killing his stepson in 1667 and the following year a man was found guilty of homicide and was transported. The acquitted woman subsequently married again. The branded man four years later signed a petition as one of the chief inhabitants of Earls Colne, asking for a schoolmaster, and the transported felon later returned to live in the village.[14] Since it is difficult to conceal a dead body, these probably constitute most of the cases of homicide. In the nearby parish of Terling, with a population of roughly half the size, over the 140 years from 1560 to 1699, there was one reported infanticide by a mentally unstable woman and one reported homicide.[15] No comparable study of an English village over the last one or two centuries has been undertaken, but it is difficult to envisage that the number of cases would be much lower.

The fact that detailed village studies fail to confirm widespread violence could be explained away, partly through the distortion created by failures to detect violence and crime, partly through the destruction of records. There are various ways we might hope to get round these problems, one of them being to use other sources which give an insight into what went on outside the official records. The account books and notebooks of petty law-enforcement officers, constables, High

[12] Walker, *Crime,* 47. (I am grateful to Mr Walker for permission to quote from his thesis).
[13] In Cockburn, *Crime,* 100, 109.
[14] The sources and methodology of this study are described in Macfarlane, *Reconstructing.*
[15] Wrightson and Levine, *Terling,* 116–17.

Constables and bailiffs are one such source, but again, in the few examples I have seen, they are strangely negative.[16] For instance, Arthur Raistrick has summarized the contents of an account book kept by Richard Wigglesworth in the 1690s in the honour of Skipton in Yorkshire. Wigglesworth acted as constable, churchwarden, pinder in charge of the village pound, bylawman and overseer of the poor. There are plenty of records of the detaining of stray animals, of the loading and transporting of poor vagrants, of the carrying out of local by-laws. Given all these law-enforcement activities, we would have expected that in this remote and wild area there would have been a good deal of opposition to his activities. Raistrick concludes, however, that 'in the years when he has served as constable his duties varied, but the area was peaceful, so his journal has no record of violence or theft'.[17]

Another promising source would be contemporary accounts of village life. The best of these is the famous description of the Shropshire parish of Myddle, written in 1700 by Richard Gough.[18] It is based on Gough's experience of life in the parish back to the first half of the seventeenth century. The extraordinary value of this account has been increased by a detailed local study by David Hey, which puts this account into the context of other records. Myddle was a parish of small pastoral farmers and tenants, with a population of about 600 persons. It is ideally situated for the study of past violence, for several reasons. It was only a few miles from the Welsh border, and hence on the margins of English society. Furthermore, a number of contemporaries in the seventeenth century stressed that of all of England, the woodland areas like Myddle were the most 'idle and lawless'. And Gough is a perfect chronicler, for, as Hey remarks, he was 'attracted by the sensational'.[19] Over a 50-year period, from memory and experience, Gough did indeed find violent incidents. He reported a homicide with a peat spade and a murder of an infant, as well as the attempts of several women who were 'weary of their husbands' to poison them.[20] He also mentions some suicides and a certain amount of theft, a good deal of it petty, and cases of bastardy and drunkenness. But the major and almost sole instance of

---

[16] An example is France, 'Register'.   [17] Raistrick, *Yorkshire*, 62–71.
[18] Gough, *Myddle*.
[19] Hey, *Myddle*, 224, 188.   [20]Gough, *Myddle*, 30, 72, 91.

physically violent behaviour apart from this was in the case of a man called William Tyler, who was a considerable trouble to the village. He resisted arrest, but was finally taken to gaol. Despite various serious crimes, he was released. During these 60 years, two persons from the community were sentenced to death, according to Gough – a thief and a murderer. Hey comments that 'vicious crime' was 'unusual'. Indeed, Hey's impression is that, although there were some notorious individuals and families, on the whole 'the crime rate seems to have been lower, and the moral code more strictly observed, than is the case in much of the England of today'.[21] Obviously such a statement, to be proven, would require not only that the criminal records for Myddle should have survived and been analysed, but also that they should be carefully compared with those for the present. Nevertheless, it is an interesting impression, which tends once again to fit badly with our expectations. In fact, standing back from Gough's account, it is the absences which are most interesting: witchcraft, feuds and factions, highway robbers, mob violence and sadism are nowhere to be seen. There is very little recorded interpersonal violence, and there is a great deal of counter-evidence in his work of warmth, humour, tolerance and kindliness, love and affection, both within the family and between neighbours.

In order to give the 'violent past' thesis every benefit of the doubt I have analysed a rather unusual set of documents. First, I have taken those records most likely to give evidence of violence, the indictments and depositions of the criminal courts, and the notebooks and papers of the Justices of the Peace. These materials, combined with local records, allow us to go beyond the more outward appearances, the gross number of cases, down to the intimate level of how violence was manifested, controlled and contained in seventeenth-century England. They enable us, furthermore, to see how violence was perceived and the degree to which it permeated thought and action.

Secondly, I have taken documents from that area of England which was thought to be among the wildest and most violent, namely Cumbria on the Scottish border. Poorer, more remote, with effective hiding places in the hills and moors for criminals, with a convenient border to slip across, if there were to be feuds, bandits and open violence anywhere, it would be here in the pastoral uplands of what used to be

[21] Hey, *Myddle*, 225, 224.

called Westmorland and Cumberland. Thirdly, I have taken a period of particular upheaval, the 1680s. The supposed Popish Plot of 1679 was succeeded by many other threatened risings, culminating in Monmouth's rebellion and the final expulsion of James II. The political uncertainties of a divided ruling class were exacerbated by the terrible weather and dearths of the 1680s in this region.

Finally, I have taken a set of events which, even within the records of the northern Assizes, were exceptional. They concerned the activities of a loose association of coin-clippers, highwaymen, thieves and others. There are few instances of other events as serious during the later seventeenth century in this area. We may wonder what impressions we obtain from the intensive analysis of this extended case-study of criminal violence in and around the northern parish of Kirkby Lonsdale in the 1680s.[22] How do the patterns of violence compare to those for selected peasantries elsewhere in the world? What does the behaviour of the Smorthwait brothers, Edward Bainbridge and their accomplices, and the reactions to this behaviour of the prosecuting Justice of the Peace Sir Daniel Fleming and other local inhabitants show us? What is revealed about the style and level of violence in the later seventeenth century, on the eve of the urban and industrial revolutions?

The nature of the crimes for which inhabitants of northern England were prosecuted is in striking contrast to that recorded for the other peasantries we have cited. Elsewhere, the major offences were physical assaults, often homicides, and included sexual assaults and attacks on children. These types of crime are almost totally absent for Westmorland. We encounter less than half a dozen persons suspected of murder or homicide during the 50 years 1650–99 for the county. Of really serious and brutal assaults involving the loss of limbs or serious injuries, there are very few indeed. Even the Smorthwaits and their associates do not kill or maim; in their worst attack they left a man unable to walk for three weeks, but normally they just pricked their victims on ears or nose. A comparison of Blok's figures for homicides in Sicily with those of Westmorland shows an entirely different world.

Nor is there much evidence of the other major offences mentioned in the studies of peasantries, namely rape, arson and large-scale cattle rustling. There are no documented cases of any of these for Kirkby

---

[22] For a fuller account of the events, see Macfarlane, *Justice*, chs 1–10.

Lonsdale in the hundred years after 1650, and scarcely a case for the whole of Westmorland in the surviving records for 1650–99. Though the Bainbridge brothers threatened to set their neighbours' houses on fire, there are no records of attacks on the haystacks or outbuildings of a hated landlord. There are no recorded assaults on young children, apart from the occasional murder of a new-born bastard child. I have not come across a single prosecuted rape for Westmorland for this period and there is not even a hint of sexual violence in the Smorthwait affair. Nor is it possible to classify the odd thefts of a single sheep, cow or horse as cattle or sheep-rustling, which involves the driving away of whole herds or flocks of animals, as described for Sicily. The 'peasant' crimes are very weakly represented.

On the other hand, what might be termed 'capitalist crimes', those to do with money and private property, are more numerous. The most obvious of these is counterfeiting coins – an offence which is not mentioned for any of the money-scarce peasant economies in our sample studies, but is of central importance in England. It presupposes a very widespread use of and demand for coinage at the lowest levels. Secondly, the various forms of theft of property were very common. This was not just a matter of stealing food or the odd handkerchief, as described for France, but premeditated theft, intended to obtain money or valuable goods which could be sold. Burglaries and highway robberies were planned to bring in hundreds of pounds, even though the robbers were often misinformed, and there were considerable sums of money, in cash, or bills and bonds, to be had. Theft, a characteristically 'bourgeois' or capitalist crime, has been the central and most prosecuted criminal offence in England since at least the fourteenth century. This is no coincidence.

The nature of the crimes is related to the motives of the criminals. Bandits or 'peasants' tend to commit crimes out of anger or present need. The physical attacks are often the result of wounded honour or as defence against supposed aggression by another party, while the occasional thefts arise out of desperation. But there is no evidence of either of these types of motive in the Smorthwait case. Superficially, if we had only the indictments, we might have believed that the thefts of veal or heifers, or even of money and clothing, were the reactions of a starving peasantry. But the added information from depositions and local documents enables us to see, from the position of those involved and their other activities, that this was far from the case. It is clear that crime was considered a short cut to greater wealth, rather than an attempt to stave off starvation. Only this can explain the involvement in such activities of people of the level of the gentleman William Foster, the wealthy yeoman William Smorthwait, or the clergyman Edmund Lodge. Their behaviour puzzled contemporaries as well. A reported conversation in 1688 concerning coin-clipping gives some clues as to the motives. A man said to another: 'I wonder you should follow this course of life having a good estate, to whom William Atkinson replies, thou art a fool in so saying, for I can live better than thee'.[23] It is perhaps easiest to interpret the crimes as stemming from a combination of greed and adventurousness. There is not a hint of the desire to steal from the rich to give to the poor, nothing of political or social criticism, beyond the fact that Bainbridge tried to claim that it was no crime to steal from Robert Robinson, possibly implying that he was rich. It seems that clipping and theft were merely thought to be easier ways to make money than other activities. The risks involved were worth taking and, as in other diversions, may have added to the pleasure. Such activities were bi-occupations: one could combine farming or blacksmithing or alehouse keeping with a little burglary or clipping, just as others would combine it with hunting or knitting stockings.

The lack of social motivation is also shown in the nature of the victims. Bandits and peasants, we are told, seldom rob from their near neighbours; they steal from landlords, townsmen or other more distant and socially superior persons. Yet the Smorthwaits and their associates did not act in this way: they stole from each other, from very close neighbours, from relatives, and from those poorer and weaker than themselves, servants and carriers and drovers. The nearest they came to stealing from the gentry was from the aged Robinson or the widow Bainbridge. It was not Sir George Fletcher's house or park that Bradrick and his associates robbed, though Bradrick had inspected the house during his supposed courtship of a servant there, but a husbandman's cottage nearby, where they stole small sums of money. They even stole from next-door neighbours, as at Old Hutton or Hawking Hall – hence the need to wear vizards and to alter their voices. Bandits are supported by their fellow-villagers and do not need to disguise themselves since they are known outlaws.

[23] Westmorland Record Office, Fleming Manuscripts, WD/Ry/57.

But the Smorthwaits carried their vizards in their pockets; they rode armed and at night, as much to avoid their neighbours as the Justices of the Peace.

Thus the pattern of violence reveals no split between town and country or between social classes. There are no hints of battles between peasants and 'landlords', as reported for the other peasantries, nor of anything similar to the seigneur-baiting of Languedoc, or the running battles between poachers and gamekeepers described for nineteenth-century France.[24] In the absence of any clear-cut distinction between 'landlords' and others in Westmorland, it would have been surprising if there had been such battles. The Smorthwaits and others were themselves landlords, though minor ones, and they did not attack any of the higher gentry; for example, Fleming or Sir George Fletcher or any of the other Justices. The difficulty of deciding who were gentry and who ordinary commoners is indicated by the fact that William Smorthwait himself was styled 'gentleman' on certain occasions and yeoman or husbandman on others.

If the violence does not highlight clashes between supposed classes, nor does it do so between family groups. The long-standing feuds and vendettas, the answering of blood with blood, which are a central feature of the situations described for France, China and Sicily, are totally absent in the English evidence. Where kinship ties are strong but national justice weak, retaliation and the keeping of the peace is often in the hands of kin, and violence and kinship are closely linked. But in the English evidence from the Smorthwait case there is no suggestion of blood feuding, long-lasting vendettas or anything of that nature. The Bainbridges and Smorthwaits do not emerge as traditional rivals of other specific families, and there is no sign that wrongs supposedly suffered in this case were passed on to be righted in the next generation. Nor is there any hint of family feuds in the other legal records for the whole period 1650–1750 for Kirkby Lonsdale. Obviously, there were animosities between specific individuals, and even between one family and another, but the character is so different from the violent, intergenerational, feuds described elsewhere as to belong to a different order of things. The absence of

---

[24] Certain parts of southern England in the early eighteenth century had something vaguely approaching these battles, which have been documented in Thompson, *Whigs and Hunters;* see also Hay, *Albion's Tree.*

feuds and vendettas is marked, central and important, and it is difficult to believe that the legal and other records would have completely overlooked such a phenomenon if it had been widely present. For example, the opportunities for retribution against the robbers or members of their families in this case are never recorded as being taken.

This situation helps to explain the apparent absence of fear of assault. Even towards the end of the nineteenth century in rural France, or up to the present in Sicily, many parts of the countryside were unsafe for travellers, especially in mountainous or forested regions and at night. The events described in the Smorthwait case seem to illustrate that, normally, this was not the case in northern England. The abnormal conditions created by the Smorthwaits, who were frightening tradesmen and others, were given as justification by Fleming for particularly stern action against the associates. A great deal of the material in the depositions suggests that it was quite usual for women to travel by themselves, or for individuals to cross the moors alone, with money and at night. This impression is corroborated by the accounts of many of the seventeenth-century travellers in this region, who seem to have journeyed without fear of assault or robbery. There is ample documentation of a vast amount of movement throughout the region, with people driving large trains of pack horses, or herds of cattle, or carrying money back from the market, without apparent fear of robbery.

Nor is there evidence that travellers or the inhabitants of remote hamlets and farmhouses lived in daily dread of bands of wandering, half-starved peasants. Such bands, some of them endemic, others caused by the terrible natural disasters chronicled for many parts of the world before the twentieth century, were a constant threat to law and order in the other peasantries examined. Moreover, it has long been held that gangs of beggars and vagabonds, partly attributed to the supposed dislocation brought about by the capitalist revolution of the sixteenth and seventeenth centuries, were a central feature of England at this time. One of the very few parish registers mentioning death by starvation comes from Greystoke in Cumberland, and it has been suggested that 'crises' of subsistence in this area lasted until at least the middle of the seventeenth century.[25] And although the worst might be

---

[25] Appleby, *Famine*, especially chs 7, 8.

over in terms of sheer starvation, it was notably in the 100 years after the Civil War that these extreme regions would have suffered the full effects of the economic revolution which had begun in the south and east. Westmorland, therefore, should have been the ideal setting for organized vagabondage, yet there is not a hint, in either the depositions or any other records, of such a phenomenon at this period. We know of no such bands entering Kendal or Kirkby Lonsdale. Given the very detailed manor court records for the latter, which list all persons trying to gain settlement in the town, the churchwardens' accounts, which give payments to the poor, the full reporting by constables to the Quarter Sessions, and the careful supervision by the Justices of the Peace, it seems certain that if there had been a perennial or recurrent problem of vagabondage, we should have heard about it. These records do show that there were individual vagrants and beggars. But there is absolutely no sign of a major threat to law and order from wandering beggars, either individually or collectively.

Another potent cause of popular disorder in peasantries – fights between gangs of youths who represent different groups within the parish, or different villages – is also absent. A central feature of many traditional peasantries is the strong boundary between neighbouring communities, with a concomitant hostility towards outsiders, most fully described in the French instances. If in Westmorland there had been similar inter-village pitched battles, or gangs of wandering youths from different hamlets, there can be little doubt that the legal records would have alluded to them. And if the activities of the Bainbridges of Mansergh had enraged the inhabitants of Killington and they had reacted with force, we would have heard about it. Yet the records of this parish over the 100 years after 1650, as well as those for the rest of Westmorland for the first 50 years of this period, give no indication of anything like the gang warfare described for France at a later time. There are no reported gangs of youths fighting after drinking or at football matches, no weekly battles. Of course there were disputes between parishes, particularly over boundaries, grazing rights, responsibility for the settlement of the poor and other matters. But these were settled in court, not by physical force. The whole dimension of battles between communities, or between groups within communities, appears to be missing in this region.

The absence of physical violence and everyday fear in Westmorland is reflected in the nature of weapons and defensive fortifications.

Widespread violence, with marauding bandits, bands of vagabonds, or family feuds, is usually accompanied by large numbers of weapons, particularly firearms, daggers and swords, fortified houses and fierce mastiffs. Such huge proliferation of firearms is described for eighteenth-century Languedoc and nineteenth-century Sicily. But if we look at the Smorthwait depositions and other local documents, it is a different picture. It is true that the Smorthwaits and their accomplices had rapiers and pistols, but their riding around armed was remarked upon as exceptional. The victims of their attacks were usually unarmed, or very lightly defended. Margaret Bainbridge's husband had an old rapier, but widow Bainbridge did not even bother to put it in her bedroom though she suspected there might be robbers. Henry Preston had a sword, and the constable of Killington had an old fowling piece. But on other occasions when assaults and burglaries occurred, there is no mention of weapons in the victim's possession, as in the robbery at Robert Robinson's or in Cumberland. None of those attacked, with the exception of Preston, defended themselves with cudgel, sword or dagger. Nowhere are we told of fierce dogs defending a house, or attacking intruders, though the barking of dogs woke the household in two of the burglaries. Nor is there any evidence that houses themselves were heavily defended, though many were remote farmhouses. The most they had were shutters on the windows, which in the Robinson house were normally left open, and an iron bar through the front door. The building of fortified houses had ended at least 120 years before the 1680s in this part of Westmorland and there is no trace in the architecture of a defensive need.[26]

To take a more detailed look at the presence of weapons, out of a sample of 412 inventories for the parish of Kirkby Lonsdale in the period 1500–1720, only 24 mention weapons; over nine-tenths of the population had no noted weapons. Looking at the inventories by decade, it is possible to see that there was no appreciable change in weapon ownership over the period. In the 33 inventories for 1610–19

[26] Thus, for example, when the antiquary Machell travelled around southern Westmorland in 1692 he found that the fortifications had long decayed: Machell, *Antiquary*. Bouch and Jones, *Lake Counties*, 36, state that 'from the middle of the sixteenth century to the end of the seventeenth the large house . . . made little or no provision for defence'.

there are no weapons mentioned. For the other periods we can express the ratio of 'weaponless' inventories to the total number of inventories mentioning a weapon as follows:

before 1590, 17:1	1660–69, 20:1
1590–99, 11:1	1670–79, 12:1
1600–09, 25:1	1680–89, 16:1
1620–29, 21:1	1690–99, 18:1
1630–39, 15:1	1700–09, 37:1
1640–49, 6:1	1710–19, 22:1
1650–59, 11:1	

As we might expect, the decade including the Civil War in the 1640s produced the highest ratio of weapons. Under-registration would be due to the fact that not all small weapons such as daggers or bows were listed, although three daggers and several bows do appear in inventories; but this is compensated for by the fact that many of the 'weapons' were obviously primarily for hunting rather than fighting. Thus, of the 16 'guns' mentioned in these 412 inventories, four are explicitly said to be 'fowling pieces' and another is an 'old' gun. Several of the swords are also said to be 'old', implying that they were basically family heirlooms.[27]

One of the reasons for this conspicuous absence of offensive weapons seems to have been their effective regulation through law. In the warrant against John Bainbridge it was stated that he 'hath divers guns, pistols and other arms (although he is not qualified by law to keep them)'. This was a reference to the laws concerning the keeping of weapons, summarized in Justice Fleming's copy of the *Statues* under 'Guns and Cross-bows' as follows (Fleming's additions are shown in italics):

I. Stat.33.H.8.6. None shall shoot in, or *use to* keep in his house or *elsewhere* any cross-bow, handgun, hagbut, or demy-hake, unless his lands be of the value of £100 per annum, in pain to forfeit £10 for every such offence. *Dags, pistols, & stonebows within this act . . .*

III. None shall travel (*save £100 men*) with a cross-bow bent, or gun charged, except in time *and service* of war, nor shoot *in a gun* within a

---

[27] It is interesting to compare this to a muster held in 1569 by the Bishop of Durham. Even for such a warlike occasion, in this border region, 'just over 4,000 out of the total number of 6,477 were without weapons of any kind' (James, *Family*, 37).

quarter of a mile of a city, borough, or market town, except for the defence of himself or his house, or at a dead mark, in pain of ten pound.

£100 *per annum* income from real estate was a high sum in this area, and it is doubtful whether more than one or two inhabitants of the parish of Kirby Lonsdale were at this level.

Fleming then summarized some of the exceptions: for example, lords spiritual and temporal and inhabitants of cities, boroughs and market towns could keep large guns. But no one was to shoot, carry or have any gun under the length of three quarters of a yard of pain of forfeiting £10. Anyone seeing such a weapon having £100 of property was to seize it and destroy it within 20 days. None below the degree of a baron was to shoot a gun in a city or town. Of course, the extent to which the law was effectively enforced requires further investigation.

The apparent absence of weapons and of frequent recourse to physical violence is related to two other notable features. The first is that there were no pitched battles between the robbers and the forces of order. This is in striking contrast to the situations described for China, France and Sicily where highly armed, often mounted, police and military forces controlled the countryside, and used to fight pitched battles with gangs of robbers and bandits. Although Fleming did at one time envisage using the trained band, an amateur organization of footmen and horsemen, there is no evidence that it was called upon. The arrests of the arch-suspects on various occasions were made by constables or justices who were, as far as we know, either unarmed or equipped only with sword or staff. The robbers sometimes fled, but there is no evidence that even William Smorthwait, who talked boastfully of being able to raise as many men as Fleming and the other justices, ever used his sword or pistol to prevent arrest. Certainly no one is reported as being wounded in any of the arrests. It has long been noted as a characteristic of England that there was no standing army and that when a regular, professional police force developed in the nineteenth century, it was without weapons apart from truncheons. This continued a tradition dating from well before the seventeenth century. Although they caused unusual alarm by being armed and riding and attacking in small groups, the robbers were basically individuals who acted separately. They, and even less minor criminals, did not present a threat which had to be met by strong punitive forces.

Secondly, people did not need to be protected from violence or given access to justice through the less formal channels of patronage and protection, as described in Blok's work on the mafia and *mafiosi* of Sicily. There, amidst the violence of everyday life, and with the huge gap between countrymen on the one hand, and the bureaucracy and power of the towns and of the landlords on the other, a set of intermediary protectors has grown up. More generally, anthropologists have documented the importance of protection by means of patron–client ties throughout the peasantries of the Mediterranean.[28] The weakness of central government and of national law leads to the importance of political protection by 'godfathers' and other patrons. There is scarcely a hint of such political patronage in the Smorthwait events, and no mention of godparenthood or other 'constructed' kinship ties being of any significance. The person who would most surely have revealed such a system in his own dealings was Fleming, who was in a prime position to act as a patron. It is true that he was once offered money for favour, and some of the letters, particularly those of Robert Robinson and Henry Smorthwait, asked for his protection. But this is a far cry from the deeply ingrained and institutionalized patterns we observe in studies by anthropologists and sociologists. And the Smorthwaits themselves, though they threatened people, apparently never took the opportunity of the fear they aroused to obtain protection money or become political patrons. When protection was needed, it was bought on the open market with cash, by the hiring of professional attorneys or barristers.

In fact, the methods by which disputes were settled outside the criminal courts is highly significant: rather than resorting to threats or force, people would use the other legal courts as well as informal negotiators. The depositions give us an unusual insight into a number of cases which normally would never have come to our attention. Here we find people hiring attorneys and taking each other to the civil courts, or settling matters out of court for the payment of cash, after influential local inhabitants had been called in to arbitrate. Both these methods are illustrated in the reactions to Bainbridge's theft. In other more minor cases, such as Scaif's pickpocketing, people were prepared to

[28] Gellner and Waterbury, *Patrons*.

accept their money back again. In general, it seems many were loath to bring criminal charges, which caused bad feeling, cost money and might well rebound. If possible they would settle out of court; if not, they would use another part of the highly elaborate judicial system. This confirms the belief of historians that many crimes do not appear in the surviving legal records. In the particular case of the Smorthwaits, it would seem that at least half the major crimes would never have been prosecuted if the case had not developed into such a serious one.

The unwillingness to prosecute, and the resort to negotiation and money fines rather than to physical violence, is again at odds with what we find in many peasantries. When supposed wrongs are righted there, the punishments are often of a physically brutal kind. The slitting off of noses and ears, the maiming and killing described for China, Sicily or France, are the natural counterpart to the viciousness of the crimes themselves. This violence is a feature both of the informal vengeance of neighbours and kin at the local level, and of the punishments inflicted by the state. Just as the cruelty of peasant rebellions is characteristically quenched by enormous brutality on the part of the landlords and the state, so the only way to check violent crimes is by savage penalties.

But in the Smorthwait affair, at the informal level, there is not a single example of 'mob' vengeance, the only trace being in the nineteenth-century legend that the people of Middleton had risen up against the Smorthwaits. This absence of popular retaliation is most marked in relation to Edward Bainbridge. He molested his neighbours for over 30 years, stealing from them, threatening them, leaving their gates open. Yet all they appeared to do was to try to reason with him, urging him to give up his evil ways or, finally, to prosecute and complain about him in the courts. There is scarcely any evidence that people used physical threats or brutal attacks to punish each other. Of course there were assaults, and there were many affrays concerned with the right to particular ownership of houses and fields. But these were on a scale and of a nature which places them in a different class to those we observe in other societies.

It could well be argued that this was because the state monopolized violence, just as the upper classes monopolized the use of serious weapons. If we read only legal textbooks and the statutes, it would appear that this was indeed so. The official penalties for what seemed to us fairly trivial offences, especially those concerned with property, were very harsh. But if the potential punishments were grave, how many people were actually convicted of such offences, how many were pardoned though convicted, and to what extent were the penalties mitigated in practice? This is not the place to undertake such a study in detail, but the Smorthwait affair lends support to the view that, while the sanctions of the law were severe in theory, in reality it bore less heavily on the population. The reluctance to convict is well shown in this case, for despite the apparently immense evidence, the major figures escaped once and Bainbridge and Thompson escaped again and again.[29] It is well known that, when convicted, perhaps half the condemned escaped execution through a reprieve or pardon.[30] Both Bainbridge and Thompson received pardons and reprieves and, according to Fleming's letter to the Clerk of assize, attempts were being made to obtain a pardon for the Smorthwaits. Gaol calendars for Westmorland frequently contain 'reprieved' or 'transported' against the names of those who one would have assumed, from the indictment, were to be executed. Even when a person was to be executed, the penalty was often lightened. For instance, clipping and coining were high treason and, in theory, a man convicted of these offences was to be drawn to the scaffold, hanged by the neck and then cut down, dismembered while alive and his entrails burnt before his eyes, and finally cut into four pieces. In practice, it would seem, those executed for this offence were hanged in the normal way, or at least hanged until dead before the later stages began. In the case of women, for whom the penalty was burning alive, they were usually strangled before being burnt.[31] Perhaps the best characterization of the formal system would be to say that a harsh legal code existed, but that a great deal of flexibility and compromise was permitted in its application. Thus for the whole of Westmorland for the second half of the seventeenth century, perhaps half a dozen persons were hanged for normal criminal offences.

[29] Baker, in Cockburn, *Crime*, 23, estimates that the acquittal rate in the sixteenth to eighteenth centuries was 'between one quarter and one half of those indicted'.
[30] Baker, in Cockburn, *Crime*, 43, citing the work of Cockburn and Radzinowicz, states that 'it has been estimated that the number of convicted felons actually condemned to death, throughout our period, was between 10 and 20 per cent; while the proportion of those condemned who were actually executed probably averaged about one half'. Taking all this and the previous note into account, it would appear that between 2.5 and 7.5 per cent of those indicted for felony were actually executed.
[31] Atkinson, 'Trial at York', 225n.

Numerous other indices could be used to point out the difference between the situation revealed in studies of rural violence and banditry in China, France and Sicily and that shown by the Smorthwait affair. For example, one of the centrally defining features of bandits as opposed to ordinary robbers, according to Hobsbawm, is that social bandits are admired and helped by their fellow peasants. While Bainbridge and the others would have liked to encourage others to support them and argued that it was no sin to rob Robert Robinson, they seem to have failed to gain popular favour. There is some evidence that a few young men went around when drunk imitating William Smorthwait, and the reluctance of the juries who were too 'favourable' to them may indicate a certain sympathy, but it would be difficult to argue that the Smorthwaits and their accomplices really approached the position described by Hobsbawm. By attacking the houses and persons of their near neighbours, frightening local women late at night, causing general dislocation and anxiety, they alienated many. While their clipping and coining may have fostered no general resentment, it is clear that they were commonly regarded as ordinary, if flamboyant, criminals, whether pickpockets like Scaif, stealing petticoats and sides of veal, or robbing from aged gentlemen, carriers and drovers. Search warrants were taken out by the villagers and local inhabitants did the prosecuting. These were not full-time bandits, shielded from the law, but part-time robbers, threatening those around them not to betray them. We are a long way indeed from social bandits.

We must now try to answer the difficult question of why the small amount of evidence we have cited, if confirmed, suggests that the English case should be so exceptional. We can find a clue in the English legal and social system, and a striking feature which differentiates it from those of the other countries which have been studied. One of the most marked characteristics of peasant societies is the opposition between the culture and controls within the local community, what is often known as the Little Tradition, and the rules and norms of the wider society and the state, of the Great Tradition. Combined with vertical gaps between the peasantry and the other estates of lords, clergy and professions, and between the county and the town, this tends to produce a very marked opposition on the part of villagers to the agencies and even the premises of the national law. For instance, in eighteenth and nineteenth-century France the formal apparatus of courts and officers was resented and kept at a distance by the villagers;

justice and gendarmes were seen as evil threats, and the central government was forced to accept that its hold over a village was weak and superficial.

The documents for Westmorland give a contrary picture. Informal mechanisms of dispute settlement might be widespread, but even they involved attorneys and recourse to courts of law. Constables might be reluctant to present cases but, when they were summoned by justices, they appeared. There is no indication of a popular opposition to national laws or to the activities of justices or other law-enforcement officers. There were many reasons for wishing to avoid appearance at court or as witness, but the system of recognizances, whereby people were bound in large sums of money to appear at court as witnesses or prosecutor, seems to have been effective in making them do so. Likewise, the technique of binding people under pain of similarly large sums not to break the peace seems also to have been observed, on the whole. Furthermore, most adult men were themselves minor legal officials. In the Smorthwait case the legal officials included the major criminals as well as the law-abiding; this means that any analysis in terms of opposition between a Little Tradition of local custom and informal control rejecting the Great Tradition of professional lawmen and law officers is mistaken. The self-policing involved in the English system had long been one of its distinguishing and crucial features.[32]

The experience which people gained of the law is reflected in the depositions and letters in this case, and these, alongside other legal records, show a very considerable awareness of how the law worked, what the laws were, and a general consensus that they were locally applicable and to be observed. There was not one law for the nation and another for the community. Occasionally we find a servant perhaps over-stressing her ingenuousness, saying that she was not

[32] Dawson, *Lay Judges*, provides an excellent account of this legal and law-enforcement system from early times. The Justice of the Peace was clearly a crucial figure here. Fleming may be exceptional, but the case does lend support to the contested theory of John Langbein; namely, that justices had important prosecutorial and investigative roles in preparing cases for judges in felony cases, as well as in cases of misdemeanour. In fact the Smorthwait affair and Fleming's activities in it are exactly what Langbein would have expected, though he himself was unable to find conclusive evidence in support of his case (Langbein, *Prosecuting Crime*, part 1).

sure whether a certain activity was unlawful. But the total impression is that the multitude of overlapping courts and laws penetrated right down to the level of the lowest inhabitants, and that ordinary people had a good working knowledge of the national system of criminal law. Such a picture certainly fits well with the other recorded legal activities of the Westmorland inhabitants at the time. In France, China or Sicily, it would be inconceivable that large numbers of villagers should personally initiate complex legal actions against their fellows to be heard in the capital city of the nation, over 200 miles away, by the highest judges in the land. Yet this is exactly what happened in Westmorland. Between 1550 and 1720, in just one of the central courts, that of Chancery, dozens of cases from Kirkby Lonsdale were heard, each one extending to a large number of written pages of evidence. They concerned small pieces of landed property and other goods in the parish. To people engaged in such litigation, not only in Chancery but in King's Bench, the court of Common Pleas, the ecclesiastical courts and elsewhere, the complexities of the Smorthwait affair would not have seemed great. English society was based on, and integrated by, two principal mechanisms – money and the law. The twin pillars of justice and economics were mutually supporting and avoided the necessity for recourse to either physical or religious persuasion. As Edward Thompson has nicely put it, the rule of the eighteenth-century gentry and aristocracy 'was expressed, above all, not in military force, not in the mystifications of a priesthood or of the press, not even in economic coercion, but in the rituals of the study of the Justices of the Peace, in the Quarter Sessions, in the pomp of Assizes and in the theatre of Tyburn'.[33]

If it is indeed true that herein lies the key to the difference between England and many other contemporary societies, we are again drawn to the peculiar and exceptional development of the common law of England from the twelfth century onwards. The system of Justices of the Peace, Quarter Sessions and Assizes was established in principle by the thirteenth century, though some features were not formally instituted until the middle of the fourteenth. This is not the place to pursue this story back to those times, but perhaps we can end with citing just one small example from an earlier period.

It has been frequently suggested, as we have seen, that banditry

---

[33] Thompson, *Whigs and Hunters*, 262.

and peasants are associated; it could furthermore be argued that bandits are only the most extreme and visible feature of a whole system of informal violence, which had disappeared in England by the time of the Smorthwaits. If we could find when banditry ceased, we might well gain some clue to the disappearance of the whole pattern of peasant violence. Hobsbawm's book on bandits is a starting point. Many bandits from throughout the world are cited, over 120 names in all, but only two English 'bandits' are included in the name index, Robin Hood and Dick Turpin. Hobsbawm willingly concedes that Turpin, whose behaviour is rather like Smorthwait's, is not a bandit at all, but a highway robber who has been accidentally romanticized.[34] This leaves Robin Hood, a particularly important figure since 'the country which has given the world Robin Hood, the international paradigm of social banditry, has no record of actual social bandits after, say, the early seventeenth century.[35] This is an interesting statement, implying that there are documented bandits for England before the early seventeenth century. Yet none is cited and I know of no historian who has ever discovered any either for the sixteenth, fifteenth, fourteenth or thirteenth centuries.[36] Of course one can play tricks with words and try to turn any robber baron or outlaw into a bandit. One can even attempt to transform the whole of feudal society into one vast system of banditry made outwardly legitimate.[37] But if we take Hobsbawm's definitions seriously, we are left with one figure for all those centuries – Robin Hood.

---

[34] Hobsbawm, *Bandits*, 39.   [35] Ibid., 19.

[36] For example, see Bellamy, *Crime*, especially ch. 3, which shows a state of affairs very different from that predicted by Hobsbawm. The robber gangs seem quite unlike the 'social bandits', and, for example, 'for the most part the leaders were drawn from the gentry, the knights, and esquires' (p. 72) and many of them were subsequently elected to Parliament (p. 82) and given local offices (p. 86). Likewise, though James Given uses the words 'bandits', 'robbers', 'burglars' and 'thieves' as synonyms, it appears that the thirteenth-century criminals he describes are very different from Hobsbawm's social bandits. For example, we are told that 'organized groups like Robin Hood's were largely a figment of myth and legend' and rather than attacking lords, townsmen and merchants, the robbers attacked 'peasants', particularly women and children who were present in the houses they robbed (Given, *Homicide*, 111 and ch. 6 passim).

[37] 'European feudalism was mainly gangsterism that had become society itself and acquired respectability through the notions of chivalry' (Barrington Moore, *Dictatorship and Democracy*, 214).

Yet even Robin Hood vanishes in our gaze. Hobsbawm himself
admits that while Robin Hood is 'in most ways the quintessence of
bandit legend', in 'many other respects ... [he] is also rather
untypical'. Moreover, 'no real original Robin Hood has ever been
identified beyond dispute'. This is somewhat deflating: we do not know
that such a person ever existed, and even if he did, or in the legends
about him, he does not behave as a bandit should. There is no explicit
cross-reference by Hobsbawm here, but he may be thinking of the
famous controversy in the pages of the journal *Past and Present*, where
an attempt to turn Robin Hood into a kind of social bandit, a hero of the
peasantry attacking the rich and giving to the poor, failed to demonstrate
that there ever was a real Robin Hood, that he was any kind of a peasant
or that his victims were the landlord class.[38]

One detailed case-study, even if it does fit well with other evidence
from travellers, diaries, village studies and other sources for the period,
cannot prove the case. Minimally what it does suggest is that there are
certain peculiarities about the patterns of English violence in the past.
These peculiarities are consistent with the view, expressed elsewhere,
that there is only very weak evidence for a massive revolution from a
medieval 'peasant' society to a modern 'capitalist' one during this
period. The evidence also casts doubt on any argument that suggests
that our ancestors were somehow intrinsically more brutal or
brutalized than we are. Comforting though it may be to believe in a
steady 'civilizing' process, an evolution from savagery to civility, the
English evidence, of which this is only a tiny part, does not appear to
support such a belief. What has been cited here tends to support the
work of the many historians, from Maitland onwards, who have been
impressed by the orderliness and control of physical violence achieved
by the earliest nation-state. Edward Thompson made a detailed study
of another apparently violent criminal episode, and concluded that 'the
notion of the regulation and reconciliation of conflicts through the rule
of law ... seems to me a cultural achievement of universal
significance'.[39] I would agree with this view and would add that the
cultural achievement appears to have been made very early. It was for
this reason that F. W. Maitland could end his great work entitled *A
History of English Law* in the year 1307.

---

[38] The controversy has been republished, with an additional and important
recantation by M. Keen (266) in Hilton, *Peasants*.
[39] Thompson, *Whigs and Hunters*.

4
Nature

Man and the Natural World

MODERN SOCIOLOGISTS have been puzzled by the innate anti-urbanism and love of 'nature' of the English. For instance, Mann notes that 'the attraction of the rural residence and urban work is very apparent'. The only explanation he can give is to follow Anthony Sampson, and argue in a circular way, that it is 'part of the Englishman's basic desire to become a landed aristocrat'.[1] This is one aspect of a wider set of paradoxes which presented the enquiring foreigner in the nineteenth century with something of a shock. England was the most urbanized country in the world, yet one where the yearning for the countryside and rural values was the most developed. Its strangely anti-urban bias was shown in the prevalence of parks, the ubiquity of flower gardens, the country holiday industry, the dreams of retirement to a honeysuckle cottage and the emphasis on 'nature' and rural values in the Romantic and pre-Raphaelite movements. One of the most acute analysts of these curiosities was the Frenchman, Hyppolyte Taine, in his *Notes on England*, based on impressions of England during the 1860s.

Taine noticed the rurality within urbanity of the English when he visited the city parks where 'both taste and scale are utterly different from ours'. For instance, 'Saint James's Park is a real piece of country, and of English country: enormous ancient trees, real meadows, a lake peopled by ducks and wading birds, cows, and folded sheep graze the eternally fresh grass ... What a contrast with the Tuileries, the Champs-Elysees, the Luxembourg!'[2] He noticed it when he visited the gardens and parks round country houses.

[1] Mann, *Urban Sociology*, 94.   [2] Taine, *Notes*, 16.

We have visited seven or eight gentlemen's parks . . . The perfect meadows shine under the sun and are richly covered with buttercups and daisies . . . What freshness, and what silence! You feel relaxed, rested: this natural beauty receives you with smooth caresses, discreetly, intimately . . . In my opinion these gardens reveal, better than any other work, the poetic dream in the English soul . . . All their imagination, all their native inventiveness has gone into their parks.[3]

He noticed it in the layout of the industrial towns. Walking round the richer part of Manchester he wrote that

Here and in Liverpool, as in London, the English character can be seen in their way of building. The townsman does everything in his power to cease being a townsman, and tries to fit a country-house and a bit of country into a corner of the town. He feels the need to be in his own home, to be alone, king of his family and servants, and to have about him a bit of park or garden in which he can relax after his artificial business life.[4]

Taine saw the same love of country over town, so contrasted to his own culture, reflected in the layout of the land. For the English, the

city is not, as it is with us, the favourite place of residence. Apart from the great manufacturing towns, provincial cities, York for instance, are inhabited almost solely by shopkeepers: the *élite*, the nation's leaders, are elsewhere, in the country. London itself is now no more than a great business centre: people meet there, for three or four months during the summer, to talk, amuse themselves, see their friends, look to their interests, renew their acquaintances. But their roots are in their 'country seats': there lies their real motherland[5]

As a literary critic and one of the foremost experts on English literature of the century, he noticed the curious obsession with the countryside, nature, the rural, in English literature. 'These people adore the country: you have only to read their literature, from Chaucer to Shakespeare, from Thompson to Wordsworth and Shelley, to have proof of this'.[6]

England was the most industrialized country in the world, the one where animal power was least essential, having been replaced by steam,

---

[3] Ibid., 147–8.   [4] Ibid., 220.   [5] Ibid., 141.   [6] Ibid., 16.

and where animals were consequently no longer central to production. Yet it was paradoxically the country where the concern for animals was most developed in the world, expressed in creative literature, in painting, in concern for animal welfare and in the widespread prevalence of pets. England was still almost the most carniverous of all societies, yet it was the most concerned with arguments for vegetarianism. It was a country in which man and animal had become separated, nature had been subdued and distanced. Yet it was in England that Darwin and Wallace finally successfully linked man and animal through the theory of the evolution of species. The heart of the paradox is that England was the most developed capitalistic and industrial society, when man lived in a largely artificial, man-made landscape, yet it was in England that the respect for, and love of, the wild and the non-artificial was most evident. How are we to explain these contradictions, many of which have become absorbed into the form of capitalism that has been exported to America, Australia, Canada and other parts of the former Empire?

One of the most impressive attempts to summarize the evidence and to explain the puzzles provides us with a very good start down the road to an explanation. This is the book by Keith Thomas, *Man and the Natural World* (1983). Thomas's central argument is that these are not real oppositions or contradictions at all, but are linked as cause and effect. It was because of the urbanism, the industrialism and the general distancing and control of nature that many of the peculiarities of the English that so struck foreigners could develop.

Keith Thomas's argument is as follows. If we compare the start and end of the period he reviews, 1500 and 1800, a series of complete changes in perception and feeling had occurred. By the end we are in such a changed world that it is not inappropriate to speak of a series of revolutions, to be placed alongside the industrial, agricultural and political revolutions charted by historians. In essence, we have moved from a pre-modern, pre-capitalistic, magical cosmology, into a modern, capitalistic, scientific one. Weber's 'disenchantment of the world' has occurred, Marx's alienation of man from the natural world is complete. In 1500 we are in an anthropocentric world of the Bible. All creatures are ordained for man's use; 'nature' is made for man alone and has no rights apart from man. 'Man stood to animal as did heaven to earth, soul to body, culture to nature'. This assumption of a man-ordained world was gradually eroded during this period. For example, species no longer came to be classified by their utility to humans, but rather by their inherent characteristics. This 'revolution in perception – for it was no less' at the upper intellectual and social levels, had a 'traumatic effect upon the outlook of ordinary people'. Basically what happened was the separation of man from nature. 'Crucial' to the older beliefs was the interblending of man and nature, 'the ancient assumption that man and nature were locked into one interacting world'. There then occurred the split between man and nature, between thought and emotion, which is part of the dissociation of sensibility. The natural world was no longer full of human significance. No longer was every natural event studied for its meaning for humans, 'for the seventeenth and eighteenth centuries had seen a fundamental departure from the assumptions of the past'.[7] That loss of innocence and of meaning in nature, reflected in Wordsworth's poetry, had occurred at a national level.

As the link between man and nature was broken, paradoxically people became more emotionally involved with particular animals and more concerned with the rights of animals in general. Thus 'a combination of religious piety and bourgeois sensibility . . . led to a new and effective campaign' in suppression of cruel sports. This was part of the general 'dethronement of man'. Thus 'the explicit acceptance of the view that the world does not exist for man alone can fairly be regarded as one of the great revolutions in modern Western thought'. This major revolution was the result of many factors. There were scientific and intellectual discoveries: the telescope expanded the heavens and diminished man in space, geological discoveries diminished man in time, the microscope brought out the complexity of nature, exploration and empire brought unimagined species to light. There were economic and social causes. 'The triumph of the new attitude was closely linked to the growth of towns and the emergence of an industrial order in which animals became increasingly marginal to the process of production. This industrial order first emerged in England; as a result, it was there that concern for animals was most widely expressed'. Kindness to animals, for example, depended on the newly created wealth; it was 'a luxury which not everyone had learnt to afford'.[8]

Just as these pressures led to a revolution in the perception and treatment of animals, so they did in relation to trees and flowers. Once

[7] Thomas, *Natural World*, 35, 70, 70, 75, 90.   [8] Ibid., 159, 167, 181, 186.

the forests had been wild and magical. As the trees were eliminated and became less important economically, people became fonder of them, emotionally involved in a new way. Similarly with flowers: as the wild world shrunk, so the domesticated version expanded. Here was another revolution. The expansion of flower gardening in the eighteenth and nineteenth centuries was so great 'as to justify our adding to all the other revolutions of the early modern period another one: the Gardening Revolution'. There emerged 'that non-utilitarian attitude to the natural world', that delight in nature for its own sake, as an end and not as a means, which is the theme of the book.[9]

At the start of the period, the English had looked to the city. 'In Renaissance times', we are told, 'the city had been synonymous with civility, the country with rusticity and boorishness'.[10] By the end of the period this was all reversed. At the start of the period and right up to the end of the seventeenth century there was a dislike of wildness; as late as the second half of the seventeenth century many travellers through mountain districts had been disgusted or terrified by the countryside. But in the second half of the eighteenth century the passion for mountains was under way. Security and control were prerequisites for this new appreciation. As agriculture became more rational, orderly and intensive, so people yearned for the opposite. New security, man's increasing control over the natural world 'was the essential precondition for greater tolerance'. Only when species defined as 'vermin' had been almost totally eliminated did they start to be protected. The irony was that the 'educated tastes of the aesthetes had themselves been paid for by the developments which they affected to deplore'.[11]

Thus it was that rapid urbanization, the replacement of animal by artificial power, growing affluence and security, a widening intellectual horizon, had led to a new dilemma. Previously the problem had been to conquer, to domesticate, the natural world. Yet as that problem was solved, a new difficulty had emerged, namely 'how to reconcile the physical requirements of civilization with the new feelings and values which that same civilization had generated'. Thus, we are told, 'by 1800 the confident anthropocentrism of Tudor

---

[9] Ibid., 224, 240.   [10] Ibid., 243.   [11] Ibid., 243, 273, 287.

England had given way to an altogether more confused state of mind'.[12]

The argument is elegant and largely convincing, the illustrative and supporting evidence apt and enlightening. Most authors would have stopped at this point. Many would have succumbed to the temptation to present us with a neat and watertight argument, which largely conforms to our expectations yet expands our understanding by explaining the resolution of the paradoxes at the heart of modern developments. Yet such is Thomas's rigour and scholarship that he has noted his doubts and difficulties. This enables us to see below the surface a sub-plot which is partly in contradiction to the main argument. For when we examine the material in more depth, the story is not so clear. Let us examine these hints and ambivalences.

Concerning the 'disenchantment of the world', it is not clear that this occurred after the Reformation, for Thomas tells us that 'since Anglo-Saxon times the Christian Church in England had stood out against the worship of wells and rivers. The pagan divinities of grove, stream and mountain had been expelled, leaving behind them a disenchanted world to be shaped, moulded and dominated'.[13] Although Thomas is right to point out that it is too simple to see this disenchantment as simply equated with Christianity, there is certainly an ascetic stress in Christianity, and particularly in the northern variety, which was hostile to the interfusion of man and nature, to 'magic' and 'symbolic thinking'. Closely related was the supposed shift from the anthropocentric classification of the world, a growing tendency to recognize the separateness and autonomy of the natural world. Having argued that this change was a central feature of the revolution in perception, Thomas continues that 'there was, of course, nothing new about the realization that the natural world had a life of its own'. The view was fully propounded in Aristotle. Furthermore, although attempts were made to classify things in a non-anthropocentric way, Thomas shows that Linnaeus himself classified dogs by their human uses, and even today lawyers impose human criteria on animals. Likewise, though there was a growing interest in the natural world for its own sake, in the exact observations which would lead to new discoveries in botany and zoology, we are

---

[12] Ibid., 301.   [13] Ibid., 22.

reminded that 'there were plenty of people in medieval England who observed the natural world very carefully'.[14]

In the section on 'vulgar errors', we find further curious features. It begins to appear that instead of an ancient 'folk tradition', an alternative way of thinking and feeling welling up from an oral culture, a cosmology appropriate to a pre-modern, peasant, society, what we really have is a jumble of out-of-fashion pieces of the 'scientific' high culture. The beliefs were in fact 'learned errors, rather than vulgar ones', many based on Pliny, Aristotle and others. 'Sir Thomas Browne in the seventeenth century and William Cobbett in the early nineteenth, both of them acute observers, held the classical writers responsible for the bulk of English rural superstitions'. Nor was the attack on 'vulgar errors' a new one, a new battle of world views in the sixteenth and seventeenth centuries, but rather the perennial attack on out-of-date ideas. 'Vehement Protestants' might attack the popular superstitions, but, as Thomas states, they were doing so 'like some of their medieval predecessors'.[15] To give one example of the ebb and flow of opinion, the belief that the barnacle goose was hatched from shells on trees was rejected in 1633. This was not a new argument. The belief had been attacked by the Emperor Frederick II in the twelfth century and by the philosopher Albert the Great in the thirteenth. John Gerard had resurrected the belief in his *Herball* in 1597.

In sum, then, the separation of man and the natural world was not a new phenomenon, invented as mankind for the first time gained complete mastery over nature. For though we are told that in the seventeenth and eighteenth centuries we see 'a fundamental departure from the assumptions of the past', in that nature was being studied in its own right, we are also told that 'this was a return to that separation of human society from nature which had been pioneered by the ancient Greek atomists Leucippus and Democritus'. Nor did the temporary return to a separatist philosophy last for long, for 'even as the older view was driven out by the scientists, it began to creep back in the form of the pathetic fallacy of the Romantic poets and travellers'. The very rocks and trees became filled with life and feeling. The same impression that rather than dealing with a change from 'traditional' to 'modern', we are dealing with constant ebb and flow, emerges from further consideration of the break with the anthropocentric view. Having stated that

---

[14] Ibid., 51. [15] Ibid., 77, 78.

this was 'one of the great revolutions in modern Western thought', the next sentence continues: 'Of course, there had been many ancient thinkers, Cynics, sceptics and Epicureans, who denied that men were the centre of the Universe or that mankind was an object of special concern to the gods. In the Christian era a periodic challenge to anthropocentric complacency had been presented by sceptical thinkers'. Nor was it all-conquering: 'as the nineteenth century debate on evolution would show, anthropocentrism was still the prevailing outlook'.[16]

We may now consider more specific side-effects of these shifts. The English are widely known as a nation of pet-keepers, as well as shopkeepers. This tradition seems to go back a long way. Thomas points out that 'pet-keeping had been fashionable among the well-to-do in the Middle Ages'.[17] We learn of lapdogs, birds, rabbits, hounds, caged birds, squirrels and monkeys, for instance.[18] About the rest of the population we have little evidence, but as soon as they become visible in the records, pets are widespread. Thus Thomas concludes that 'it was in the sixteenth and seventeenth centuries that pets seemed to have really established themselves as a normal feature of the middle-class household'.[19] Thomas gives evidence of monkeys, tortoises, otters, rabbits, squirrels, lambs and caged birds. To these may be added many others. Thomas Ady in 1656 listed rats, mice, dormice, rabbits, birds, grasshoppers, caterpillars and snakes, as both 'lawful and common among very innocent and harmless people' as pets. He even told of a Gentleman who 'did once keep in a Box a Maggot that came out of a Nut, till it grew to an incredible bigness'.[20] The range was very wide, therefore, and it may be mistaken, as Thomas argues, to believe that taste in pets grew more catholic in the eighteenth century.[21] It is more difficult to obtain some idea of the incidence of pets, but two indications of the extent of the keeping of domestic animals can be given. In his pictorial encyclopedia for children, Comenius gave a picture of a house and its animals, these included the dog, cat, and squirrel, ape and monkey which 'are kept

---

[16] Ibid., 90, 91, 91, 166, 169.   [17] Ibid., 110.
[18] Salzman, *English Life*, 100–2.
[19] Thomas, *Natural World*, 110.   [20] Ady, *Candle*, 135.
[21] Thomas, *Natural World*, 110.

at home for delight'.[22] Defoe, in his late-seventeenth-century reconstructed *Journal of the Plaque Year* descibes how almost every house in London had a dog and several cats,[23] though here, as elsewhere, we face difficult problems of defining what exactly a 'pet' is. If it is regarded as non-utilitarian, like a flower garden, we nevertheless find that by the sixteenth century in the large middling ranks of society many had rabbits, weasels, ferrets, monkeys, parrots, squirrels, muskrats, toy dogs, and other pets.[24] If it is certainly the case that by '1700 all the symptoms of obsessive pet-keeping were in evidence',[25] it could well be argued that strong indications of such an obsession were present several centuries earlier, as soon as we have sufficient documentation to be able to note pets. It is clear from this that the phenomenon developed well before urbanization and industrialization could have had much effect. Widespread pet-keeping is a by-product of something deeper than the changes of the eighteenth century.

A sentimental involvement with animals shown in pet-keeping is closely associated with the topic of cruelty to animals. The picture here is also not a straightforward one. At first we are told that the English were once notorious for their cruelty to animals, eating bloody meat to an unusual degree, engaging in animal fighting and bloody sports. Later, England became the home of the League Against Cruel Sports and the Royal Society for the Prevention of Cruelty to Animals. The transformation appears to be sudden and revolutionary. Thus a section of Thomas's book is headed 'New Arguments'. Yet we are immediately told that 'there was, of course, nothing new about the idea that unnecessary cruelty to animals was a bad thing'. Thomas very properly avoids the Whiggish view that men gradually became intrinsically more humane: 'what had changed was not the sentiment of humanity as such, but the definition of the area within which it was allowed to operate'. But even this watered-down view is challenged, for classical and medieval authors are cited who had used a classification which allowed humanity and kindness to be shown to animals. A striking example is the poem 'Dives et Pauper', written in England not later than 1410. This is quoted at length and

[22] Comenius, *Orbis*, 55. [23] Defoe, *Journal*, 137.
[24] Pearson, *Elizabethans*, 19.
[25] Thomas, *Natural World*, 117.

Thomas concludes that 'this is a notable passage and a very embarrassing one to anybody trying to trace some development in English thinking about animal cruelty'.[26]

Thomas then makes the remarkable statement that the 'truth is that one single, coherent and remarkably constant attitude underlay the great bulk of the preaching and pamphleteering against animal cruelty between the fifteenth and nineteenth centuries'. He proceeds to summarize this attitude and to conclude that 'so far as their main arguments were concerned there was a notable lack of historical development', the 'position was constant'. So much for 'New Arguments'; what of the next section headed 'New Sensibilities'? Again we are soon told that 'of course, spontaneous tender-heartedness, as such, was not new'. A considerable amount of literature is cited to show the 'new sensibility' at work before 1700. What happened in the eighteenth century was not a radical novelty, but a spreading of the feelings; they 'seem to have been much more widely dispersed' and were 'much more explicitly backed up by the religious and philosophical teaching of the time'.[27]

If we turn from animals to plants, we may consider first the 'Gardening Revolution'. It is indeed true that the English are unusually enthusiastic domestic gardeners. It is also true that the content of their gardens altered dramatically over the centuries. We are told that 'in 1500 there were perhaps 200 kinds of cultivated plant in England. Yet in 1839 the figure was put at 18,000'. But because there were few cultivated species to choose from before 1500, this does not mean that flower-gardening was uncommon. There were commercial plant sellers from at least the thirteenth century and we are assured that 'more flower-gardening had gone on in the Middle Ages than is sometimes appreciated', even though the 'repertoire seems to have been fairly limited'.[28] This repertoire was limited by what was native to England and Europe, but it is symptomatic of the innate enthusiasm that as soon as it became possible to vary the plants by importing exotic species from newly discovered America and the widening contacts with Africa and Asia, people enthusiastically did so. William Harrison in the later sixteenth century marvelled at the English garden which had been 'wonderfully' increased in its beauty not only with flowers but also with 'herbs, plants, and annual fruits' which 'are daily brought unto us from

---

[26] Ibid., 150, 150, 152.   [27] Ibid., 153, 154, 173, 174.   [28] Ibid., 226.

the Indies, Americas, Taprobane (Ceylon), Canary Isles, and all parts of the world'. As a result 'there is not almost one nobleman, gentleman, or merchant that hath not great store of these flowers'. Harrison, an Essex vicar, concluded by boasting a little of his own garden, 'which is but small and the whole area thereof little above three hundred foot of ground, and yet, such hath been my good luck in purchase of the variety of simples, that, notwithstanding my small ability, there are very near three hundred of one sort and other contained therein, no one of them being common or usually to be had'.[29]

The enthusiasm for gardening, from the small cottage garden to the large garden of the gentry house, which is such a striking and characteristic feature of England even up to the present, was clearly indicated from the earliest detailed records of the sixteenth century. We are told that 'Elizabethans did not spend any more time indoors than necessary, for they were lovers of gardens if they loved their homes', and Pearson provides extensive accounts of the gentry and merchant gardens of the time.[30] Contemporary treatises on gardening began to be published as soon as printing became common; for instance, Thomas Hill's *A Most Briefe and Pleasaunt Treatyse, Teachynge howe to Dress, Save and Set a Garden* in 1563. The poetry of the Elizabethans, and in particular Spenser and Shakespeare, as well as the central motif of the Garden of Eden as the fount of innocence and pleasure, all indicate the very widespread absorption with natural beauty in the shape of flowers and trees. As the philosopher Bacon argued in his essay 'Of Gardens' in the early seventeenth century, 'God Almighty first planted a garden. And indeed it is the purest of human pleasures. It is the greatest refreshment to the spirits of man, without which, buildings and palaces are but gross handyworks'.[31]

Such appreciation was not limited to the very wealthy. There is evidence that ordinary, middling, folk were keen gardeners. Writing of the English yeoman in the later sixteenth and early seventeenth century, Mildred Campbell concluded that 'already gardens, that happy result of the Englishman's climate and his skill, added beauty and colour for a part of the year to the farm and village scene'.[32] She

---

[29] Harrison, *Description*, 265, 270–1   [30] Pearson, *Elizabethans*, 58ff.
[31] Bacon, *Essayes*, xlvi.
[32] Campbell, *English Yeoman*, 241.

alludes to the record made by a neighbour of all the flowers that were
in bloom in the garden of a certain 'Goodwife Cantrey', a
Northamptonshire yeoman's wife, on 28 July 1658. These included
'double and single larkspurs, double and single Sweet Williams, three
kinds of spiderwort, lupin in four colours, purple and white scabious,
marigolds, Life Everlasting, London pride, Hollyhocks and many
other flowers', as well as medicinal flowers like fennel, camomile and
white lilies.[33]

It is, of course, difficult to know how widespread gardening and the
love of flowers was, but Thomas gives several pieces of evidence to
suggest that it was indeed spread down to very ordinary people in the
seventeenth century. He quotes John Worlidge who in 1677 wrote
that 'in most parts of the southern parts of England', there was
'scarce a cottage' which was without 'its proportionable garden, so
great a delight do most of men take in it'. A few years earlier, a book
on flower gardening intended chiefly for 'plain and ordinary
countrymen and women' had been published and the first impression
was sold out in three months.[34] We can be sure that the widespread
and enthusiastic interest in flowers and gardens is present well
before the growth of cities and industrialism in the second half of the
eighteenth century. Again, we must try to explain it by something that
is present in England before the seventeenth century.

From flowers, we may turn to wilds, and particularly mountains. At
first sight we are faced by a revolutionary perceptual change in the
period between 1660 and 1760, when mountains and wilds became
attractive instead of intolerable. But a closer examination shows that
many of those who wrote in the period up to the end of the
seventeenth century did not feel enthusiastic about the wilder scenery
less because of instinctive aversion than because of the uselessness of
such areas. Thus Daniel Defoe was oppressed by the mountains of
north-west England because, unlike the Peak district, the Alps, the
hills around Halifax, or even the Andes, all was 'barren and wild, of
no use or advantage either to man or beast'.[35] As Thomas shows,
there were throughout the seventeenth century defenders of mountains such as George Hakewill who supported them for their 'pleasing
variety', and many of those who lived among them, such as Sir Daniel

---

[33] Fussell, *English Countrywoman*, 65.   [34] Thomas, *Natural World*, 228.
[35] Defoe, *Tour*, 549.

Fleming of Rydal Hall in the late seventeenth century, or visited them, such as the antiquary Thomas Machell from Oxford, found them perfectly pleasing and interesting.[36] What *is* true is that the mystic reverence of the Lake Poets, and the Romantic ardour of the tourists of the later eighteenth century, does seem to have been of an added intensity.

In his account of the changing attitudes to trees and forests, Thomas shows an ancient pattern. Wide-scale admiration of trees and planting of trees occurred from the middle ages onwards. At the upper level this was not spurred on by urbanization or industrialization, but by 'social assertiveness, aesthetic sense, patriotism and long-term profit'. It is true that, as with flowers, many new varieties were brought in from the expanding empire. But there was 'no dramatic shift from tree-destruction to tree-preservation'. The earlier liking for trees was shown in the way in which the English, from well before the eighteenth century, tried to make their cities as much like the country as possible by filling them with parks and trees. This occurred very early, and Thomas gives much evidence to show that other cities were, like Norwich in the sixteenth century, 'either a city in an orchard or an orchard in a city'. The idea of the 'Garden City', we are told, was not invented by Ebenezer Howard, but by John Evelyn in 1661.[37]

The desire from an early date to make the towns into countryside is curious for it shows an early anti-urbanism. The more conventional argument is the one pursued elsewhere by Thomas, namely of a great change some time in the seventeenth and eighteenth century. We have quoted him as saying that at the Renaissance 'the city had been synonymous with civility, the country with rusticity and boorishness', a view that still prevails in much of Europe. Why did the English come to change from this view? Thomas argues that they did so in revulsion from a too-rapid growth. Smoke, dirt, noise, overcrowding, drove the earlier city-lovers into becoming country-lovers. As the cities and industrial activities rapidly developed, so, in direct proportion, did the amount of criticism and complaint: 'there was no real precedent for the volume of late eighteenth-century complaint about the disfiguring effects of new buildings, roads, canals, tourism

[36] Fleming, *Description*, Machell, *Antiquary*.
[37] Thomas, *Natural World*, 209, 197, 205, 206.

and industry'. Certainly the volume of complaint increased, but Thomas is also aware that the arguments themselves were not new. The strange attitude that what was useful and productive was 'most likely to be ugly and distasteful', he remarks, 'had a long pre-history', stretching back to at least the sixteenth century.[38]

This criticism of town vices is part of that pro-rural, anti-urban, bias which, we have seen, Taine observed in the nineteenth century. As Thomas points out, 'the preoccupation with nature and rural life . . . is certainly something which the English townsman has for a long time liked to think of as "peculiarly English"'. Whether it is or not, 'much of the country's literature and intellectual life has displayed a profoundly anti-urban bias'.[39] This bias was strongly manifest in the eighteenth century when, for instance, Adam Smith assumed that the 'natural inclinations of man' would lead everyone to want to live in the country.[40] Yet the curious desire of the English to spend as little time in towns as possible goes back much further than that.

Thomas tells us that 'even in the twelfth century it had been customary for the rich citizens of large towns to hold rural property nearby', providing them with country houses to which they could retreat.[41] In the fifteenth century, Fortescue compared England to France, where he had spent a number of years, and found a great difference. In England the countryside was 'so filled and replenished with landed men, that therein so small a thorpe [village, hamlet] can not be found wherein dwells not a knight, an esquire, or such a housholder, as is there commonly called a frankelyn, enriched with great possessions'. He thought that 'after this manner . . . none other realms of the world' were so inhabited. For though there were rich and powerful men elsewhere, they lived in 'cities and walled towns'.[42]

Moving to the early sixteenth century, Thomas Starkey, 'lamented that it was impossible to persuade them [i.e. the nobility] to make their chief residence in town and deplored the "great rudeness and barbarous custom" of dwelling in the country'.[43] Foreigners 'were astonished at the love of the English gentry for rural life', Trevelyan remarks. Visitors noted in amazement that 'every gentleman flieth into the country. Few inhabit cities and towns, few have any regard of

[38] Ibid., 243, 286, 286.   [39] Ibid., 14.   [40] Smith, *Wealth*, I, 403.
[41] Thomas, *Natural World*, 247.
[42] Fortescue, *Learned Commendation*, 66–7.   [43] Thomas, *Natural World*, 247.

them'.[44] An author in 1579 observed that 'whereas in some foreign countries gentlemen inhabited "the cities and chief towns", "our English manner" was for them "to make most abode in their country houses"'.[45] Taine quotes the traveller Poggio, who wrote in the sixteenth century that 'among the English the nobles think shame to live in the towns; they reside in the country, withdrawn among woods and pastures; . . . they give themselves to the things of the fields, sell their wool and their cattle, and do not consider such rustic profits shameful'. As Taine observes, 'the contrast between this rural life of the English nobility and the urban life of the Italian nobility' was 'very great', and he adds 'it is not less so for a Frenchman'.[46] From this evidence it again looks as if the phenomenon to be explained, namely the pro-rural bias, is both unusual and had developed long before the industrial and urban revolution. It is an added irony that the most anti-urban of countries should be the first major urban and industrial nation in the world. It is worth remembering this internal contradiction in sentiments and attitudes which has persisted up to the present.

If it is indeed the case that much of what occurred in the seventeenth and eighteenth centuries was merely an accentuation, an increase in volume and pace, rather than a complete break, we may wonder how we are to explain the patterns that already seem to have been established by 1600, and sometimes well before. Industrialism, urbanism, the political dislocation of the seventeenth century, and even the Reformation seem, in themselves, too late or too little to explain those deep-seated peculiarities which Thomas has reminded us of. These are a curious attitude to animals, to gardens, to the city and to other natural phenomena. One central suggestion made by Thomas is that as man gained control over nature his attitude could become more positive. When there is a battle for survival against the wild, then sympathy and tenderness are difficult; but once mastery is gained, a feeling that care and protection is needed can grow. Instead of animals being dangerous, they are endangered. If we pursue this explanation, there are good grounds for believing that the domestication of the natural and human world that allowed a relaxed attitude was already achieved well before 1600.

---

[44] Quoted in Trevelyan, *Social History*, 127.   [45] Thomas, *Natural World*, 247.
[46] Taine, *Notes*, 141.

The landscape, the physical world of forests, marshes, moors and meadows had been early conquered and brought into the full control of man in England. As Thomas shows, following the work of H. C. Darby and historical geographers, the physical landscape had been tamed and ordered by the eleventh century, if not earlier. The shape of the fields and hedges, of the roads and paths, of the majority of human settlements, had been laid out by the eleventh century and was to change little over the next 700 years. Dangerous wild animals, which still roamed over much of continental Europe or Scotland until the eighteenth and nineteenth centuries were destroyed very early. In the sixteenth century Harrison thought it one of the important blessings of God on England 'that it is void of noisome beasts, as lions, bears, tigers, pards [leopards], wolves, and suchlike, by means whereof our countrymen may travel in safety and our herds and flocks remain for the most part abroad in the field without any herdmen or keeper'.[47] He compared this with the situation beyond the Tweed, where fierce animals abounded. The perceived safety of the countryside went back much earlier. In the early thirteenth century the English monk Bartholomaeus Anglicus noted that in England there were 'few wolves or none' and as a result sheep could be securely left 'without ward in pasture and in fields'. This, he said, went back to Anglo-Saxon times, and had been a phenomenon noted by Bede.[48]

Even more dangerous than animal predators are human ones, and it is they who usually make it necessary for armed shepherds to guard the flocks. As important as the control of the physical world of nature was the control of human violence through political and legal means. Here again it would seem that England had been early tamed. England was a unified nation-state in Anglo-Saxon times and the continuing uncertainties, regional oppositions and over-mighty subjects were, in the main, eliminated by the strong governments of the Normans and Angevins. Internal warfare and invading armies, which made much of Europe dangerous and led to a weapon-carrying population and the defensive fortifications of nobility and cities up to the nineteenth century, had largely been eliminated by the early medieval period in England. The power of the King's Courts, the absence of a standing army, the freedom from foreign invasions provided by sea boundaries, these and other factors combined to give a very early and continuous

---

[47] Harrison, *Description*, 324.   [48] Anglicus, *Properties*, II, 734.

peace. Of course it was broken occasionally, as in the Wars of the Roses, or in Stephen and Matilda's reign. But the contrast with the devastations of France, Germany, Spain or Italy through the centuries is very marked. The differences in political structure, if further investigated, would help to explain the curious fact that the English gentry were happy to live in undefended manor houses in the country, while in most countries they sheltered within huge chateau fortifications or, preferably, within the city walls. Towns and castles were the refuge of 'civility' and 'civilization' when times were violent, and hence were far more important on the Continent. It is for these reasons that Freeman, for instance, when trying to explain the absence of 'capital' cities in England, ascribed it to political factors. The 'princely' and the 'civic' element show themselves in greater splendour in French rather than English cities 'simply because in England the kingdom was more united, because the general government was stronger, because the English earl or bishop was not an independent prince, nor the English city an independent commonwealth'.[49] Edinburgh or Durham were the nearest British equivalents to such a phenomenon.

This relative political security provided by a powerful and early nation-state was an essential background to an economic world which was also unusually secure, and over which ordinary people had an unusually developed control. The wealth of medieval England is still impressive to us today in its numerous surviving churches and houses. Accounts of the population at the time both from literary sources such as Chaucer, or from economic historians, suggest a world which had already escaped from the subsistence level of periodic famine which dogged much of Europe until the eighteenth century. There is no documented national, or even large regional, famine for England from the Norman Conquest onwards. The clothing, the food, the housing, the amount of personal goods and money that are revealed by the records from the thirteenth century onwards suggests that this was a relatively affluent agricultural society. Disease was the great uncertainty, but this is an insecurity with which we still live. This was not a desperate world ceaselessly poised on the edge of starvation, unable to 'afford' the luxury of appreciating natural beauty as an end in itself in its desperate struggle to survive. It was from very early on,

[49] Freeman, *Essays*, 42.

in Thomas's terms, a society which had the wealth and leisure to treat animals and flowers and trees as ends and not merely as means, as things to joy and delight in, as well as to use.

The economic security was part of a particular mode of production whose later refinement we call capitalism. It is worth considering whether, as Marx and Weber both in their own ways suggested, this mode of production produces a curious and paradoxical attitude to the environment, a contradictory attitude of alienation on the one hand and sentimental attachment on the other. In capitalism, land and human labour are treated as means to an end, as commodities to buy and sell on the market. In theory, everything has a price and is placed on one scale in the market. Yet, paradoxically, as most relations become contractual and commercialized, as farming is pursued almost solely for profit, as the business ethic intrudes into all relations, a counter tendency builds up. A stronger and stronger boundary is erected between this utilitarian approach to most things and certain reserved areas which are carefully kept outside the market mentality. It is emphasized that flowers and pets, favourite trees and mountains, have no price and cannot be measured by the usual standards. Their uselessness is their value, they are particularly treasured because they are of no commercial utility. Thus pets must not be eaten, trees must not be cut down and burnt, mountains are bare and desolate, flowers are transitory and like the lily of the field neither do they weave nor do they spin. The human heart caught in the restless striving of constant calculative capitalism rejoices in these havens of non-utility.

Since the peculiarities we are trying to understand pre-date rapid urbanization and industrialization, but are parallel to the early development of a particular form of individualistic capitalism in England from the middle ages, it seems more likely that the explanation lies in some 'elective affinity' between the spirit of capitalism and the love of certain parts of nature. It would seem that the very early development of money relations, markets and capitalistic relations of production in England not only helped to provide the wealth and security which was a necessary precondition for the disinterested appreciation of nature, but also those curious ambivalences which make capitalist societies simultaneously the most exploitative and the most protective towards nature.[50]

---

[50] For some similar arguments see Williams, *Country and City*, 295ff.

A closely related feature was the nature of literacy. The widespread dominance of money and contractual relations from early on was made possible by the very developed use of writing on parchment or paper. One of the powerful messages of Keith Thomas's book is the way in which the growth of printing and a public which devoured the literature devoted to 'nature' powerfully influenced the development of an interest in the countryside. But the impact of written communication went deeper than this, for it seems likely that a very developed use of writing to record and transmit information from at least the thirteenth century in England influenced the concepts of the natural world. The use of the written mode had spread so widely that it helped to undermine the normal opposition between urban, literate, high culture, and a rural, illiterate, oral 'little community'. Hence the widespread 'learned errors' to which Thomas has drawn our attention, hence the rapid spread of new fashions and tastes with regard to natural objects, hence the relative absence, as compared to much of Europe, of great regional diversities in taste. These effects of literacy in breaking down oppositions and in exerting control have been well analysed by Jack Goody.[51] Their later development at the popular level of a very large chapbook literature has also been documented.[52] Just as the political and economic and physical worlds had become tamed, controlled and ordered, so the world of information and thought had been reduced to orderliness on parchment and paper.

At one point Thomas links the psychological function of pets to their attractiveness within a modern, atomistic, kinship system.[53] This intriguing suggestion could be broadened. In the majority of societies, a combination of early marriage, constant childbearing, the close physical and emotional presence of numerous kin, together provide the emotional satisfactions which many people now find in their pets. Now that we know that this individualistic kinship and marriage system is very old in England, probably dating in its central features to at least the thirteenth century if not before, it is not difficult to see that pet-keeping and a fondness for nature are very early and related phenomena. Just as English children were

[51] Goody, *Domestication*.   [52] Spufford, *Books*.
[53] Thomas, *Natural World*, 119.

luxuries, regarded as superior pets,[54] so English pets were luxuries, regarded as alternative children. The boundaries between the animal and the human, and between the exploitation and preservation of species are complex. We see in England over the centuries that through a careful classification of the world into tame and wild, edible and inedible, it was possible for our ancestors, as it still is for us, to be great meat-eaters and yet greatly devoted to particular animals and concerned with animal cruelty.

A final strand of the explanation of the peculiarities undoubtedly lies in the religious system. Keith Thomas, following Weber, rightly lays considerable stress on this. Christianity in general has a curiously ambivalent attitude towards the relations between man and nature. On the one hand it stresses an exploitative attitude; all creatures were made by God for man, and can be used for his own good. On the other hand, all creatures were created by God, and man should respect His creation and see His hand in its beauty. The myth of the Garden of Eden is an aspect of the rural emphasis of the religion. Within Christianity, the proto-Protestant and Protestant versions that dominated England stressed an anti-magical, disenchanted attitude towards nature which Weber noted. Long before the Reformation, many of the uncertainties, mysteries and extensive ritual confusions had been eliminated. An overlap of the material and spiritual worlds common in most cultures was absent. The attack on those popular errors which indicated a fear and awe of nature, the undermining of a belief in divine presences in natural phenomena, had begun long ago under the Anglo-Saxon Church. It was carried to its logical and final limits by Protestantism. An ascetic, anti-magical tendency in Christianity thus fitted with the other forces, political, economic, social, which separated the world of man and nature, bringing nature under absolute control, and then allowing a sentimental re-integration on man's own terms. This disenchantment of the world is the central theme of Thomas's work and he summarizes the process thus: 'in place of a natural world redolent with human analogy and symbolic meaning, and sensitive to man's behaviour, they constructed a detached natural scene to be viewed and studied from the outside'.[55] In Keats and Wordsworth and Shelley we see the last fading of the links, 'fled is that music, do I wake or sleep?'.

---

[54] Macfarlane, *Marriage*, 54–6.   [55] Thomas, *Natural World*, 89.

If we return to the paradoxes with which we started, which surprised
visitors to England in the nineteenth century and still lie deep in
English society and in many of the parts of the world where British
culture was exported, we have an explanation at two levels. By 1500,
and even more obviously by 1650, the preconditions for the peculiar
attitudes to animals, plants and the countryside were already established. This was a result of the political, economic, social and religious
factors briefly mentioned above. There may also have been other
cultural factors which cannot be pursued here, but are worth mentioning. It is well known from the earliest descriptions by Tacitus that
the Germanic invaders of the essentially town-based Roman civilization preferred the countryside to the towns. In much of Europe these
rural peoples were absorbed into the Roman world, and finally the
town-dominated world of Rome re-established itself with Roman law,
religion, language and cities. England and northern Europe were less
influenced by Rome, and in England the law, language and settlement
patterns were almost exclusively Germanic through the three waves of
Anglo-Saxon, Viking and Norman settlers. That Germanic preference
for the countryside was never erased and has, curiously, been preserved in the midst of the first industrial and urban society.

These early preconditions and deep cultural preferences were then
given a particular twist by the events after the sixteenth century. In a
period which saw unprecedented population growth in England from
the 1730s, the mastery of a new and artificial form of production in
industrialization, the first rapid urbanization in the world, and the
exploration and domination over half the world, these earlier tendencies were not wiped out but, in some ways, became stronger. Rather
than quenching the love of animals, trees, country living, the effects of
cities and industries and a growing dominance of market values was to
emphasize these feelings. The period of most rapid growth of the new
features in the later eighteenth century also saw the height of the
alternative tendency in the Romantic movement. The extraordinary
increase in the volume of emotion and interest in the natural world thus
fits with the growth of an apparently hostile environment. Rather than
trying to eliminate the contradictions, it is more useful to understand
how the dilemmas arose and why many felt pulled in opposite
directions. The struggles of the tendencies in capitalism have reached
global proportions and the outcome in Amazonia, the Himalayas, the
world's oceans will affect us all.

5
Evil

The Root of all Evil

THE WORD 'evil' is of Teutonic origin. The *Oxford English Dictionary* distinguishes between a strong and a weak meaning. In the strong meaning, 'evil' is used to mean the antithesis of good in all its principal senses; morally depraved, bad, wicked, vicious. This strong sense of evil, the *OED* tells us, is 'little used in modern English'; when applied to persons it is 'obsolete'. The word is nowadays used only in the weak version, meaning to cause discomfort and/or pain, to be unpleasant, offensive and disagreeable, to be 'not good'. It is interchangeable with 'bad', 'unpleasant', 'harmful'. I shall be concerned here with the strong sense of 'evil': how, when and why did it become obsolete? The disappearance of evil as a concept is one of the most extraordinary features of modern society. That it is no longer generally possible to conceive of an abstract force of evil is clearly of great interest to historians and anthropologists.

The essence of evil lies in a combination of several features. First, it is shadowy, mysterious, covert, hidden, not fully understood; hence the association with night, darkness, black, secrecy. Secondly, it is an aggressive or, as the *OED* puts it, a positive force. Evil tries to destroy the integrity, the happiness and the welfare of 'normal' society. It is aggressively, if insidiously, undermining, the worm in the bud. Witches are evil because they attack society, causing illness and death. These attacks are not justified; either they are motiveless, or the motives are perverted. God or the ancestors are not evil when they afflict man, for their ends are good: to improve the afflicted. They correct mankind as a loving father corrects a child. Yet when havoc falls out of a clear sky and strikes down an individual or a society, there evil is at work.[1] Evil is an inversion of good, the moral standards of society are turned upside down. The ultimate representatives of evil are witches and heretics, who are believed to eat human flesh, engage in sexual perversions, worship the Devil, and go naked to their monstrous meetings by flying through the air.

When misfortunes occur they tend to be explained by a set of factors. The causes are placed on a continuum, from an extreme of very human, personal causes, through rather abstract, half-human ones to the mechanical and inhuman. Among these are the following: ancestors, witches, fairies or other small spirits, God or the Devil, the stars, 'science', fate and chance. Usually a society will have available a set of two or three of these explanations. The choice of a particular explanation will reflect an individual's location in relation to the unfortunate event; for example, whether there was thought to have been some earlier wrongdoing. One of the most puzzling problems has for long been why different societies should have opted for different sets of explanations and also why such sets should change. This essay is a brief attempt to suggest a few of the background factors that lie behind the choice of explanatory frameworks.

The nature of a world in which real evil is all around can be partially diagnosed. First, there is the secrecy. Things are not what they seem: the smiling face conceals hatred, the friendly gesture leads to downfall. The same person is both a neighbour and possibly a member of a secret, subversive, organization. This is a world of limited good, envy, the 'Evil Eye'. Although the forms will differ with the religious system, if we survey all human societies, it does seem roughly to be the case that the strong concept of immanent evil flourishes in the middle range of human societies. Often the concept is weakly developed or absent in hunter–gatherer societies. In many tribal societies, in so far as there is evil, it is usually members of other distant groups who are evil, or abstract, non-human spirits. It is in the

---

[1] I am grateful to Professor David Parkin and other members of the 'Evil' seminar for their comments on drafts of this essay. Among these was the suggestion that we still use 'evil' in the strong sense, for instance to describe the Nazi holocaust, mass torture, sadistic crimes. This is perfectly true. Yet I would maintain that the *Oxford English Dictionary* is correct in saying that the word when applied to persons is 'obsolete'. The precise combination of horror, terror and condemnation that combines beliefs about supernatural as well as natural threats is almost, if not totally extinguished at present in much of western Europe and North America.

densely settled agrarian societies that anthropologists have had to label as 'peasant' – China, India, parts of South America and Catholic Europe – that evil has developed as a massive moral and practical problem. Each of these civilizations has an intricate theodicy in which evil is given a formal place in the system of explanation, with the curious exception, perhaps, of certain forms of Buddhism.[2] Though the location and attributes of evil are infinitely varied, evil and the concept of evil are of central importance.

It could thus be argued that the moral economy of peasant society has, as one aspect, the economy of evil. A great amount of energy is spent in trying to hold back and defeat evil through the use of that 'magic' that is built into practical religion in Catholic, Hindu, Muslim and Confucian societies. Life and happiness are thought to be constantly threatened, by women, by death, by secret evil, by diffuse and invisible powers. There is a never-ending war, both within the individual and against external dark forces. An archetypical example of such a world can be seen in much of continental Europe between the fifteenth and eighteenth centuries. In the *Malleus Maleficarum*, or 'Hammer of Evil', written by Sprenger and Kramer and published in 1486, we are provided with a compendium of possible evil and a directory of how, through torture, interrogation and trickery, evil was to be eliminated. Throughout Catholic Europe the Holy Office of the Inquisition, in alliance with the state, set up an elaborate machine for seeking out and destroying secret evil. In that 'everlasting bonfire',[3] thousands were burnt to death for their supposed evil works and many thousands of others were imprisoned and tortured.[4] The world later satirized by Goya, that world of constant threat and evil whose roots Norman Cohn has unmasked in *Europe's Inner Demons*, is one that is now becoming fully documented. There was believed to be a vast conspiracy of Evil abroad: relapsed Jews, gypsies, freemasons,

[2] Parkin, *Evil*, ch. 8.   [3] Pollock and Maitland, *English Law*, II, 659.
[4] An early estimate by a Secretary of the Spanish Inquisition (Llorente, *Inquisition*, 583) put the numbers punished by the Spanish Inquisition as follows: 'Number of persons who were condemned and punished in the flames – 31,912; Effigies burnt – 17,659; Condemned to severe penances – 291,450'. Even if, as later writers have argued (e.g. Bennassar, *L'Inquisition*),these figures are likely to be inflated, the toll of the Spanish and Portuguese Inquisitions was still enormous. In Portugal there were reputedly almost 900 public *autos-da-fés*, in which approximately 30,000 persons were sentenced, over 1,000 of them being publicly burnt (Adler, *Auto da Fé*, 169).

witches, Lutherans – all were sought out as agents of Evil. Evil was then purged from them by fire and the rack. The Devil was alive and well and hovered over much of Europe. It is clear that, from rural peasant to Dominican inquisitor, few doubted the daily reality of Evil, the Evil One and evil beings. There was a Holy War for four centuries.[5]

Contrast this with the world of industrial, capitalist society in the later twentieth century, the world of Benedorm and Monte Carlo, of 'Jeux sans Frontières' and the Eurovision Song Contest, the European Economic Community and butter mountains. Though 'evil' titillates in the films, television, science fiction and children's stories, in ordinary life the concept and the reality have largely been banished. Most people move in a one-dimensional world that has expelled Satan, witches, the Evil Eye and fairies. The supernatural dimension is dead, except as 'fantasy'. It appears that 'science' and 'chance' have largely replaced personalized explanation. As Keith Thomas has argued, the reasons for this transformation are still a mystery.[6] In many ways the world of evil and anti-evil, of witchcraft and magic, are psychologically much more appealing than the acceptance of capricious fate. This, then, is the problem: how has evil, however temporarily, been almost abolished?

The conventional wisdom may be briefly summarized as follows. The world of evil was first abandoned in a part of north-western Europe, the same area where the rise of Protestant, capitalist, rationalistic societies emerged. This was part of Max Weber's 'disenchantment of the world'. The turning point was in the sixteenth to eighteenth centuries. There was then a revolutionary movement, from the mystical, magical universe of medieval Catholicism to the

---

[5] It has been suggested that the sense of evil among the ordinary population of Europe may have had little developed, and that it was really only in the minds of a small number of the clerical elite and the persecuted heretics that it was a daily reality. Clearly, the extremes of terror came in waves, and it would be unlikely that people could sustain a constant alarm, yet a reading of the recent works by Baroja (*World*), Cohn (*Inner Demons*), Henningsen (*Witches' Advocate*) and Larner (*Witchcraft*) will indicate how widespread the alarm was and how it penetrated to the lowest levels of society. Symbolically, the expulsion of evil at the *auto-da-fé* involved not just the inquisitors, but the whole population, all of whom took part in the rite. I have here drawn on unpublished work on the Inquisition processes in Portugal, currently being undertaken by a joint project sponsored by the Gulbenkian Foundation in Lisbon and King's College, Cambridge.

[6] Thomas, *Religion* and *Natural World*.

clockwork, mechanical cosmology of eighteenth-century rationalism.
There was an expulsion of the concept of evil, first among the elite
and then, increasingly, among the hitherto 'superstitious' folk. The
process paralleled and was linked to other attacks on 'irrationality',
the irrationality of despotic government, peasant ownership, familistic
sentiments.

The causes of this massive change are notoriously difficult to
establish. Once we have abandoned a belief in the necessary progress
of 'enlightenment' and rationality, we are forced to argue that the
social and other frameworks that had nourished the roots of the
concept of evil had changed. Max Gluckman suggested a few of the
possible underlying connections between a changing social and
economic world and changes in the moral and explanatory theories.[7]
He argued that there was a basic change from a world in which most
good things arrive through other people (multiplex, face-to-face
communities) to a world in which good arrives by way of impersonal
forces, through the exchange of money, contracts, labour, short-term
manipulative relationships. As good things come in this new form, it
is no longer tempting to believe that evil also flows along personal
networks. Thus, a change from a deeply rooted, multiplex, face-to-
face community to those highly mobile, 'modern' societies would lead
to the decline of witchcraft and evil. This is another dimension of that
famous movement from status to contract, from *gemeinschaft to
gesellschaft*.

Another interesting suggestion lies behind Keith Thomas's two
major works, namely that it is increasing security, arising from greater
control over the natural world, that frees men from terror and hence
from evil.[8] Through technical, technological, organizational and
other changes, man's vulnerability is decreased. The mysterious is
eliminated, or else is so contained that people can believe that one day
all will be explained. Through improvements in the standard of living,
through insurance, through the triumphs of exploration and
discovery, men became confident. Risk was minimized, shocks were
less frequent, logical patterns emerged. A planned, controlled,
human-constructed world emerged. There is little place for evil in
the polite orderly world of Jane Austen and Capability Brown. The

[7] Gluckman, *Custom*, ch. 4 and *Politics*, ch. 6.
[8] Thomas, *Religion* and *Natural World*.

neat, systematic, mercantile world of the seventeenth-century Dutch landscape painters finally eliminated the demons that had infested Europe from the fall of Rome to Hieronymus Bosch. Though the romantic movement and gothic revival tried to re-introduce the mystery and some of the horror, the world of Frankenstein, the Pit and the Pendulum and Sir Walter Scott was a fantasy world, a literary genre like science fiction today. Essentially, the argument is that the tree of evil was destroyed when the roots were exposed through the rise of bourgeois capitalism. The process was circular, for it was the elimination of 'evil' that enabled people to investigate the real causes of pain and misfortune. In other terms, 'science' replaced 'magic' in the older Frazerian formula.

There is something intrinsically attractive and plausible in this account. It feels like our own life-experience leading up to the present. There seems a natural progression from the childhood of the world, where men feared the dark, ghosts and witches, to the more prosaic world of adulthood, where caprice, chance and psychological or sociological explanations are offered for disaster. This is a world in which people believe that, if only one knew enough, all could be explained. The extension of the argument is that where the social and mental institutions of northern Europe were exported, and later reinforced by a similar ideology in northern America, there evil withered. There were pockets of resistance and accommodation, yet basically mobility, money, markets and improved technology would be more powerful than the missionaries. Much of anthropology's task has been to study and document this ripple effect.

Before accepting the chronology and the explanation, however, let us look a little more closely at the first European escape from this evil-threatened cosmology. This occurred in England. The first thing to establish is when evil as a practical possibility was abolished. This is not easy, for it is notoriously difficult to penetrate to the level of ordinary behaviour and belief in the past. All we can do here, when considering a country of four to five million persons over a period of four centuries, is to start by looking at one tiny microcosm, one parish. How did the situation there compare with that on much of the Continent, Scotland and in some contemporary peasantries?

During the last 12 years we have assembled, transcribed and indexed all the known surviving records for the parish of Earls

Colne over the period 1380–1750.[9] This was a parish with abut 700 inhabitants, on average, situated near Colchester in Essex. It has very detailed records, manorial, ecclesiastical and civil, which enable us to begin to analyse ordinary village life and concepts.[10] All these records have been put into a computer database system so that they can be searched instantaneously by word or subject from any direction. We may survey what they reveal about the concepts of evil and related topics.

The first striking fact is how infrequently the word 'evil' is used. In the 10,000 pages of transcribed documents, it occurs (if we include 'evilly' and 'evils') only 27 times. This is despite very full ecclesiastical and equity court records where people were frequently abusing each other. The word occurs six times in a set of ecclesiastical depositions concerning a case of adultery and only once elsewhere in the ecclesiastical courts. It occurs 12 times in three disputes over property in the Court of Chancery. Otherwise, there is a single reference in each of the following: in a manorial jury presentment, in minutes of a Friends Quarterly Meeting, in memoranda of the Quarter Sessions and in one or two other sources. In all of these sources, the word appears to have been used in the weaker and not the stronger meaning.

Although the records are much less ample in the fifteenth than in the sixteenth to eighteenth centuries, there is as yet no evidence of either a rapid increase or decline in the usage of the word over these centuries. Nor is there any evidence that it radically changed its meaning as the centuries went by. Its first use in the fifteenth century was in relation to people who broke into other people's property and were termed 'evil doers'. Its last use, in the eighteenth century, was when it was used to describe debtors who had fled to avoid paying their debts and who were called 'evil persons'. These two uses were

[9] I am grateful to other members of the Earls Colne project (a project funded by the Social Science Research Council), namely Sarah Harrison, Jessica King, Tim King and Charles Jardine, for the work from which these results are drawn. All the documents for Earls Colne have now been published on microfiche by Chadwyck-Healey Ltd and are available in a number of university libraries and the British Lending Library. The references to 'evil' and similar words are listed in the subject index included in that microfiche, where the full context of the use of the word may be seen.
[10] Macfarlane, *Reconstructing* and *Guide*.

characteristic and they illustrate the most important conclusion of all. 'Evil' as a word was always used in the weaker, 'modern', sense of being synonymous with 'bad', 'criminal'. It was never used in the strong sense of being totally anti-social. This important conclusion can be illustrated by looking at the phrases in which it occurred.

A suspected adulteress was accused of leading an 'evil or dishonest life', and it was claimed that she never performed any 'evil or dishonest act'. A man was warned by the ecclesiastical court 'for keeping an evil woman in his house'. Intruders, persons who made wagers and defrauded others and those who failed to pay their debts – all were referred to as of 'evil conversation', of 'evil disposition and narrow of conscience' and as 'evil doers'. Evil was used to describe ordinary secular criminal acts. Thus, people were warned against 'felonies, trespasses and other evil acts . . .'; people claimed that they had been 'very sore hurt and evil treated by the complainant', that riots had been caused by 'evil persons that are the secret authors or abettors of such tumultuous disorders', that people 'did assault and evil entreat' others. This is a use of the word 'evil' in its widest sense, just as we might today describe something as bad or wicked in a loose way. There is apparently nothing of the association with the Devil, with spiritual darkness, with another moral dimension.

It is always dangerous to work from absences in the records, since the documents were usually created in formal settings. Yet it is striking that, when the word was used, it was always used in the weaker sense. There is certainly no evidence here that evil in the stronger meaning was an important force in the life of the village. This first impression is supported by other related features. One of these concerns those associated concepts in Christian eschatology, the Devil and hell. It is likely that, if this was a world where evil was widely feared, the Devil would not have been far away and people would have been in constant mindfulness of the pains of hell. This was particularly to be expected in an area of East Anglia that was famous for its strident puritanism. It is curious, then, that a search of the immense number of words that have survived in the records for Earls Colne does not reveal a single use of either the words 'Devil' or 'hell' (or their derivatives). Never, it seems, did people in their bitter wrangling allege, at least in writing, that their opponents were in league with the Devil, that they would go to hell. If we were to judge from local and legal records, this was a prosaic world in which evil, the Devil and hell were of marginal significance from at least the middle of the sixteenth century. Since the threat of evil, of the Devil and of hell is such a useful sanction in societies where it is strongly present, this seems strange. Yet again it fits more widely with other features of the society as revealed in the documents.

Where evil is an ever-present threat and reality, people are constantly seeking protection from it. They engage in a thousand forms of activity to ward it off, protecting their houses, their loved ones, their animals. Although Keith Thomas has documented a good deal of this activity in general,[11] it is striking that so very little evidence survives at the village level for ritual and magical protection against evil. A certain amount of the burying of objects, hanging up of horseshoes, wearing of parts of the Bible round the neck as amulets would no doubt go unnoted in formal records. Yet it is significant that the church itself was very anxious to extirpate such magical protections, which were thought superstititious and unnecessary. Thus, in Earls Colne an astrologer who used magical books was prosecuted by the church authorities. It seems likely that, if there had been much magical activity, it would have been noticed in the church courts or by the puritan vicar of Earls Colne, who has left a detailed diary covering the period 1640–83.[12] Ralph Josselin does occasionally mention superstitious practices, such as erecting a maypole. Yet he never reports charms, amulets, magical words or signs that were designed to protect mankind against evil. The only protection was prayer and an upright soul.

While individuals do not appear to have had a wide repertoire of antidotes to evil, the formal authorities provided even less. Since the work of Robertson Smith,[13] anthropologists have been aware that, in a cosmology where evil is a constant threat, mankind tries to ward it off by various types of ritual activity that will avert the dangers. Among the most powerful of these are the ritual of sacrifice and exorcism. Sacrifice, the ritual destruction of an object and the giving of part of it, often the blood, to gods, ancestors or spirits, is a powerful technique in the battle against evil. Sacrifice acts as a lightning conductor, for the sacrificial animal takes upon itself the sins of the world and carries them away, thus diverting disaster. Man is protected from various evils, merited and unmerited, by sacrifice. It

---

[11] Thomas, *Religion.* [12] Macfarlane, *Ralph Josselin.*
[13] Robertson Smith, *Lectures.*

could almost be asserted that sacrifice and developed concepts of evil are necessarily intertwined. Looked at from this perspective, the total absence, as far as we know, of animal or other sacrifice in Earls Colne throughout the whole period is significant. Even the symbolic sacrifice of Christ on the cross was minimized by the Protestant emphasis on the fact that communion was not a ritual act, a sacrifice of blood and flesh, but merely a commemorative and communal act 'in remembrance of me'. There is no evidence that the rituals of the Church provided an effective shield against evil.

The weakness of ritual is also apparent in the absence of exorcism and possession. Although the rite of exorcism was available in the Anglican Church and was sometimes used during this period, there is no evidence in these village records that it was of any practical importance. There is not a single case of diabolic possession recorded and no known instance of exorcism. Physical manifestation of the Evil One seems to have been minimal. The overwhelming impression from all types of documents is of a secularized world where people were concerned primarily with money, power and social relationships. It was not, as far as we can see at present, a world darkened by the overcasting shadow of menacing evil. Consequently it is not surprising to find an absence of any indication of evil times or evil places. There is no hint that certain days were evil in themselves, that the churchyard or other places were intrinsically evil. Of course, there were unlucky days; it was best not to set out on journeys on them, marry on them or undertake business on them. Yet bad luck and fortune are different from true evil.

Another apparent absence is the concept of the Evil Eye. Just as in Essex as a whole,[14] so in Earls Colne, there is no evidence for the developed belief that envy, in a world where good things are limited, endangers all life. In almost all other peasantries, it is believed that certain individuals are born with an evil eye; whenever they look with envy on a thing, it withers and dies. Such beliefs were strongly developed in parts of Scotland, Mediterranean Europe and elsewhere. Yet there is not a single hint, in all of our Earls Colne or wider Essex material, of such a concept, so closely linked to an idea of evil.

More complex is the reality and importance of witchcraft and fairy beliefs. In a general work I have surveyed witchcraft beliefs and prosecutions in Essex over the period 1560–1680, and there showed

[14] Macfarlane, *Witchcraft.*

that Essex was one of the most witch-conscious of counties and that the sixteenth and seventeenth centuries saw the peak of beliefs and prosecutions.[15] Yet when we place witchcraft beliefs and accusations within the context of all the events within one parish, they become less impressive. In Earls Colne, there were literally hundreds of cases of recorded sexual misdemeanours, hundreds of accusations concerning economic affairs. Yet not a single person was condemned as a witch. The nearest to a formal prosecution occurred in the archdeaconry court in 1581, when Mary Green was accused by the churchwardens of Colne of being 'vehemently suspected of sorcery and witchcraft'. She failed to produce neighbours to swear an oath on her behalf and was thus excommunicated. We hear nothing more of her, so that she probably moved. The wording, alluding to 'sorcery', suggests that she was probably a 'white' witch; that is, someone who was illicitly curing people or searching for lost objects. Apart from several references to a local wizard or astrologer at the same period, this is all we would hear of witchcraft from the records. Nor is there any mention of any other evil or half-evil spirits. There is not a single reference in any of the documents to fairies, goblins, brownies or any of the host of spirits that peopled the high literature of Elizabethan England.[16] There are no allusions to stories, myths, beliefs in the fairy world. It is a curiously flat, matter-of-fact world that is indicated by the local records.

We may pursue this question a little further, for the nature of English witchcraft is curious not only quantitatively, but also qualitatively. The epitome of evil in many soceties is the witch. Beliefs about witches provide us with one of the few accurate mirrors of popular concepts of evil. In much of the witchcraft belief system of continental Europe throughout the fifteenth to seventeenth centuries, in Scotland in the sixteenth and seventeenth centuries, or in contemporary witchcraft beliefs in Africa, the witch represents the antithesis of society, pure evil.[17] In every way she (for witches are most often thought to be women) inverts the values and customs of society. Witches are believed to constitute an organized and alternative evil empire, threatening the whole of civilized, human,

---

[15] Idem.   [16] Briggs, *Hecate's Team*.
[17] Cohn. *Inner Demons;* Larner, *Enemies* and *Witchcraft*, especially vii, viii, 52, 54, 75; Mair, *Witchcraft*.

'society'. They work closely with the Devil, engaging in a satanic compact whereby they exchange their soul for temporary power in this life. They meet at 'sabbats' where they worship the Devil, rather than God. They invert the holiest of rituals, the holy sacrament, undertaking black masses with desecrated food and prayers that are spoken back to front. They operate at night, when Christian people are asleep. They engage in sexual perversions, both with each other and with the Devil in the shape of *incubi* and *succubi*. They eat the most forbidden of foods, the flesh of human beings. They reject the decencies of clothes, dancing lasciviously naked. They travel to their meetings in strange ways, flying through the air or walking upside down. Thus they represent horrific caricatures of normal values, inverting human behaviour in relation to time, space, sex, eating, clothing. These were the attributes of many witchcraft beliefs through much of Europe and Scotland. How do these nightmares compare with what we know of English witchcraft beliefs in the same period?

English witchcraft beliefs and the evidence brought forward in prosecutions suggest a very different attitude. Basically, witchcraft was not seen as a form of heresy. Despite the attempts of Margaret Murray to introduce them into the records, there is little evidence of a belief in a large, alternative, heretical organization of witches based on 'covens' or 'sabbats' at which the Devil was worshipped.[18] The key concern was with the effects of *maleficium*, not the causes, in a supposed compact with the Devil. English witches acted singly, as individuals, rather than in groups. If they wanted a link with the Devil it was not through weekly or monthly meetings with him, but rather by keeping a small domestic pet, thought to be his 'imp' or 'familiar', which the witch would feed. Even in witchcraft, the English obsession with pet-keeping emerged. There is scarcely any evidence of alternative rituals, black masses, worship of the Devil, sacrifice of animals and so on. This was not a secret alternative organization that was threatening to bring down godly society. Witches were the enemies of specific individuals, not of society as a whole.[19] Their motives were prosaic. They did not seek great power, great wealth, the downfall of Christ's kingdom on earth. They were thought, instead, to have been angered by some small act of unkindness by a

---

[18] Macfarlane, *Witchcraft*, 10; Larner, *Witchcraft*, viii.
[19] Rowland, 'Fantasticall'.

neighbour. The quarrels were petty ones over disputed boundaries, differences over loans, muttered curses.[20]

The reputed behaviour of supposed witches in England also lacked the inverted horrors of their continental and Scottish counterparts. Their sexual behaviour was not remarkable. There is a conspicuous absence of a sexual element in English witchcraft. Although it is true that the majority of those accused were women, there is no strong evidence of a belief that they were particularly licentious, that they copulated with the Devil or other witches, that they engaged in sexual intercourse with animals or in forbidden ways. Essex witchcraft beliefs, and indeed those for England as a whole, were very decorous. The absence of immodesty is also shown in their clothing. While elsewhere witches showed their evil nature by throwing off their clothes and exposing their buttocks and genitals in a provocative way, English witches were thought to remain fully dressed. They were similarly restrained in their eating habits. There is very little evidence of communal eating by supposed English witches who sometimes met to eat a roast cow or sheep. There is no evidence that when, infrequently, they were thought to meet, they broke any food taboos. In particular, the sacrifice and eating of human flesh, especially that of Christian babies, was not one of their supposed habits. The hunger and food motif, the lust for food as well as sex, which is characteristic of witch beliefs through much of the world, is absent. Feasting and cannibalism are not important features. Nor were witches thought to travel across England in mysterious and threatening ways. Like ordinary people they walked to their work. They did not travel on broomsticks, anoint themselves with magic' potions, or fly up through chimneys, through keyholes, or travel upside down.

The English witch was in popular thought a curiously tame and homely creature. Unpleasant, vindictive, a criminal even, but not a member of a deep and concerted attack on society, a terrifying intrusion of evil into this world. Why this should have been the case it is difficult to say. Part of the answer for the peculiarities lies in the nature of English law. Norman Cohn and others have successfully shown how the popular and less sensational beliefs in daily evil, *maleficium*, were turned into diabolical witchcraft in the context of the system of inquisition and torture used under the Roman law of the Church and

---

[20] Macfarlane, *Witchcraft*, 196.

state in Europe.[21] The absence of torture as a formal part of the law, and of leading questions based on inquisitors' manuals, helped to prevent many of the more sensational beliefs from becoming incorporated into the final, formal, confessions. Yet this alone cannot be a total and sufficient explanation of the differences. It is clear that witchcraft beliefs in Europe reflected the attitudes of both the inquisitors and also popular beliefs.[22] In England, the absence of an inquisitorial framework was paralleled by an apparent absence among the populace of beliefs in really evil, satanic, individuals. In the earliest witchcraft trials, for instance those in the county of Essex in the 1560s, we can observe the highest legal officials in the land being taught about popular beliefs by Essex villagers.[23] The ideas they received, which were then reinforced in later trials, were very far indeed from the nightmare inversions which we find in Scottish and continental witchcraft. It would seem that at the level of popular cosmology, in the villages and hamlets of sixteenth and seventeenth-century England, there was a singular absence of the concept of pure evil as personified in the witch.

Such a picture of practical life is a useful corrective to the exclusive use of literary sources. Yet there are clearly dangers in using only impersonal, often formal records. Fortunately for Earls Colne, we are not just left with such material; for one of the richest sources on past beliefs, namely diaries and autobiographies, is well represented by the extensive 600-page diary of the vicar of Earls Colne, Ralph Josselin. The full diary has been analysed and published,[24] and we may mention some of the conclusions to be drawn from this source covering the middle of the seventeenth century. The projection of the distinction between good and evil into strong beliefs in heaven and hell does not show itself in this diary:

belief in the after-life does not play an important part in his private thoughts as recorded in the Diary. There is not a single direct reference to hell or to damnation. It thus seems that a Puritan clergyman, who might have been expected to use heaven and hell as threats or inducements to himself and his congregation, showed the most tepid interests in both.[25]

[21] Cohn, *Inner Demons*.   [22] Henningsen, *Witches' Advocate;* Ginzburg, *Cheese.*
[23] Rosen, *Witchraft*, 72–82.   [24] Macfarlane, *Ralph Josselin* and *Family Life.*
[25] Macfarlane, *Family Life*, 168.

Josselin was preoccupied with misfortune, illness and insecurities of various kinds. There are consequently many moving passages on death and disease. Yet what is striking in the diary is the conviction that all suffering was derived from God. In Josselin's thought there emerges very clearly 'the principle that pain and evil came from God. There is no hint in the Diary that Josselin envisaged an alternative source of evil, Satan for example. Again and again he traces his own and the nation's troubles back to God'. Basically, 'Josselin seems to have accepted that pain was either divine purge, as in the story of Job, or a punishment'.[26] Guilt strikes us throughout the diary, for Josselin blamed himself for much of the suffering of those around him; in the most famous instance, he linked too much chess-playing to illness and death. Thus, the roots of evil were ultimately in his own corrupt heart. It was no use blaming other people. The cause was either a loving God testing him, or his own, or the nation's failings. There is no suggestion that Josselin blamed witches, Satan or anyone else.

Interestingly, however, Josselin also believed in the possibility of diabolic intervention and of witchcraft. He never encountered the Devil himself, but he seems to have accepted the stories concerning two of his parishioners who had encountered the Devil. One had been tossed into a river by 'one in the shape of a bull', whom it was rumoured was the Devil. Another man visited Josselin to tell him that the Devil had appeared to him: 'the greediness of money, made him desire it, and God suffered it; he [i.e. the Devil] appeared in a black gown, and then in red; he took his blood on white paper'. A few days later Josselin was with the same man and there was fear that the Devil might appear, but he failed to do so.[27]

Josselin also believed in the possibility of witchcraft and reported two cases. In the first of these, 'one J. Biford was clamoured on as a witch, and Mr C. thought his child ill by it'. Josselin took the suspect 'alone into the field, and dealt with him solemnly, and I conceive the poor wretch is innocent as to that evil'. The following year he heard from a neighbouring minister that a woman was a suspected witch, who had acted in a suspect manner near a grave. Josselin 'pressed her what I could; she protests her innocency'.[28] Josselin also believed in the power of cursing.

[26] Ibid., 173, 174. [27] Ibid., 190–1. [28] Ibid., 191–2.

In this and other respects a personal diary helps to provide an added spiritual dimension to the local records. It shows a world of symbols, signs and visions that are absent from court records. Yet in many ways the diary complements the other records in its central impressions concerning evil. Evil, the Evil One, the evil eye, the force and danger of evil, are largely absent. The world revealed by the diary is not one of a constant battle between the forces of good and evil, of imminent destruction and threat from evil-minded persons or evil-minded spirits. Ultimately the individual, through his own purity of heart and through understanding God, can control the world. This is a world fully consistent with that we shall examine in relation to Josselin's great contemporary, John Milton, where evil and good are interchangeable. Josselin is primarily concerned with practical problems; with making money above all, and secondarily with establishing good relations with his neighbours, his family and God. The quality of this world can be most startlingly shown if we compare the atmosphere of this diary, cosy and suburban in many ways, with the feeling portrayed by a fictional account of the mental world of another branch of Calvinism, the horrific account of the Devil and pure evil in James Hogg's *The Private Memoirs and Confessions of a Justified Sinner* (1824). There is portrayed a world where hell, the Devil, real evil and darkness are a felt reality; that account leaves the landscape of Josselin's Earls Colne seeming a sunny, open and this-worldly one. Evil is never entirely banished, of course, but it is just a shadow on the edge of this English world, not a central pervasive feature, as it is in many cultures.

These are impressions based on one small example. Yet they are consistent with other contemporary evidence for the sixteenth to eighteenth centuries. Those familiar with the most detailed English diaries and autobiographies of this period, for example those of Samuel Pepys, John Evelyn and Oliver Heywood,[29] will know that there is very little in them about evil in the strict sense. Occasionally there are strange intrusions from another dimension – ghosts, poltergeists, the odd witchcraft trial. Yet the tone of all of the diaries is this-worldly, prosaic, not soaked in evil. The same is true of another genre, letters, which have survived in considerable numbers from the fifteenth century. The famous collections of the Pastons, the

---

[29] Latham and Matthews, *Diary;* De Beer, *Diary;* Horsfall Turner, *Autobiography.*

Celys and the Verneys have scarcely anything in them suggesting an interest in evil in the strong sense.[30]

The absence of a horror of and concern with evil is also clearly indicated by English proverbs. The various dictionaries of phrase and fable and handbooks of English proverbs contain very little about evil. For instance, the *Oxford Dictionary of English Proverbs* (1952) contains only a few proverbs under the title 'Evil'. In almost all of these it is clear that the word is being used in the weaker sense. For example, there is the proverb 'Evils (Harms, Ills, Mischiefs), of two/choose the least', which is first quoted for Chaucer (using the word 'harms'). Another is that 'Of Evil (ill) manners, spring good laws'. Hell is equally lightly treated. There are only 11 proverbs cited, including 'From Hell, Hull and Halifax, good Lord deliver us'; 'Hell and chancery are always open'; 'Hell or Connaught' and other frivolous ones. None is concerned with the horrors of hell, how to avoid hell and so on. Hell is a place that is 'full of good meanings and wishes', 'paved with good intentions'; 'He that is in hell thinks there is no other heaven'. The Devil receives more attention, but again is treated with a frivolous lightness which is significant. 'The Devil always leaves a stink behind him'; 'The Devil gets up to the belfry by the vicar's skirts'; 'The devil is a busy bishop in his own diocese'; 'The Devil is an ass'; 'The Devil makes his Christmas-pies of lawyers' tongues and clerks' fingers'; 'The Devil will not come into Cornwall, for fear of being put into a pie' and many others. In sum, 'The Devil is not so black as he is painted'; he is a joker, God's ape, puny and weak, a trickster in a safe world.

Of course, the majestic prose of the Bible gives us a vision of a society where evil, hell, the Devil and all his works were very important. It would be foolish to overlook this dimension, and we can represent it here by one quotation. The Lord's Prayer included the phrase 'And lead us not into temptation; But deliver us from evil'. In his catechism, one of the sixteenth-century Protestants, Thomas Becon, quoted this slightly differently as 'But deliver us from the evil'. What was 'the evil'? It was 'our arch-enemy the devil, author of all evil'. Becon referred here to St Paul, who had equated the evil and the Devil. Satan, Becon tells us, brings about two major species of evil, of the soul and of the body. The evils of the soul include 'incredulity, misbelief, doubting, . . . uncircumcision of heart, corruption of judgement, error, heresy,

---

[30] Gairdner, *Paston Letters;* Hanham, *Cely Letters;* Verney, *Memoirs.*

schisms, controversies in religion, sects, pride of the mind, obstinancy in wickedness, fleshly lusts' and many others. There were also many evils of the body, including 'sudden death, plague, pestilence, unwholesome weather . . . famine, hunger, battle, dearth, beggary, loss of goods, infamy, shame, confusion, madness . . .' and a host of others.[31] It is essential to remember that, at least nominally, this was a Christian civilization based on the premise that there were tangible evils, the Devil and hell; catechisms, sermons and much of education were founded on these beliefs. Yet, just as Keith Thomas has shown the amazing amount of religious ignorance and even stark atheism in this period and country,[32] so it may be that, while people knew little of God and Christ, they also knew little of the Devil, and cared less.

A satisfying explanation of the absence of absolute evil, the Devil and hell will need a fuller treatment. It is clearly no coincidence, for example, that England was the only major European nation to have no Catholic Inquisition and no inquisitorial process under law. The terror of evil was not encouraged. Another part of the solution, as well as further evidence on the nature of the problem, is provided by two of those who wrote in England during the period under consideration. They have provided two of the best accounts of the problems of evil and good known to us, namely Shakespeare and Milton.

One of the most striking features of both authors, making them seem very 'modern' and relevant to us, is that they are concerned with a grey world where good and evil are interchangeable; where it is impossible to be certain, to have absolute moral standards; where nothing is entirely black or white. This is clearly the case in Shakespeare's treatment of all his central characters – Hamlet, Brutus, Prospero, Macbeth and even Iago. For them, the choices are difficult, there is no absolute standard, things are not what they seem. Shakespeare even suggests reasons why good and evil have become blurred. Money, he shows, could change one into the other. Here he is touching on a central paradox. In a capitalist society, evil becomes good, good evil. Karl Marx quoted Shakespeare approvingly because he had seen this central feature.[33] A passage from *Timon of Athens* (Act IV, scene 3) is worth quoting at greater length than that in Marx's work. Timon digs in the ground and finds gold.

[31] Becon, *Works*, 196.   [32] Thomas, *Religion*, ch. 6.
[33] Marx and Engels, *German Ideology*, 102; Marx, *Grundrisse*, 163.

What is here?
Gold? yellow, glittering precious gold? No, gods,
I am no idle votarist. Roots, you clear heavens!
Thus much of this will make black, white; foul, fair;
Wrong, right; base, noble; old, young; coward, valiant.
Ha, you gods! why this? What this, you gods? Why, this
Will lug your priests and servants from your sides;
Pluck stout men's pillows from below their heads:
This yellow slave
Will knit and break religions; bless the accurs'd;
Make the hoar leprosy ador'd; place thieves,
And give them title, knee, and approbation,
With senators on the bench: this is it
That makes the wrappen'd widow wed again; . . .

Thus, gold transforms everything, from black to white and back again; it brings together as equivalents things that are not really on the same plane and divides things that are naturally together. Man is no longer able to discriminate between what is good, what evil.

This confusion at the heart of life is echoed in Milton's greatest poem. The central theme of *Paradise Lost* is the battle between good and evil. Yet the struggle is not between two opposed sides, but within the same principle. The poem is an attempt to state the paradox that good and evil are entirely separate, yet also entirely the same. It grapples with the problem of how evil emerged at all, for it arose out of goodness. The problem is given one formulation in the myth of the Garden of Eden, where evil was present even in a perfect paradise. Once evil has emerged as distinct from goodness, having become separated, the problem for both is to prevent their mutual contamination and a tendency to become joined again. The attempt to foil God's attempt to bring them back into his mercy is the subject of many of Satan's famous lines in the poem. 'If then his providence/Out of our evil seek to bring forth good,/Our labour must be to prevent that end,/And out of good still find means of evil' (book i, line 157). The world has to be redefined in order to achieve this. 'So farewell hope, and with hope farewell fear,/Farewell remorse: all good to me is lost; Evil be thou my Good' (book iv, line 108). Yet, just as evil has emerged out of the principle of good, so it is possible for good to emerge from evil. This is the constant threat to the fallen angels; that God may win them back and turn their evil into good, for the power of goodness is very great: 'abashed the devil stood, And felt how awful goodness is' (book iv, line 846). Ultimately, good and evil are not separable. Heaven and hell, the Devil and God are in essence different aspects of the same power.

Milton's poem could be seen as the eloquent expression of the tragic recognition that the simplicities of a childlike black and white vision are not sufficient. It is all a matter of how we look at things, a subjectivist world in which man cannot depend on any external, eternal, objective, moral laws. Milton needed to justify the ways of God to man; as a result, each man would act as a judge upon God, rather than the reverse. Morality was in the eye of the beholder. As Pope would put it, 'Pleasure, or wrong or rightly understood/Our greatest evil, or our greatest good' (*Essay on Man*, epistle 2, line 91).

Pope, indeed, represented the culmination of a trend towards ethical relativism which argued from growing evidence that every civilization had its own appropriate moral system. Pascal had summarized this view in the seventeenth century. 'We hardly know of anything just or unjust which does not change its character with a change of climate. Three degrees of polar elevation overturn the whole system of jurisprudence. A meridian determines what is truth . . . There is not a single law which is universal'.[34] Pope took the next step:

All nature is but art, unknown to thee;
All chance, direction which thou canst not see;
All discord, harmony not understood;
All partial evil, universal good;
And, spite of pride, in erring reason's spite,
One truth is clear, Whatever is, is right.
Essay on Man, epistle 1, line 289

Beyond this lay extreme cynicism, as expressed for instance by Charles Churchill:

Keep up appearances; there lies the test;
The world will give thee credit for the rest.
Outward be fair, however foul within;
Sin, if thou wilt, but then in secret sin.[35]

[34] Pascal, *Pensées*, II, 126ff. [35] Churchill, *Poems*, I, 71.

In a short essay such as this, it is possible only to raise a few questions and hint at an answer to the problem of the origins of the disappearance of pure evil. Both the answer and the problem are encapsulated in St Paul's warning that 'the love of money is the root of all evil' (1 Timothy 6, v. 10). This dismissal of avarice is one of the central pillars of that Judaeo-Christian tradition upon which western civilization is based. Yet, it could equally well be argued that the love of money – the famous propensity to barter, trade, accumulate – is an equally important pillar of this civilization. Adam Smith most clearly exposed this foundation of modern society, a feature without which capitalist societies would immediately collapse. As he put it, 'the division of labour, from which so many advantages are derived . . . is the necessary . . . consequence of a certain propensity in human nature . . . the propensity to truck, barter, and exchange one thing for another'.[36] This division of labour and all that flows from it is thus based on a propensity that is, in the ethical terms laid down by the formal theology, evil. The foundations are laid on individual acquisitiveness, the love of money and pursuit of profit. Thus, good and evil are mixed in the roots of modern society.

Yet money, and all it symbolizes, is the root of all evil in a deeper sense than this. Viewed from outside the system, money can be seen to do something even more insidious. It subtly eliminates the very concept of evil. Or, rather, it makes it impossible to discriminate between good and evil, throwing people into that confusion that cast the angels from paradise and afflicted Shakespeare's central characters. 'Money', which is a shorthand way of saying capitalistic relations, market values, trade and exchange, ushers in a world of moral confusion. This effect of money has been most obvious where a capitalistic, monetary economy has clashed with another, opposed, system. Thus it is anthropologists, working in such areas of conflict, who have witnessed most dramatically the effect of the introduction of a monetized economy. They have noted how money disrupts the moral as well as the economic world. As Burridge, for example, writes of the effect of money in Melanesia: money complicates the moral order, turning what was formerly black and white into greyness. Money, he argues, 'reveals the vice in cultivated virtues, allows no vice without some virtue, concedes an element of right in wrong-doing, finds the sin of pride in an upright fellow. . . money invites a complex differentiation and

[36] Smith, *Wealth*, book 1, ch. 2: 17.

multiplication of the parts and qualities of man'.[37] More broadly, it is
money, markets and market capitalism that eliminate absolute
moralities. Not only is every moral system throughout the world
equally valid, as Pascal noted, but, *within* every system, whatever is, is
right.

The consequences of money and the mentality associated with it
are equally apparent to the major sociological thinkers. One of the
most eloquent descriptions of the way in which money destroys moral
polarities, qualitative difference, is in Simmel's essay on the
'Metropolis and Mental Life'.

By being the equivalent to all the manifold things in one and the same way,
money becomes the most frightful leveller. For money expresses all
qualitative differences of things in terms of 'how much?' Money, with all its
colourlessness and indifference, becomes the common denominator of all
values; irreparably it hollows out the core of things, their individuality, their
specific gravity in the constantly moving stream of money. All things lie on
the same level and differ from one another only in the size of the area which
they cover.[38]

The consequences of this moral revolution were already apparent to
people in the most developed capitalist economy, England, by the
eighteenth century.

What had happened was that capitalism had fully triumphed: to
modify Swinburne, 'Thou hast conquered, O pale Capitalism; the
world has grown grey from thy breath'.[39] It has now become clear that
what was considered to be the root of all evil, namely the love of
money, was also the root of all that was good, namely the bargaining,
market principle of Adam Smith. This paradox was so horrifying in
its implications that, when it was pointed out starkly, there was fierce
condemnation. The man who made the unspeakable truth known was
Bernard Mandeville, a Dutchman who had settled as a doctor in
London, in his *Fable of the Bees*. The subtitle of the work summarized
the theme: it was 'Private Vices, Public Benefits'. The work,
published in 1714, went alongside a doggerel poem entitled 'The
Grumbling Hive: or, Knaves Turn'd Honest', first published in 1705.

---

[37] Burridge, *New Heaven*, 45.   [38] Simmel, *Sociology*, 414.
[39] Swinburne's original (in *Hymn to ·Prosperpine*) referred to Christ, 'O pale
Galilean', rather than capitalism.

The theme of the poem was that it was out of the private passions and
vices of the citizens – their lusts, acquisitive spirits and aggressive
competition – that public benefits flowed. As Mandeville rhymed,

> Thus every part was full of Vice,
> Yet the whole Mass a Paradice;
> Flatter'd in Peace, and fear'd in wars
> They were th'Esteem of Foreigners,
> And lavish of their Wealth and Lives,
> The Balance of all other Hives.
> Such were the Blessings of that State;
> Their Crimes conspired to make 'em Great;
> And Vertue, who from Politicks.
> Had learn'd a Thousand cunning Tricks,
> Was, by their happy Influence,
> Made Friends with Vice: And ever since
> The Worst of all the Multitude
> Did something for the common Good.[40]

Out of vice and evil passion came forth wealth and goodness. Evil lay at
the heart of good in a capitalist society, just as evil had lain at the heart
of good when the good angels had arisen to build a new world in the
midst of Paradise. Mandeville's message was that, if one tried to be
privately virtuous, the public world would collapse. Right at the end of
the *Fable* Mandeville concluded that:

After this I flatter my self to have demonstrated that neither the Friendly
Qualities and kind Affections that are natural to Man, nor the real Virtues he is
capable of acquiring by Reason and Self-Denial are the foundation of Society;
but that what we call Evil in this World, Moral as well as Natural, is the grand
principle that makes us Sociable Creatures, the solid Basis, the Life and
Support of all Trades and Employments without exception: That there we
must look for the true origin of all Arts and Sciences, and that the moment Evil
ceases, the Society must be spoil'd if not totally dissolv'd.[41]

This was Mandeville's central message, and it was incorporated in the
great work that was written by the very moral Adam Smith, and which
would outline the basis of the capitalist system: 'Without any

[40] Mandeville, *Fable*, 67–8.   [41] Ibid., 370.

intervention of law, therefore, the private interests and passions of men naturally lead them to divide and distribute the stock of every society, among all the different employments carried on in it, as nearly as possible in the proportion which is most aggreeable to the interest of the whole society.'[42] Thus private vice, passions and interest have merged into public good.

Ironically, the foundations of Paradise were laid in hell, and hell in Paradise. The serpent of desire propped up the tree of the knowledge of good and evil. Or, to put it another way, the serpent was also the tree. By being that tree, he led to the ultimate confusion, the inability to distinguish between good and evil. When the fruit was tasted, it was found that, rather than containing the new knowledge that enabled man to discriminate good from evil, it contained the deadly knowledge that it was now impossible to distinguish the two.

If the thesis advanced here has any truth in it, namely that capitalism and a money order were fatally intertwined with an inability to distinguish good and evil, it is clearly necessary to go futher. We need to probe deep into the origins of capitalism in order to seek out how it had eliminated the opposition of good and evil. Such an adventure is for another occasion. What is clear is that, at least at the popular level in England, the ambivalences and contradictions were present back to the start of the sixteenth century. From other work on related themes, it seems likely that they were present much earlier, at least back to the thirteenth century.[43] It is possible to argue that ordinary people in England had for centuries been accustomed to a world not of absolutes, but of relative good and evil, where all could be changed by money. It is appropriate and hardly fortuitous that Shakespeare should have provided the most exquisite expressions of that uncertainty in the midst of the period, or that in its full flowering Pope should have summarized the indecision and confusion so grandly:

> Placed on this isthmus of a middle state,
> A being darkly wise, and rudely great:
>
> . . .
>
> He hangs between; in doubt to act, or rest;
> In doubt to deem himself a god, or beast;
>
> . . .

[42] Quoted in Hirschman, *Passions.* 110–11.   [43] Macfarlane, *Individualism.*

Chaos of thought and passion, all confused;
Still by himself abused, or disabused;
Created half to rise, and half to fall;
Great Lord of all things, yet a prey to all;
Sole judge of truth, in endless error hurled:
The glory, jest, and riddle of the world!

An Essay on Man, epistle 2

6
Love

Love and Capitalism

L OVE BETWEEN men and women as the basis of marriage is a central feature of modern industrial societies.[1] Such love is a powerful cultural component with large implications both for the societies themselves and the civilizations they are affecting. Yet this association of love and marriage is neither universal nor automatic. The majority of people in most societies believe that marriage is too important a matter to be left to the individuals concerned. Hence the personal feelings of the prospective marriage partners, their 'love' attraction, is largely irrelevant to arranging a marriage. This is not to argue that 'love' or deep affection between members of the opposite sex are unknown outside modern industrial societies. There is plenty of evidence for these emotions in simple societies, and to a certain extent in tribal societies 'love matches' may be recognized as a basis for marriage.[2] Yet if we distinguish between love outside and within marriage, there is a certain peculiarity of the western pattern. It is unusual to find that the person one marries should be the person one has previously loved, and reciprocally that the person one loves should be the person one marries. In many societies, love affairs occur before and outside marriage, but marriages are nevertheless arranged. In many societies the arranged marriages lead to companionate love within marriage. What is extraordinary is the fact that the decision to marry should be based on the premise that love

---

[1] A number of individuals at the conference on 'Love' at the University of Virginia, Charlottesville, Spetember 1986, made helpful comments on a draft of this essay. Several of the suggested modifications have been incorporated.

[2] Westermarck, *Marriage*, II, ch. 21.

and marriage are indistinguishably united. Thus particularly in peasant societies, marriage is largely based on arrangement by kin or other wider groups and the personal feelings of an often very young couple are not of concern. Love marriage, the romantic love complex, may therefore be seen as a culturally peculiar institution. This strange pattern whereby love between a man and a woman before and during marriage becomes the basis for the familial and emotional system of a whole complex civilization has naturally attracted the attention of anthropologists.

Ralph Linton summarized the findings of cross-comparative research thus: 'all societies recognize that there are occasional violent attachments between persons of the opposite sex, but our present American culture is practically the only one which has attempted to capitalize these and make them the basis for marriage'.[3] E. A. Hoebel came to the same conclusion, suggesting that 'few people are so given to romantic love as are Americans. In our individualistic sentimentalism we exalt the ideal of marriage based on love – that mysterious psychophysiological reaction'.[4] Robert Redfield concluded that 'not many societies have been able to afford some approximation of romantic love as realized in marriage; peasant societies are certainly not among them'.[5]

It was Robert Lowie who most forcefully and caustically summed up the extensive anthropological evidence. In most human societies 'practical points of view are foremost in inaugurating and maintaining the conjugal state. They eclipse romance not only among aborigines, but virtually everywhere except in small circles of Western society. Romance need not be absent, but it is held inessential for that serious part of life which is marriage'. Elsewhere Lowie went further, arguing that 'individual attraction, we repeat, is not the basic factor; our own immediate ancestors and virtually every other society in human history would have rejected contemporary Western conceptions as absurd and vicious in principle.' He wrote ironically, 'but of love among savages? . . . Passion, of course, is taken for granted; affection, which many travellers vouch for, might be conceded; but Love? Well,

---

[3] Linton, quoted in Hunt, *Love*, 308.   [4] Hoebel, *Primitive*, 214.
[5] Redfield, *Human Nature*, 317.

the romantic sentiment occurs in simpler conditions, as with us – in fiction'.[6]

A recent survey of friendship and love by a British anthropologist finds only slight evidence of the 'romantic love complex' in non-western societies and the author concludes that 'the combination of spiritual love, frustrated sex, and marriage is a uniquely Western contribution'.[7] Here he is echoing the earlier views of the literary critic C. S. Lewis, who wrote that the love poetry of England from the sixteenth century onwards was 'a highly specialized historical phenomenon – the peculiar flower of a peculiar civilization, important whether for good or ill and well worth our understanding'.[8] It is indeed important to understand both the causes and the functions of this peculiarity, to know 'what are the social and cultural factors that have led us – unique among the societies of the world – to marry for love?'.[9] This essay will consider some of the alternative solutions that have been suggested to this problem with particular reference to the case of England.

Having roughly tied down the association between love and marriage in space, the next step is to locate it in time. Any explanation of the causes of this unusual association will depend heavily on when it is believed that it first emerged. One view is that the complex is very recent, that the harnessing of the mysterious passion of 'love' to marriage was a relatively recent invention, probably occurring about the same time as the supposed rise of 'modern' industrial civilization in western Europe and northern America. This would locate its origin in the second half of the eighteenth and first half of the nineteenth century, appropriately coinciding with the Romantic Movement in literature and art. The argument is plausible enough. The anomie or rootless lack of consensus and values caused by rapid industrial and urban growth, combined with the emergence of the impersonal relations of market capitalism, were bound to create a new emotional structure. One side-effect of the first urban and industrial revolution was a new sentiment and a new marriage system, appropriately based on individualism in its most extreme form. In answer to Keith Thomas's question as to whether it is true that 'romantic love is the

[6] Lowie, *Social Organization*, 220, 95, and quoted in Goode, 'Love', 40.
[7] Brain, *Friends*, 222.
[8] Lewis, *Allegory*, 360.   [9] Brain, *Friends*, 245.

product of a poorly integrated society, in the way that the literary form of tragedy is said to be', most historians, sociologists and anthropologists would answer 'yes'.[10] Depending on how one regards the 'romantic love complex', it could be seen as one of the compensations for the loneliness and isolation of a disintegrated, associational, society, or as yet another curse produced by the disintegration of the old community bonds.

Robert Lowie, we have seen, thought that 'our own immediate ancestors' would have rejected contemporary western ideas on love marriage. A. R. Radcliffe-Brown believed that 'we must remember that the modern English idea of marriage is recent and decidedly unusual, the product of a particular social development'.[11] Brain believes that it was 'in the middle of the eighteenth century [that] romantic love ceased to be a frenzy or a tragic condition and became a desirable state . . .'.[12] The view that love connected with marriage is an 'invention of modernization' and, in particular, the result of events in north-western Europe in the eighteenth and nineteenth centuries, is based on the work of a number of historians.

It seemed plausible to guess that if individualistic 'love' was somehow associated with capitalism, with an individualistic philosophy, and possibly with changes in standards of living and changes in the means of production, then the roots of this phenomenon should be located centrally in the eighteenth and nineteenth centuries. Furthermore, it seemed likely that the oddness of love could be linked to the growing oddness of England as the first industrial and urban society and the prototype of market capitalism. The supposed bourgeois revolution of the seventeenth century in England, the changes in the relations of production, would lead to changes in the ideology, to an affective revolution. This discovery of love and its uses as a basis for marriage could then be seen, as Lawrence Stone has described it, as 'perhaps the most important change in *mentalité* to have occurred in the Early Modern period, indeed possibly in the last thousand years of Western history'.[13] The widely accepted model of a revolution in social, economic and political life in England and parts of western Europe, when a peasant and feudal society was

---

[10] Thomas, 'History', 15–16.   [11] Radcliffe-Brown, *African Kinship*, 43.
[12] Brain, *Friends*, 247.
[13] Stone, *Family*, 4.

transformed between the sixteenth and eighteenth centuries into a 'modern' and capitalistic one, fits well with the view that there must also have been a simultaneous revolution in sentiment. Indeed it is almost essential that there should have been this tremendous change in ideology.

It is widely believed that there was a growth of individualism during the period between the sixteenth and nineteenth centuries in Europe and particularly in England. This involved the transformation of a traditional, group-based, kinship-dominated society into the modern capitalistic system. These changes were described in the work of such historians as R. H. Tawney and Christopher Hill, building on the work of Marx and Weber. In the period between 1400 and 1750 the following major changes are thought to have occurred: the invention of private, absolute property and the destruction of group ownership; the elimination of the household as the basic unit of production and consumption; the growth of a money economy; the rise of a class of permanent wage-labourers; the growing dominance of the profit motive and the psychological drive towards endless accumulation; the rise of modern industrial production; the growth of large urban centres, the elimination of those 'magical' and 'irrational' forces which prevented the rational pursuit of economic gain; the undermining of small, closely-meshed communities with the growth of geographical and social mobility. England, it is argued, changed from a society in which the individual was subordinated to a group of some kind, whether the family, village, religious congregation or estate, to a land of almost autonomous individuals, bound together by money, paper and allegiance to the new nation-state.

The ideology of romantic love, 'vicious in principle' because it places the wishes of the individual above those of the wider group, could be predicted to emerge. It is the affective dimension of this major transformation. As the political, economic and social structures went through a revolution, so, we would expect, there would be a revolution in mentality and sentiment. Peasantries, as Redfield pointed out, are not characterized by the ideology of romantic love. Many argue that England was a peasant society until about the seventeenth century. It was only when a peasant society became transformed into a capitalistic one that the new marriage system based on love could emerge.

This connection between capitalism and the 'modern' marital system was made long ago by Engels, extending Marx's theories. He pointed out that monogamy was a necessary if not sufficient cause of modern 'sex-love', as he called it, but that it took time for such monogamous marriage to develop into our modern individual-choice marriage. In medieval society, Engels argued, 'the question of fitness was unconditionally decided, not by individual inclination, but by family interests. In the overwhelming majority of cases the marriage contract thus remained to the end of the middle ages what it has been from the outset: a matter that was not decided by the parties most interested'. Then a new capitalistic world began to emerge in the later fifteenth century. This created a new order: 'by changing all things into commodities, it dissolved all inherited and traditional relations and replaced time hallowed custom and historical right by purchase and sale, by "free contract" '. In order to make valid contracts people must be, nominally, 'free' and 'equal', and hence 'the creation of these "free" and "equal" people was precisely one of the main functions of capitalist production'. Engels argued that while marriages became 'contracts', legal affairs, the principle of freedom to contract inevitably if gradually placed the decision in the hands of those who would have to honour the contract – the couple themselves. 'Did not the two young people who were to be coupled together have the right freely to dispose of themselves, of their bodies, and the organs of these?' So the 'rising bourgeoisie', especially those in Protestant countries where freedom was greatest, recognized the 'freedom of contracting a marriage'. In short, 'the love match was proclaimed as a human right'.[14]

Thus romantic love could be seen as one of the side-effects of the dissolution of feudal, peasant society and the emergence of the market principles of capitalism, of increasing individualism and individual property. Since this occurred, according to a widely accepted chronology, in north-western Europe from the end of the fifteenth century, reaching its climax in the seventeenth and eighteenth centuries, it is then that we should find the birth of the 'romantic love complex'. The model gives the causes and predicts the timing.

More recently, a second type of argument has led people to expect that the so-called revolution in sentiment must have occurred recently: this was the argument from a change in the physical environment. It is widely accepted that one of the major transformations in world history has been the rapid reduction in infant, child and adult mortality during

---

[14] Engels, *Origin*, 95–8.

the so-called 'demographic transition' which many date from the middle of the eighteenth century.[15] Most human societies for most of history have experienced high mortality. This, it has been suggested, had a considerable effect on emotional relations.

The French historian Philippe Ariès, in his study of childhood, was one of the first to suggest a direct connection between love and death. He stated that 'people could not allow themselves to become too attached to something that was regarded as a probable loss. This is the reason for certain remarks which shock our present-day sensibility . . . Nobody thought, as we ordinarily think today, that every child already contained a man's personality. Too many of them died'.[16] The argument was soon extended from the relations with children to those between men and women. Husbands and wives, it was suggested, dared not invest strongly in their emotional relationships because of the threat that one of them would die. The subsequent cruelty of husbands to wives led to further mortality and increased insecurity. More widely, it began to be argued that the callousness within the family arising from demographic insecurity led to whole societies in the past being inhabited by cold and aggressive individuals, incapable of feeling love and affection. The birth of affection, joy in another's presence, spontaneous warmth, the romantic love complex, came to be linked with the supposed demographic revolution which started to reduce mortality in the eighteenth century.

The most forceful exponent of this view is Lawrence Stone. In a large book on the family he repeatedly argues that affection and love were, on the whole, impossible before the eighteenth century because the conditions of pre-industrial life were so insecure that people did not dare to enter into a deep relationship for fear of it abruptly ending. Marriage based on love was impossible until mortality dropped. Stone argues that marriages only lasted for an average of 17 to 20 years in 'Early Modern England', and thus they were 'statistically speaking, a transient and temporary association'. Consequently, he claims, relations between husband and wife lacked affection, both before and during marriage. The conjugal family, based on unloved children and unloving husband and wife, was therefore 'very short-lived and unstable in its composition. Few mutual demands were made on its members, so that it was a low-keyed and undemanding institution

which could therefore weather this instability with relative ease'. This
demographic insecurity was exacerbated by economic insecurity.
Stone argues that sentiment cannot thrive in poverty. Writing of the
eighteenth century, he suggests that there 'are levels of human misery
at which the intensity of the struggle to satisfy the basic need for food
and shelter leaves little room for humane emotions and affective
relationships'.[17] Thus the majority of the population, who lived in such
conditions up to the end of the eighteenth century, could not 'afford'
love.

According to the general theory, love is a consequence of
demographic, industrial and capitalistic revolutions, coming to a head
in the eighteenth century in England. The first wave of historians to
devote themselves exclusively to family history, and particularly
marriage, found what the model predicted they would find, the
invention of sentiment and the 'romantic love complex' in the
eighteenth century. The situation at the end of a decade of work in
1980 has been well surveyed by Michael Anderson in a chapter
summarizing the 'Sentiments Approach' to the history of the western
family.[18] He outlines the work of Ariès, Shorter, Stone and Flandrin,
and points out that their views were all in accord with one another, and
that they all believe in an affective revolution located predominantly in
the eighteenth and early nineteenth centuries. The agreed general
view can be illustrated in the work of Edward Shorter.

Shorter argued that the family has broken loose from its
surroundings, the 'traditional' embedded family giving way to the
separate nuclear family. Marriage has changed from being arranged by
kin to the modern system of choice and affection; 'popular marriage in
former centuries was usually affectionless, held together by considerations of property and lineage'. Within marriage 'the prospect of death
seemed to arouse no deep sentiments between spouses'. All this
changed in a revolutionary way towards the end of the eighteenth
century. There was a 'sexual revolution' when 'young people began
paying much more attention to inner feelings than to outward
considerations, such as property and parental wishes, in choosing
marriage partners'. At the same period 'a rush of sentiment swept over
mating and dating', replacing the 'lack of romance in peasant
courtship' in the traditional society with the new ideology of romantic

---

[17] Stone, *Family*, 55, 60, 476.   [18] Anderson, *Approaches*, ch. 3.

love. Courtship was transformed, 'the most important change in nineteenth and twentieth century courtship has been the surge of sentiment'.[19]

The cause of the revolution was the development of capitalism: 'market capitalism was probably at the root of the revolution in sentiment'.[20] According to Shorter, capitalism broke down the small, economically self-sufficient communities that had been universal in the 'traditional' societies existing up to the eighteenth century. Markets opened up, mobility increased, people were caught up in a new and open environment with money and market values dominant. Secondly, capitalism improved the standard of living. This altered the material conditions of life. Thirdly, capitalism, or more particularly its manifestation in a particular industrial form, led to the break-up of the rural communities. People were sucked into an urban and industrial proletariat.

The ways in which these changes caused the 'romance revolution' are partly indicated by Shorter. The changes led to the ethic of individualism and competition. Thus ordinary people were forced into the market-place and 'this egoistical economic mentality spread into various noneconomic domains of life, specifically into those ties that bind the individual to the surrounding community'.[21] As Engels had argued long before, the desire to be free in one sphere led to a desire to be free in emotional life. Furthermore, an improvement in material standards, Shorter argues, allowed maternal love to flourish with new-found leisure, and the same argument could well be applied to conjugal love.

There seemed strong grounds for arguing that capitalism and industrialism, with connected demographic and social changes, were the causes of the peculiar pattern of romantic love. As predicted, they caused a revolution in sentiment in the eighteenth century, from which our modern world has developed. A challenge to this position would throw into question the model of the origins of modern civilization. If it turned out to be the case that romantic love was not basically an invention of the eighteenth and early nineteenth centuries, we would have to reassess our way of thinking about the transition from 'pre-modern' to 'modern'. This seemed an unlikely eventuality.

[19] Shorter, *Modern Family*, 55, 57, 79, 141, 148.   [20] Ibid., 255.
[21] Ibid., 258, 259.

In fact, it has become increasingly clear that the connection between love and the rise of capitalism is much more complex than this. Already in the late 1960s and 1970s the work of historical demographers, and in particular John Hajnal, Peter Laslett and E. A. Wrigley, showed that many of the most unusual structural features of the north-west European family and marriage patterns were very old.[22] Variously dated back to the start of the sixteenth century, or several centuries earlier, it was now clear that most people had married at a relatively late age, or not at all, and that married children had lived apart from their parents in small households. There was little evidence in the newly discovered listings of inhabitants and the evidence beginning to emerge from parish register reconstitutions that there had been a structural transformation in the demographic and marital patterns in the sixteenth, seventeenth or eighteenth centuries. Some of the main characteristics of this pattern, enduring from the sixteenth to nineteenth centuries, were specified by Peter Laslett in 1977. These included the nuclear family form, the late age at marriage, a small gap between spouses, 'marriage tending towards the companionate', and the presence of large numbers of servants. Thus Laslett suggested that the pattern of family and marriage was basically 'the same in the 1550s as it was in the 1820s'. Largely on the basis of work by Richard Smith, he suggested that this pattern probably went back to the fourteenth century at least. If these demographic parameters had changed little, Laslett inferred 'that Western marriage has always tended to be companionate'. But he admitted that 'only the attitudinal or ideological evidence we need so much to discover could vindicate the claim'.[23] It was during the 1980s that such evidence began to be published.

The orthodox positon on sentiment was challenged in an article in 1979,[24] but it was only in the 1980s that convincing evidence was produced to show that the predictions of the capitalist revolution model were totally wrong. Some of the major works were written by historians, others by anthropologists and sociologists. We may very briefly summarize a number of the landmarks in this surprisingly rapid overturning of a whole school of thought.

[22] Hajnal, 'European Marriage'; Laslett, *Family Life;* Wrigley, *Population.*
[23] Laslett, *Family Life,* 13, 27, 42.
[24] Macfarlane, 'Review'.

The anthropologist Jacqueline Sarsby examined the development
of romantic love in England using literary, autobiographical and local
materials. Her historical chapters flatly contradict the developmental
story as embodied in the 'rise of sentiment' school.[25] Ferdinand
Mount considered the evidence without a pre-commitment to a belief
in the capitalist and other revolutions which should have caused a late
invention of love, and his work supports Sarsby's. Through an
examination of a wide variety of sources dating back to Anglo-Saxon
England he suggests that 'most of what has been written until recently
about the family in times past must now be dismissed or questioned'.[26] He finds strong evidence for the romantic love complex as
far back as the historical records extend. On a related topic, Linda
Pollock found that the theory of the invention of parental love in the
eighteenth century was equally questionable.[27]

Finally, among those who were not full-time historians, the
anthropologist Jack Goody argued that the basic structural shape of
'modern' marriage had been attained in England by the eleventh
century at the latest, and in all probability between the fourth and
ninth centuries. The emphasis on the conjugal pair, on consent, a
high status for women, and many of the other preconditions for the
romantic love complex were already present in late Anglo-Saxon
England. He argues that the 'love match' was encouraged by the
Church's insistence on consent and affection in the early middle ages.
This institution in essence owes 'little to the later transformations of
feudalism, mercantile capitalism, industrial society, Hollywood or the
Germanic tradition'.[28]

These views are now supported by a number of full-time historians
who have come to the same conclusion. In a collection of essays on
marriage in England, the contributors challenge the orthodoxy.
Christopher Brooke shows how important consent and affection were
in medieval marriage, Martin Ingram shows the presence of love in
ecclesiastical court litigation from the sixteenth century and Kathleen
Davies shows that the ideals of family life changed very little as
between the fifteenth and seventeenth centuries.[29] In one of the first
syntheses of the new historical research on early modern England,

[25] Sarsby, *Romantic Love*, 35, 36, 66.   [26] Mount, *Subversive Family*, 123.
[27] Pollock, *Forgotten Children*.
[28] Goody, *Family*, 155.   [29] Outhwaite, *Marriage*, chs 1, 2, 3.

Keith Wrightson devotes two chapters to the family, drawing on a very wide range of published and unpublished sources. He concludes that below the level of aristocracy, gentry and urban elite 'there is no doubt whatever that . . . the initiative in selecting a spouse already lay with the young people concerned' in the period between 1580 and 1680. In the motivation of those getting married, he can discern no significant shift in this period. Thus he concludes that 'there is little reason to follow Professor Stone in regarding the rise of the companionate marriage as a new phenomenon of the later seventeenth and eighteenth centuries. It seems to have been already well established'.[30]

A particularly interesting study on the English family from 1450 to 1700, by Ralph Houlbrooke, covers the central period of the supposed birth of the 'modern' world of capitalism and individualism. It is exclusively devoted to the family and marriage and heavily based on the excellent church court records, which are among the best sources for the study of marital sentiment and behaviour. A whole section in the book, drawing on many sources, shows the importance of love in marriage. On the question of a revolutionary change in the marital and family pattern in this period Houlbrooke is unequivocal. 'Between the fifteenth and eighteenth centuries there was little change in familial forms and functions'.[31] His picture is one of continuity in a system based on personal choice and a mixture of love and economic considerations from the fifteenth century onwards. This view is also the one which I have argued for, using a number of different sources, over the period 1300–1840.[32] The book corroborates the views of Sarsby, Mount, Goody, Pollock, Ingram, Davies, Wrightson and Houlbrooke that it is a mistake to believe that affection and lover were inventions of the sixteenth and seventeenth centuries, let alone the eighteenth.

Two major problems emerge from the overturning of the orthodox view that the romantic love complex was largely invented in the eighteenth century. One is historiographical; namely, how did so many historians manage to make such very considerable errors? Various explanations may be mentioned. First, there was the strength of the predictive model. As Shorter and Stone, in particular, show,

---

[30] Wrightson, *English Society*, 74, 79, 103.   [31] Houlbrooke, *English Family*, 253.
[32] Macfarlane, *Marriage*, especially ch. 9.

the paradigm of a capitalist revolution, later reinforced with industrial, urban and demographic revolutions, should have led to the situation which they thought they found in the historical materials. If Marx and Weber are right in their timing, then the ideological effects of the Protestant Reformation and capitalist revolution, alongside the rise of a supposed new political and individualistic order, should indeed have been matched by a new family and marriage system whose central pivot was the conjugal unit. The model predicted the revolution in structure and sentiment, and the revolution was duly found.

A second reason for error lies in a conflation of evidence from different countries. While most writers accept in principle that the experience of England and that of France, Germany and other continental countries may have been, and probably was, very different, in practice they tend to overlook this. If we were to put on one side all evidence from outside England for the moment, then almost all of the proof for the work of Ariès, Flandrin, Shorter, Stone and others would fall away. Other reasons for error include the taking of material out of context, the jumbling of chronology, false arguments that absence of the expression of emotion means the absence of emotion, deductions about the bulk of the population from the elite and other logical, technical and historical errors.[33]

Yet in rejecting the revolutionary interpretation of family structure and the neat causal link with rapid changes in the eighteenth and nineteenth centuries, we create other problems. We are forced to wonder whether a paradigm that so conspicuously failed to predict what appears to have happened and led to so much error is of much value. We have to question the whole theory of the transition to capitalism and 'modernism'. Furthermore, we are left once again with the problems of trying to explain the causes of the peculiar marriage system.

If the romantic love complex was strongly present in the sixteenth century or earlier in England, we clearly have to reject industrialization and urbanization as causes. It is also clear that the demographic argument, from insecurity to the absence of sentiment, is wrong. This is an important finding. If it had been established that in this case high death rates, constant sickness and poverty had made 'love' impossible, it might well have been suggested that all our ancestors, and all those

[33] Macfarlane, 'Review'.

living in such conditions in the Third World, were loveless, brutalized and without affection. Of course, an enormous amount of anthropological research in tribal and other societies has documented the tenderness of parents towards their children, affection within marriage, and spontaneity and depth of feeling which is perfectly compatible with high infant and adult mortality and grinding poverty. But all this might have been brushed aside by the supposed dramatic case of the birth of 'modern' society in Europe and North America. As it happens, however, even this case shows how shallow and naive deductions from the physical and demographic world do not help us to understand the way in which humans think and feel.

It now seems certain that the romantic love complex was widespread in England by the fifteenth century and probably long before. How are we to explain its presence if we can no longer rely on traditional theories concerning the urban and industrial revolutions and the supposed effects of the rise of capitalism and the Protestant Reformation of the sixteenth century onwards? One widely accepted theory is that there was a diffusion of a new concept of marriage outwards from southern France. The work of C. S. Lewis, De Rougemont, and more recently Georges Duby, has suggested that out of the adulterous philanderings of courtiers, or possibly as a result of a new view of woman that emerged with Catharist heresy, a new sentiment emerged.[34] Thus C. S. Lewis argued that 'French poets, in the eleventh century, discovered or invented, or were the first to express, that romantic species of passion which English poets were still writing about in the nineteenth century'.[35] There are, however, numerous difficulties in using this theory to explain the presence of the romantic love complex in England by the later medieval period.

No one, as Lewis admits, has been able to explain satisfactorily why something should have been suddenly invented in twelfth-century France. The Germanic, Celtic, Byzantine, classical, Arabic or Cathar theories are all unsatisfactory in one way or another. This may be because, as Peter Dronke and others have argued, much that was taken by historians and literary critics to be new in the later eleventh century, is not, in fact, new at all.[36] Furthermore, it is now clear that

---

[34] Lewis, *Allegory;* De Rougemont, *Passion;* Duby, *Knight.*
[35] Lewis, *Allegory,* 27.
[36] Dronke, *Love Lyric.*

the portrayal of courtly love as being initially concerned exclusively with extra-marital love is incorrect.[37] A further difficulty is to show how the writings of southern French poets concerning the delights of adulterous love in the courtly circles in which they moved can have suddenly inspired millions of ordinary people within a relatively short time to feel a new and overwhelming emotion and alter centuries-old marriage practices. Life may mirror art, but this is rather an extreme case. Accidental literary origins for such a dramatic and powerful peculiarity are unlikely.

It seems much more plausible to suggest that there were major social, economic and ideological features of parts of Europe well back into the middle ages which made a certain kind of marriage both possible and desirable. It is an axiom of anthropology that everything is linked to something else, and consequently the ideology of romantic love as the basis for marriage would be part of the whole pattern of kinship and marriage. It will be linked to concepts of the purposes of marriage, the demography of marriage, ideas of the individual, the rules of marriage and so on. These patterns, in turn, will be linked to the economic, social, political and religious foundations of a society. In order to explain the origins and persistence of romantic love we need to show how it was linked to such other institutions. There is something attractive in the suggestion of Marx, Engels, Weber and their followers that there is some association between the ideology of love marriage and the individualistic and capitalistic structure of northern societies. Although the precise link in the sixteenth to eighteenth centuries does not fit the observed presence of the ideology, there is an alternative to rejecting the association altogether.

If we accept the theory that was dominant between 1880 and 1940 in England, then the distinctive features which form the background to romantic love were present in England well before the sixteenth century. As I have argued elsewhere, the individualism, market mentality, high mobility and other features which we associate with capitalism were present in England by at least the start of the thirteenth century and perhaps long before.[38] If this is correct, then the evidence concerning love falls into place. It is part of a very ancient system, both an indicator of such a pattern, and a consequence of it. It would seem that there were characteristics of the way in which kinship, religion,

[37] Mount, *Subversive Family*, ch. 6.   [38] Macfarlane, *Individualism*.

law, politics and economics were organized within the Germanic peoples who conquered western Europe which led to a pattern of which romantic love and companionate marriage are a part. Such a pattern never died out in England, whereas in much of Europe it was largely submerged by old and renovated features of the preceding Roman civilization. Being an island, one of the few areas which almost totally rejected Roman language, law and religion, England harboured a peculiar ethic of romantic love which had been more widespread earlier. Thus the ultimate origins are probably cultural and thousands of years old. Here we may end by briefly sketching a few of the ways in which such an ideology fitted functionally with some other parts of the society.

One important component was Christianity. As Jack Goody has argued, the distinctive pattern of Christian marriage was early established, the basic features being present by the ninth century.[39] This was a religion that enjoined celibacy, monogamy, a freedom of choice in marriage, and a severe sexual code prohibiting sexual relations before and outside marriage. Such a formal marriage regime enjoined by the dominant religious system was an ideal background for that peculiar romantic love ideology, which combined frustration, eroticism and desire. The ideals of celibacy, the late age at marriage, the battle between biological desire and religious injunctions are clearly a part of the pattern of romantic love. Passion was herded into marriage, sex and marriage were synonymous in a way that is unusual in world civilizations. Biological urges were channelled, sublimated and hence coloured the world. These special features were present in western Europe many centuries before the Protestant Reformation.

Romantic love also fitted with the kinship system. Talcott Parsons, when comparing the kinship system of the United States with more kinship-dominated societies, suggested that the 'structural isolation of the conjugal family tends to free the affective inclinations of the couple from a whole series of hampering restrictions'. In closely-knit, interdependent, kinship-based societies 'any considerable range of affective spontaneity would tend to impinge on the statuses and interests of too many others, with disequilibrating consequences for the system as a whole'.[40] When wider kinship is strong, marriages are arranged and affection between husband and wife is a secondary force.

[39] Goody, *Family*.   [40] Parsons, *Essays*, 187–8.

As Sjoberg has written, 'romantic love is, of all things, an expression
of individualism, and as such it is at variance with the maintenance of
a well-integrated extended kinship unit'.[41] Hence sociologists have
linked the rise of individual love marriage to the degree of
involvement of the conjugal family in wider kin ties, and to a lessened
set of obligations to parents after death.[42] We now know that the
cognatic kinship system which isolates out the husband and wife in
terminology and residence was present in England from Anglo-Saxon
time onwards. There is little evidence that wider kinship groupings
were important in everyday life among the mass of the population.
Romantic love was an appropriate ideology which could both flourish
and hold together this individualistic system.

The cohesive importance of romantic love in a society where
formal kinship is weak can be explored a little more. If kinship groups
do not arrange marriages why marry at all? One reason for marrying,
we have already seen, was that the ethical and social system was such
that to have sexual relations outside marriage was considered a
serious offence. As Thomas More pointed out in his *Utopia*,
premarital sex should be harshly punished for 'very few people would
want to get married ... if they weren't carefully prevented from
having any sexual intercourse otherwise'.[43] This links up with the
frustration theory, and has been repeated in other words by Robert
Brain who writes that 'perhaps without the passion of romantic loving
or its stimulation, along with the withholding of sexual access until
after marriage, people might not marry at all'.[44] There is a second
theory introduced here: namely, that the 'passion of romantic love'
binds people together in long-term associations which would
otherwise not occur. This also has been suggested by Greenfield:
'rational, profit-seeking, individuals would never marry at all except
for the "institutionalized irrationality" of romantic love'.[45] A socio-
biologist might, therefore, see romantic love as a necessary drive to
ensure the survival of the human race at a level above mere
short-term sexual couplings.

The romantic love ideology may be seen as appropriate, even
necessary, in a society where the external pressures on permanent

[41] Sjoberg, *Preindustrial City*, 153.   [42] Goode, *Family*, 39,52.
[43] More, *Utopia*, 103.
[44] Brain, *Friends*, 46.   [45] Quoted in Lasch, *Haven*, 144.

unions through kinship are largely absent. The intense emotion of love can also be seen as culturally induced or exaggerated by the religious and social ideology which equates sexual and marital relations. We can take these 'elective affinities' further by looking at the way in which such an ideology seems entirely appropriate, in a paradoxical way, for a capitalistic and individualistic society.

Intuitively there seems to be something plausible in the idea that the individualism of love marriage is linked to the individualism of modern society and of the 'free' person operating within a monetized, market, capitalistic system where he, or she, has individual property in his or her own body. The link which Marx and Engels made between certain relations of production and this ideology seems right; it is merely the timing of the association that is wrong. A world of individual private property, of contract, of high social and geographical mobility, of decisions made by the individual rather than the family, of constant choice and weighing of advantages, fits well with individual-choice marriage on an open market.

Even the apparent paradoxes support the association. The greatest of these has been noted by Greenfield, that between the supposed 'rationality' of capitalism and the 'irrationality' of love. This has been resolved by Weber, who delicately shows how it is not merely that frustration creates the passion of love, but that passion is sustained by the loneliness and alienation created by this particular form of society. Weber showed that the central emotional feature of 'love' is a necessity where capitalist economic structures have developed most fully. At first sight, sexual passion and 'love' seem to be totally at variance with what is needed by capitalism. Weber, summarized by Watt, observed that 'being one of the strongest non-rational factors in human life' sexual drives are 'one of the strongest potential menaces to the individual's rational pursuit of economic ends'.[46] Yet, by a subtle shift, love and sex were domesticated, the force was channelled, and love became one of the central dynamic elements in the capitalist system. Romantic love is, of course, possible and present outside capitalism, but only in capitalist, or capitalist-influenced societies, is it made the cultural pivot of the ideology.

Weber saw that as societies became more bureaucratic and 'rational', so at the heart of the system there grew an impulsive, irrational and

[46] Watt, Novel, 74.

non-capitalistic emotion at the level of the individual. We can see the same paradox in the treatment of the natural world. As things become more orderly, a desire for disorderliness and wildness grows; as the world is conquered by money and calculations of profit and loss, certain areas become reserved as totally outside any calculations based on profit. So it is with the growing desire for the totally overwhelming, irrational escape into romantic love. Just as he had caught the paradox of other-worldly mysticism leading to capitalistic accumulation, so Weber hints at the way in which love marriage lies at the heart of rational capitalism:

the erotic relation seems to offer the unsurpassable peak of the fulfilment of the request for love in the direct fusion of the souls of one to the other. This boundless giving of oneself is as radical as possible in its opposition to all functionality, rationality, and generality. It is displayed as the unique meaning which one creature in his irrationality has for another, and only for this specific other . . . The lover . . . knows himself to be freed from the cold skeleton hand of rational orders, just as completely as from the banality of everyday routine.[47]

Romantic love gives meaning in an otherwise dead and cold world. It promises that fusion with another human being which is so conspicuously lacking in the lonely crowds of autonomous individuals. It overcomes separation and gives the endlessly choice-making individual a rest, a categorical imperative which resolves all the doubts and indecisions. Furthermore, the emotion of desire, to have to own, to possess, fits very well with those similarly irrational desires to accumulate, possess and own which are the basic drive in the economic sphere. In the modern world it is obvious how consumer society has harnessed the romantic passions to sell goods, and how its enormous emphasis has raised love to a high cultural pinnacle. Love provides the promise of freedom, meaning and a return to Eden.

The opposition between the seeming 'rationality' of modern society and 'irrationality' of love is, of course, more complex than this. To start with, we need to distinguish between the irrational, passionate, love that helps in selecting a partner, and companionate love that maintains a relationship. Choice, whether in the market of marriage or other goods, is always difficult. The information is always so insufficient, the variables

---

[47] Gerth and Mills, *Max Weber*, 347.

so complex that some external force of desire is needed to help the individual to make a choice. Hence passionate 'love' overwhelms and justifies and provides compulsive authority. But the love within marriage is not necessarily as passionate or 'irrational'. It can be calm, calculating, ends and means closely connected, very like any other 'work'. If a decision has to be made to sever a relationship, the loss of mysterious 'love' is given as the justification. Love thus seems to be at its most intense when uncertainty and risk are greatest, in that phase when humans have to choose. When they make the most momentous decision of their lives, which will turn a contractual, arbitrary relationship into the deepest and most binding of a person's life, love steps in as though from outside, blind and compelling. The heart has its reasons, even if the mind is perplexed.

If we combine all these arguments, we might suggest that the romantic love complex, both before marriage and within marriage, is the result of a number of forces. The biological urge to mate, based on a deep attraction between males and females, is universal. But the way in which cultures encourage, use, or discourage it varies enormously. In the majority of societies, the feelings have not been encouraged, marriage and individual sentiment are not connected, and marriages have been arranged. This has made it possible to maintain the cohesion of wider groups of which the individual is not a separated part. Something about the kinship system in parts of Europe, and the way it interlocked with politics, economics and religion, gave the biological drives a great deal of freedom. Indeed the economy and society seemed positively to stimulate the natural emotions.

Thus it would seem that the peculiarity of romantic love which anthropologists noted in the twentieth century is a very old feature of western Europe and is particularly marked in England back to the middle ages. Through the writings of some of the greatest poets and novelists of love, and through the apparently new, individualistic, capitalistic, social, economic and political system that was dispersed from England, via America, from the seventeenth century, it has spread. What was once a cultural oddity is now very widely disseminated, and we tend to assume that it is natural, rather than cultural. It has now crossed the boundaries of political systems and is widely accepted in communist as well as capitalist societies. Only such a long and continuous history really makes it possible to understand why it has had such a vast impact and how deeply embedded it is in the way we think and feel. Indeed, it is difficult to imagine how western civilization, and consequently the world as it is, could have developed without the ideology and practice of romantic love. If love can exist without capitalism, it is more questionable as to whether capitalism could have existed, or could continue to exist, without love.

7
Revolution

Socioeconomic Revolution and the
Origin of the Modern World

IN THE early nineteenth century De Tocqueville contemplated the
differences between France on the one hand and England and
North America on the other. He came to the conclusion that he was
witnessing the emergence of an unprecedented phenomenon, a new
and 'modern' world compounded of democracy and individualism.[1]
For an inhabitant of France, the shock of the contrast was enormous.
A similar shock had jolted those eighteenth-century Scotsmen whose
observation of the contrasts between England and Highland Scotland
had led them into speculations which laid the foundations for
economics, sociology and anthropology as we know them today. Yet
the contrasts would have been magnified a hundredfold if De
Tocqueville, Millar, Kames, Adam Smith and others had come not
from adjacent regions, but from the great civilizations that flourished
elsewhere in the world. If they had come from India, or China, for
example, as yet little affected by European culture, they would have
been even more struck by the extraordinary civilization which was
flourishing in England and North America. Concentrating for the
moment on England, what were the most outstanding features of this
brave new world?

Our hypothetical oriental visitor, male or female, would have found
a peculiar legal system, based on unwritten codes and precedents,
known as the 'common law', combined with a separate and equally
strange system known as 'equity'. This legal system had many unique

---

[1] De Tocqueville, *Democracy* and *L'Ancien Régime*, of which there have been
numerous editions.

features; for instance, the use of juries, the absence of judicial torture, the concept of equality before the law. The law enshrined an obsession with property, which was conceived of as virtually private, rather than communal. These procedures and concepts of the law were linked to political and constitutional peculiarities. The most important of these was the idea of the sovereignty of the people and the supremacy of law. The Crown was under the law and answerable to the people in Parliament; this was not an absolutist state but a limited monarchy. England was a state with representative government and a constitution, even if only a small part of the people were yet enfranchised. Political power was widely dispersed and seemed to be diffused through much of the society. There was only a small standing army, no armed police force, no huge centralized bureacracy or court. This was far from the despotism that still existed over much of continental Europe or in much of Asia. It was a balanced constitutional system.

There were linked social peculiarities. Although very steeply ranked, with infinite gradations of status and occupation, there were no exclusive castes or orders. The fourfold orders of priests, warriors and rulers, townsmen and peasants, were muffled by numerous more important divisions. There were no legally separate orders of nobility or slaves, little differentiation between townsmen and country-dwellers, no endogamous enclosures within certain ranks. There was an unusually large and prosperous 'middling' band, lying between the very rich and the very poor. There was easy and frequent social mobility. Furthermore, there was a high rate of geographical mobility: people were constantly on the move, to London and other towns, to markets and fairs, throughout the life-cycle. One set of institutions which helped both kinds of mobility was the market for paid labour. Instead of family labour providing the basis for production, most labour was purchased in the market; the institutions of servanthood, apprenticeship and wage labour were very widespread to a degree unknown elsewhere.

There were many striking features in the realm of production and economic relations. Already there was a rapidly developing use of non-human energy through steam and machinery; associated with it there was a concentration of people into new and unusually compact groupings, urbanism and factory organization. Throughout town and country there was a pervasive emphasis on monetary values, on trade, profit and accumulation. The acquisitive ethic was dominant, the division of labour was far advanced and England was truly a nation not only ruled by shopkeepers but with a generalized shopkeeper mentality. Her overseas possessions were run principally for profit, rather than for their military or political value.

There were associated features in the demographic and familial structures which would have been equally surprising to a visitor from the Orient. Above all, kinship seemed very weak; people were early independent of parental power and most relied mainly on their own efforts. Even that crucial function of kinship, in dealing with accident and old age, was largely eroded, for there was a highly developed and non-kinship-based Poor Law. The weakness of kinship showed itself in the household structure; this was nuclear, on the whole, with few joint or extended families. The marriage system also reflected the unimportance of wider kinship. Marriages were based for the most part on personal initiative rather than parental arrangement, on a mixture of psychological and economic considerations of an unusual kind. Marriages occurred at a relatively late age and it was not seen to be absolutely necessary to marry. Only one partner at one time was allowed, divorce was almost impossible, yet remarriage after the death of one partner was extensive.

An oriental visitor would probably have been saddened at the mixture of wealth and squalor, comradeship and loneliness, tolerance and aggressiveness of the civilization. Yet he would have been impressed by the demographic and economic achievement. The population was rising rapidly, yet the usual positive checks of famine, war and disease were not operating. Somehow the country had escaped from the shadow of demographic crises. Wealth was conspicuously rising, even if it was unfairly distributed, and an affluence and material ascendancy was emerging unknown elsewhere in the world. Here was a land where the fortunate and the energetic, at least, could found dynasties, and where certain traditional forms of generalized 'misery' were being eradicated.

Other differences would have struck such a visitor; in religion and ritual, in art and aesthetics, in concepts of time and space, in attitudes to the natural world. Yet enough has been sketched in to make the point that for such a visitor, and for us, there is something which needs explanation. Much of what had emerged by the first half of the nineteenth century in England and North America has now permeated the world and is part of the air which many nations breathe. Time has accustomed us to it. Yet to the French, Scots and our hypothetical observer, something decidely strange seemed to have occurred in one small corner of the world. England and North America were the extreme case of many of the tendencies throughout Europe, and particularly in north-western Europe. To understand how this happened is perhaps the most important of all historical questions.

For simplicity's sake we may distinguish two ways of answering this question. The first is the 'revolutionary' theory of history. 'Revolution', of course, is a mis-use of the word, for it literally means a state where things come back full-circle, as in the 'revolution' of a wheel. Thus Ibn Khaldûn's cyclical view, or Edmund Leach's pendulum theories of change in highland Burma are true 'revolutionary' theories.[2] Yet as normally used by historians, when they talk of the 'French Revolution', the 'Industrial Revolution', and so on, they mean that *A* has moved to *B*, which never existed before. There are two constituents to the concept, newness and suddenness. Although it would be possible to talk of 'revolutions' that last for thousands of years, for instance, the 'neolithic revolution', usually the word and concept is used by modern historians to describe changes which occur over a year, decades, and sometimes up to a century or so. The speed of the 'revolutions' will vary with which of Braudel's three levels of time we are dealing with. 'Geographical time' moves very slowly, over millenia; social time moves in a century or less; individual time, including political time, often moves in a year or less.[3] In this essay we are mainly dealing with the 'social' level. The element of newness, of rejection of the past, often leads to a violence in the process; it is not a rebirth, a gentle renaissance, or even a rebellion, which ultimately changes only the personnel. The rules of the game are changed, and usually many players object; hence bloody struggle. An added feature of true revolutions is that they tend to be multi-stranded. That is to say, a change in one part, whether we ascribe it to superstructure or infrastructure, will be connected to changes in other parts. For instance, a revolutionary change in demographic structures is likely to be linked to equally revolutionary

---

[2] Ibn Khaldûn, *Muqaddimah*, various editions; Leach, *Political.*
[3] Braudel, *Mediterranean*, 20–1.

changes in familial, economic, legal and other structures, since all are connected.

Given this preliminary specification of revolutionary models of change, we may ask how well they work for one of the most interesting of all cases, that peculiar birth of the 'modern' world on a small island off Europe by the early nineteenth century. Those historians and philosophers who have espoused revolutionary theories in this instance have come up with a rather mixed set of answers. The major prophets of the revolutionary view, Marx and Weber, roughly dated the 'revolution' from 'feudalism' to 'capitalism', another way of labelling what we have described, as having occurred between about 1475 and 1700. One of their principal historical exponents, R. H. Tawney, therefore concentrated on the sixteenth century in England as the 'watershed' (his metaphor) between the 'medieval', 'peasant', 'pre-capitalist' world and the 'modern', 'individualist', 'capitalist' one. Hence the sixteenth century is known affectionately as 'Tawney's century'.[4] In the next generation, Tawney's successor, Christopher Hill, moved the revolution forward a century. Now the seventeenth century was the 'Century of Revolution', with many of the revolutionary developments occurring fairly suddenly in 1640.[5] More recently still, there has been a move to bring the 'revolution', or at least its familistic dimensions, forward another century, into the eighteenth century, when there was invented and propagated 'affective individualism'. This was 'perhaps the most important change in *mentalité* to have occurred in the Early Modern period, indeed possibly in the last thousand years of Western history', and it was particularly linked to the rise of a particular family system from the middle of the seventeenth century, which predominated in the eighteenth.[6] The fact that there is so much uncertainty as to when the major revolution occurred, combined with a strong view that whatever did occur before the nineteenth century was a failed revolution,[7] makes us a little uneasy. Surely it should not be difficult

[4] 'Tawney's Century' is the title given to the first essay, by Fisher, in *Essays*.
[5] Hill, *Revolution*.
[6] Stone, *Family*, 4–7; see also Shorter, *Modern Family*, who even more specifically dates the change to the eighteenth century.
[7] The failure of the English revolution of the seventeenth century to change the social structure is stressed by Perry Anderson and Tom Nairn; see Thompson, 'Peculiarities', especially 314.

to pin down the birth of the modern world in such a well-documented society?

Our uneasiness with this interpretation increases when we look briefly at the strands elaborated above in a little more detail. Shortage of space will force me to set boundary dates, indulge in simplification, and omit the supporting evidence for the assertions. Elsewhere I have tried to discuss many of the topics, briefly surveyed here, in more detail.[8] The central question is at what point, roughly, can we be certain that the features we have elaborated did not exist in the English past. Having located this 'other' world, we will be in a position to date and perhaps to search for plausible reasons for the revolutionary transformation.

We may start with law and government. The common law is known to have reached a mature stage of development by the end of the thirteenth century at the latest.[9] Of course the law changed, but its basic structure and principles were laid out by that time. Thus many of the peculiarities of the law, particularly in the process and in the concepts of property, were present by the thirteenth century. Likewise, the central political feature, namely that England was not an absolutist state, that the Crown was responsible to Parliament and under the law, was established before the time of Magna Carta in 1215. It was maintained thereafter, despite some attempts in the sixteenth and seventeenth centuries to introduce a continental style absolutism. The related features of little central bureaucracy, no standing army, no armed police, the tradition of non-paid local administration and justice, the self-policing local community, were all very ancient. They all went back to the thirteenth century and before. Never did a revived Roman Law sweep away the older customs and laws, as happened on the continent.

The ancient legal and political foundations were early associated with social peculiarities. Late medieval society of the thirteenth and fourteenth centuries had a very ranked yet relatively open social structure. There was no legally privileged nobility, a great contrast with France, and there were no slaves. Serfs were 'free' men and citizens, except in relation to one person, their master. Even he had only limited rights over them. There was already a very large and

---

[8] See chs 1–6 above, and Macfarlane, *Individualism* and *Guide*.
[9] An excellent outline of English common law history is Baker, *Introduction*.

prosperous middling section of townsmen, traders, artisans and yeomen, based largely on the flourishing international wool trade. There is little sign of a fourfold division of society, or of strong oppositions between townsmen (*bourgeois*) and countrymen (*paysans*). There was clearly extensive geographical mobility, again linked to the widespread and fully developed institutions of servanthood and apprenticeship. Wage-labour was highly developed, with probably more than half the population working for wages rather than as family or serf labour by the fourteenth century.

Obviously there were huge technological differences between the thirteenth and nineteenth centuries. Though wind and water power were widely used, steam power and machinery were yet to come, and to this extent England in the late medieval period was different from the early nineteenth century. Yet behind the differences of technology there lay deeper similarities. Manorial account rolls, estate manuals and other records, show that throughout town and country the use of money was widespread. Almost everything could be represented in monetary terms and almost everything could be bought in the extensive and ubiquitous markets and fairs of medieval England. This was a trading nation, with a highly developed market structure, thriving towns, and a keen interest among its inhabitants in profit. Land and labour were seen as commodities; there was a great emphasis both in law and in life on possession. Most services had long ago been commuted for cash and the estates were farmed for profit. The 'shopkeeper' mentality, that is, the interest in accounting, in producing for exchange rather than direct consumption, the desire to make economic profits, was widespread. Whereas later the Puritans and other Protestant groups would vehemently attack usury and the interest rates would be brought down to very low levels, in the later middle ages moneylending and mortgaging at interest were widespread and interest rates were higher. Accounting methods, though crude in comparison to later developments and lacking double-entry book-keeping, were sophisticated enough to make it possible to keep a check on profit and loss.

The basic features of the kinship system seem to have been early laid down. The kinship terminology was in the twelfth century as it was to be in the nineteenth, a bilateral 'eskimo' system that isolated out the nuclear family. The concepts of descent were already formed into the mould that has persisted to the present. Descent was traced through both males and females, a cognatic system that we have today. The method of computing kinship was the canon law method, based on Germanic custom. The inheritance laws were fixed in their major principles by the thirteenth century. Male primogeniture was already a distinguishing feature, with rights reserved for widows. The central principle was that inheritance was not automatic, that 'no man is the heir to a living man'. There was therefore no natural, automatic, family property, no *restrait lignager*, this was firmly outlined by Bracton in the early thirteenth century. Likewise the idea that property always descended and never ascended, that parents were never the automatic heirs of their own children, was accepted; there was vertical rather than lateral inheritance.

The weakness of kinship in this egocentric, network-based kinship system is everywhere apparent from at least the thirteenth century. In economics, ownership, production and consumption were not based on kinship groupings. Religion did not reinforce kinship through ritual or ancestor beliefs. Political life below the level of the aristocracy was run on non-kinship lines with few indications of proper blood feud, vendetta, mafia or clan warfare. The care of the sick, the poor, the old, had already been largely taken over by non-kinship institutions, by the parish, manor, guild and religious fraternities. The weakness of kinship showed itself in the household organization. There is no sign of a fundamentally different household structure, with a wide-scale presence of complex households, as far back as the documents will take us, which is the fourteenth century.

All this fits with an early developed and peculiar marriage system. We shall outline this system in a little more detail. Marriage is the crucial link between economics and biology, between the individual and society. As such, it is not only a good reflection of deeper features of the economy and society, but also the crucial determinant of demographic patterns. A 'revolution' in the socioeconomic system, for instance from a 'pre-capitalist' to 'capitalist' form in the sixteenth to eighteenth centuries, could hardly have occurred without a concurrent revolution in the marital system, which in turn would have altered the demographic regime. We may look at the constituents of what I shall term the 'Malthusian marriage pattern', so named because it is the one that Malthus advocated in the early nineteenth century.

If we consider the major rules which constrained marriage in England in the early nineteenth century, most of them can be found in operation in the fourteenth century and often well before. Age at marriage is very difficult to estimate before parish registers and therefore there is considerable guesswork in all work on the period before the sixteenth century. Yet the relatively late age at marriage for both men and women was probably a very old characteristic in England. The late age at marriage is mentioned as a characteristic of the early Germanic peoples who brought their culture to England and there is certainly no strong evidence to show that women ever universally married at puberty, as they have done in much of the rest of the world. It has been impossible to find a revolutionary change to that 'unique west European marriage pattern' which Hajnal documented.[10] A second rule of marriage is that of single marriage, or monogamy. This is again cross-comparatively rare and is clearly a pivot of the marriage system. It is also demonstrably ancient. Again the Germanic peoples who invaded England had long been monogamous and the Christian Church, despite minor lapses, reinforced this cultural premise. A substantial change introduced by the Church, almost amounting to a 'revolution', was a growing intolerance of divorce. Yet this was a change that had occurred well before the fourteenth century. A further, informal rule which allowed widespread remarriage after the death of a spouse was also clearly established by the thirteenth century at the latest.

The rules concerning whom one should and should not marry were probably also very early established. Jack Goody has shown that the widened rules of forbidden marriage were established in Anglo-Saxon England.[11] Of the positive, prescriptive, rules about which kin one must or should marry, there is little sign. There is thus no sign of a transformation of what Lévi-Strauss has termed 'elementary structures' of kinship into the 'complex structures' which existed in the nineteenth century.[12] Certainly, such elementary structures, if they had ever existed, were gone by the thirteenth century. To put it in another way, marriage in England from very early on was based on a contractual relationship, not on a status, that is kinship, tie. This was also true of another aspect of birth status, namely rank. There is little sign of endogamous groups based on blood or other criteria in the thirteenth and fourteenth centuries. The bond could patently

[10] Hajnal, 'European Marriage'.   [11] Goody, *Family*.
[12] Lévi-Strauss, *Elementary Structures*, xxiii.

marry the 'free' and did so, the gentry could marry the aristocracy, the trader could marry the landowner's daughter.

The customs concerning the all-important question of marriage payments and the economic negotiations at marriage are particularly well documented. England in the eighteenth and early nineteenth century exhibited a curious pattern of marital economics. The features included the payment of a 'portion' with a girl as a sort of 'dowry', which was to balance the jointure or common law 'dower', or the customary widowright, which she would receive from her husband. There is no sign at that date of either a full-fledged 'bridewealth' or 'dowry' system as described for India, Africa and southern Europe.[13] Furthermore, the relative rights of the partners in this conjugal property were of an unusual kind. They followed neither the complete merging, the 'community' of property, nor the absolute separation, the 'lineality' of possessions, both of which were found in the customs of France and Scotland. This marital property complex was clearly very old, many elements dating back to the thirteenth century and earlier.

These formal rules and customs are consistent with the early establishment of a particular view of the purposes and nature of marriage. This was based on four central premises. The first was that marriage was ultimately of concern to the couple themselves, that it was founded on the mutual consent of bride and groom, and not on the arrangement by others. This was a widespread view in the early nineteenth century, but its curiosity is easily seen when we compare it to the majority of peasant societies which have arranged marriage. There, marriage is seen as too important a matter to be left to the personal whim of the partners. This central feature is of very ancient standing. It had been formally accepted into the Catholic view of marriage by the twelfth century and was probably based on much earlier customs.

A second feature of the attitude to marriage was equally important, namely that to marry, or not to marry, involved a choice. Hajnal has rightly seen this as the other major feature of the unique European marriage pattern, indicated by the very large proportion of females, rising to one in six on occasions, who never marry. By the eighteenth century in England there were large numbers of elderly bachelors and spinsters and it was widely accepted that marriage was optional. To the

[13] Goody and Tambiah, *Bridewealth*.

majority of societies, where marriage is seen as a 'natural', automatic, life-cycle stage, a universal experience, this would seem strange. Unfortunately the statistical sources for identifying precisely how old this feature is are again defective. All that we can say for certain is that there is plenty of evidence for non-marriage and no conclusive evidence of universal marriage in the later medieval period. This is consistent with a particular view of the married estate early adopted by the Catholic Church. Marriage was a second best; the continent, celibate life was the highest calling, following in the steps of the bachelor Christ. Marriage was for those who failed, a remedy for lust, something for the weaker brethren. A sacrament, no doubt, but of a lower order than a life of non-marriage. This downgrading of the marital state, the making of marriage into an optional, 'cultural' event, rather than its celebration as the highest, necessary and 'natural' state as in Hindu, Muslim or Confucian religion, is of an early and striking importance. This view was clearly well established before the thirteenth century.

A third premise was that marriage was above all to be entered into for the mutual benefits to be achieved from the husband–wife relationship, rather than as a means to produce heirs. Marriage in the nineteenth century was clearly viewed as a partnership of mind and body. The husband–wife bond superseded all others; the contractual and selected relationship which it established curiously overrode all the relations of blood, with siblings, with parents, with children. This is decidedly unusual cross-comparatively, and again it is a view of marriage that is very old in England, as well as in other parts of Christian Europe. Early on in England we see the mingling of two traditions. On the one hand Christianity emphasized the conjugal bond, admonishing believers that in Paradise Adam had realized that the creation of Eve meant that 'therefore shall a man leave his father and mother, and shall cleave unto his wife: and they shall both be one flesh' (Genesis 2, v. 24). This view fitted well with the old uxoriousness of the Germanic peoples whom Tacitus described in the first century sharing their lives and cleaving closely to each other. Whatever the origins, certainly the companionate view of marriage seems to have been widely accepted by the fourteenth century. As soon as relevant documents begin, marriage seems to have been concerned more with the mutual relationship than with procreation. The absence of stress on producing children is consistent with the late age and non-universal nature of marriage and with the absence of any formal adoption procedures.

Finally there is the cultural premise that marriages are to be based on mutual attraction or 'love'. There is a considerable discussion about when 'love' marriage originated. Some place the origins in the twelfth century, some earlier, some later. What appears to be very likely from the snatches of surviving poetry, the depositions in ecclesiastical courts, from descriptions in early encyclopedias, is that by the fourteenth century at least there was a widespread acceptance of 'love' as a powerful constituent of marriage among ordinary people. Certainly, when the evidence crowds in during the sixteenth century, 'love' is widely accepted as a powerful emotion linked to marriage. There is no strong indication that this association was something suddenly invented in the fifteenth or early sixteenth centuries. Of course there were many other motives for marriage, as there were in the eighteenth and nineteenth centuries. Yet mutual liking, and preferably 'love', was widely viewed as an essential component of marriage. This distinguishing feature was not something invented as a result of Protestantism or a growing individualism of the sixteenth to eighteenth centuries, as shown in chapter 6, above.

The marital system was a mediating institution which gave rise in England to a peculiar demographic regime. A number of indications of its presence can be seen if we compare England in the seventeenth to nineteenth centuries to other parts of Europe, for instance with Sweden or France, as Wrigley has done.[14] In the mortality statistics there were two outstanding features. First, England from the Black Death onwards seems to have escaped from the 'crisis' regime whereby every few generations there would be a massive rise in mortality, usually caused by a war that dislocated an already threshold-treading economy. Such warfare would lead to massive famine and disease. In England there were, of course, continued epidemics up to the seventeenth century, and there were signs of famine deaths in Cumberland up to the same period. Yet in relation to the cataclysms which the painful history of much of continental Europe, India, China, Russia and elsewhere shows up to the eighteenth century and later, the English 'crises' are relatively insignificant in the 400 years between 1350 and 1750. A second notable feature of mortality was its relatively low perennial level. While much higher than today, as compared to many 'pre-transition' populations we have here one of the two features

[14] Wrigley and Schofield, 'English Population'.

of what Wrigley has termed a 'low-pressure' demographic regime.[15] Infant, child and adult mortality were not as high as they are in many pre-industrial populations, a feature that is apparent from at least the fifteenth century.

The fertility rates were also controlled and below their theoretical maximum. This can be seen in several ways. First, there was a curious absence of those spurts of population after a period of high mortality which happened in France and other 'high-pressure' regimes. In many societies, when an 'ecological niche' is freed by mortality, it is quickly filled by a new individual. Likewise, when there is an expansion of resources, this is rapidly converted into a growth in population. This is the well-known Malthusian trap. Yet England seemed to have escaped from both these phenomena from the fourteenth century onwards. After the Black Death the population did not surge back, but continued to fall back for another century. During the years of economic growth between the middle of the sixteenth and eighteenth centuries, population did not rapidly rise to absorb the growing resources. This was related to the unusually controlled fertility rate. That is to say, not only was marital fertility moderate, but the overall fertility rate was well below the theoretical maximum for such a population. We now know that in the seventeenth century, when this was most evident, the lowered fertility was caused by late and selective marriage, rather than by contraception or abortion within marriage. The effect of this medium-level fertility was that it balanced the medium-level mortality; over the centuries between the fourteenth and the eighteenth population grew very slowly indeed, allowing the country gradually to grow wealthier.

This last feature is one aspect of an even more interesting demographic peculiarity of a very long-lived kind. This was the way in which fertility somehow adjusted to economics, rather than being inflexibly linked to biological pressures. It has recently been shown by Wrigley and Schofield that there was a long-term association between fertility rates and real wages between the sixteenth and nineteenth centuries.[16] With a curious 20-year lag, when real wages rose, so did fertility. The lag allowed a certain economic growth to occur and the association meant that population adjusted to economic forces in a beneficial way, producing the labour supply that was needed for a

---

[15] *Ibid.*, 184.   [16] Wrigley, and Schofield, 'English Population', esp. 183.

varying economy. When hardly any growth in labour supply was needed, through the fifteenth to the early eighteenth centuries, fertility was severely controlled. So powerful were the inhibiting pressures that in certain parts of England at this period the mean age at first marriage for women rose as high as thirty years; women had put off childbearing for about 15 years after puberty and many did not marry at all. Then, when there occurred that spurt in productivity and demand for labour which we term the 'Industrial Revolution', the fertility rate responded. Marriage age fell and England for a century had the fastest rate of population growth in the whole of Europe. This flexible demographic system, one part of the Malthusian marriage pattern, was not a new creation of the seventeenth or eighteenth centuries, it would seem, but is evident from the fourteenth century at least. This makes it difficult to talk of the 'demographic transition' occurring in England. To a certain extent, it had already happened before the Reformation, although the equilibrium of births and deaths established at the medium level by the seventeenth century would drop to a much lower level at the end of the nineteenth.

It is clearly necessary to add qualifications to this very brief sketch of some of the central features of English history from the fourteenth to nineteenth centuries. Some might argue that the dating of many of the traits is either too late or too early. Yet a very strong case can be made for saying that most of the central legal, political, economic, social and demographic premises that were observable in the early nineteenth century were already formed by the fourteenth century at the latest. If this is true, it is not surprising that early modern historians have been undecided as to whether the 'revolution' occurred in the sixteenth, seventeenth, eighteenth or nineteenth centuries. A second obvious qualification is to stress that we are here looking at the middle-level, 'social', changes, not at the deepest-level geographical time, nor at the ripple of events. Even so, we also need to bear in mind these other levels, for they are all interconnected. There were numerous political economic and religious 'events' that had a profound influence, positive and negative, on the characteristics we have isolated. Many of these 'events' could have reshaped the whole situation which we have discussed. Cultural premises are shaped by the ripples, as much as the other way round. To stress continuity is not the same as believing in inevitability. The 'shape of Cleopatra's nose' school of history is perfectly compatible with a realization that things did, in a particular

Revolution

case, change less in their fundamentals than many suppose. To take one instance. The success of the Spanish Armada, bringing in its wake Roman law, Roman religions and Roman absolutism, might well have created a genuine revolution which would have broken all those continuous strands which we have elaborated. Nevertheless, as it was, the Armada was defeated, Charles I was beheaded, and through a curious set of fluxes and chances, England remained a peculiar land which became a revolutionary force in the world not because it had undergone a revolution, but precisely because it had not done so. There is nothing inevitable about this, except in the distorting mirror of hindsight. We are not forced to return to a revised Whig evolutionism.

Nor need we argue that there was no change. Clearly many things did change. The oriental visitor stepping back from the early nineteenth century to the early fourteenth would have found many differences in the physical landscape, the technology, the arts and crafts, the language, the overseas dominions, the world of thought and belief. Even those features which we have looked at were constantly fluctuating, growing more complex or simple, or withering away. Nevertheless, the most accurate way to conceive of this history is not through the 'revolutionary' metaphors of sudden and catastrophic breaks which have become so fashionable during the last 50 years. While such models may be helpful and appropriate for the history of many other European nations, applied to England they set up false expectations and distort the evidence.

Yet historians require ways of conceiving of change and if we are persuaded that the revolutionary models are of only very limited use in English history, how are we to explain that very unusual world which had emerged by the early nineteenth century? An alternative approach is provided if we consult those who studied the history of England in the later nineteenth and early twentieth century. At that time a number of historians for the first time systematically investigated and began to translate the massive records of later medieval England. They were unparalleled in their command of the historical sources, which is the essential craft skill of the historian. They also had other advantages. First, there was still sufficiently little published, and sufficiently little specialization in the subject, for them to be able to take a total view of English history, from Anglo-Saxon times up to their own generation. They did not suffer from the growing temporal and subject specialization which means that most historians now become 'sixteenth-century' or 'sixteenth-century economic' historians. This inevitable compartmentalization easily feeds into a 'revolutionary' interpretation, for it is easy to believe that everything suddenly changed either just before or just after one's period, or even more excitingly, during it. The great historians who dominated the subject between about 1870 and 1920 could gaze on the whole of English history and were hence in a position to assess more fully whether there had been any revolutionary breaks.

A second advantage of these writers was that they still suffered under what we might now consider to be a delusion, namely that what the oriental visitor found so surprising was in fact not surprising at all. These English historians, whatever their acquaintance with the works of comparative law and anthropology, still really believed that it was the *others* who were peculiar. The full impact of comparative anthropology and the unsettling influence of Marx and Weber had not yet been felt. The capitalist and individualistic system of England was recognized to be different from that of the rest of Europe, yet its full curiosity at the level of world civilizations was not yet really apparent. This belief was helpful for the historian. It meant that what an Englishman did was not seen as so odd that the historian was forced to assume that it could only be explained by some very violent transformation, some revolutionary break with the more usual human customs, the view to which Marx moved. The easy self-confidence of the later Victorian historians led them to be prepared to accept that what they themselves believed in might indeed have very ancient foundations, almost be 'natural'.

Thus the greatest of these historians, Stubbs and Maitland, approached English history with a long and broad vision, with an unrivalled grasp of the technicalities of the documents and the institutional world that had produced them, and no prejudice against believing that nineteenth-century England might have its roots in medieval, or even Anglo-Saxon England. Nor were they inspired by a zeal to show that their own world was the recent product of a revolutionary change which had such shallow roots that another revolution would easily shift it. Instead, they laboured with care and high intelligence and emerged with that vision of continuity which we are now rediscovering. Of course it is not difficult to brush them aside as irrelevant and misguided. Thus Perry Anderson asserts that 'the transition from the mediaeval to the early modern epochs thus corresponded in English history – despite all local legends of unbroken "continuity" — to a deep and radical reversal of many of the most characteristic traits of prior feudal development'.[17] Legends, however, are of interest to historians, nor are they necessarily 'untrue'.

The legend told by Stubbs is indeed one of unbroken continuity. In his majestic *Constitutional History of England* he securely laid the foundations of the English social system very early on, in Anglo-Saxon England. On this foundation, a great deal had been built by the thirteenth century. 'The great characteristic of the English constitutional system is the continuous development of representative institutions from the first elementary stage . . . The nation becomes one and realizes its oneness . . . It is completed under Henry II and his sons'. Stubbs is of course aware that there are turmoils ahead and that political and constitutional changes of considerable importance will occur over the next six centuries. Yet he believes that the basic rules change little.

The constitution which reached its formal and definite maturity under Edward I . . . the continuity of life, and the continuity of national purpose, never fails: even the great struggle of all [sic], the long labour that extends from the Reformation to the Revolution (i.e. 1688), leaves the organization, the origin of which we have been tracing, unbroken in its conscious identity, stronger in the strength which it has preserved, and grown mightier through trial.

There is no notion of any 'revolution' in Stubbs' work, no hint of a cataclysmic change from a 'medieval' to a 'modern' world. This was not because he was blind to changes when they did occur. He noted that the sixteenth and seventeenth centuries 'witnessed a series of changes in national life, mind, and character, in the relations of the classes, and in the balance of political forces, far greater than the English race had gone through since the Norman Conquest'.[18] These changes he listed as the Reformation, the 'transformation of the baronage of early England into the nobility of later times' and the 'recovered strength of the monarchic principle . . .'. Yet he did not believe that the continuity was broken.

[17] Anderson, *Lineages*, 113.
[18] Stubbs, *Constitutional History*, I, 584–5, 682; III, 3.

The continuities were strongest in the middling and lower ranks in which over 99 per cent of the English population lived. 'As we descend in the scale of social rank the differences between medieval and modern life rapidly diminish', he wrote. Stubbs was aware that the balance of ownership changed, yet there were always the same major groupings, the gentry, the tradesmen and artisans, the labourers, and that peculiar middling English estate known as the 'yeomanry'. Two features of the ancient yeoman tradition especially struck Stubbs, their wealth and their social mobility. He wrote that

the wills and inventories of the well-to-do freeholder and farmer furnish similar evidence of competency; and these are an irrefragable answer to the popular theories of the misery and discomfort of medieval middle-class life ... The house of the freeholder was substantially but simply furnished, his store of clothes and linen were ample, he had money in his purse and credit at the shop and at the market.[19]

This is no miserable subsistence peasant, but a small capitalist farmer whose cash and credit indicates his involvement in the market economy.

The second major feature Stubbs noted is the early and easy social mobility.

Before the close of the middle ages the rich townsmen had begun to intermarry with the knights and gentry, and many of the noble families of the present day trace the foundations of their fortunes to a lord mayor of London or York ... It is probable that there was no period in English history at which the barrier between the knightly and mercantile class was regarded as insuperable.

This was a society of closely spaced ranks with no insuperable barriers between them from very early on. 'The city magnate formed a link between the country squire and the tradesman; and the tradesman and the yeoman were in position and in blood closely akin. Even the villein might, by learning a craft, set his foot on the ladder of promotion'. One final feature of a 'medieval' world that looks surprisingly like that of the seventeenth and eighteenth centuries is the widespread use of

[19] *Ibid.*, III, 570, 573.

wage-labour and craft activity; there were, Stubbs tells us, 'whole classes of labourers and artisans, whose earnings never furnished more than the mere requisites of life'.[20]

Here then is a legend of unbroken continuity, a vision of a guiding set of principles or rules, a generative structure, which provided the set of customs that would shape the history of England up to Stubbs's own day. These principles were combined with important changes, but these changes were not deep enough to alter the underlying rules. The legend is told by a man about whom his most stringent and detailed critics have written: 'All that we know of Stubbs inspires confidence, confidence in the solidity and extent of his knowledge, the honesty of his criticism, the sureness of his judgement, the depth of his practical experience of men and things'.[21]

The same legend is told by F. W. Maitland, whose credentials are even more impressive than those of Stubbs. He is widely acclaimed, as a 'giant' who, with Marc Bloch, is one of the 'two greatest historians of recent times'.[22] He is 'one of the immortals', 'Mount Maitland' whose genius overtops all other English historians.[23] Maitland was familiar with continental scholarship and with contemporary anthropology, he effortlessly spanned history and law, was prodigiously learned and became one of the greatest editors of medieval documents. His high intelligence and erudition are not in doubt and like Stubbs his vision encompassed all of English history from Anglo-Saxon England up to the nineteenth century. In his many works we look in vain for any sign of a belief that a vast and revolutionary change had occurred at some specific point in English history, dividing off 'medieval' from 'modern' England. Instead, his view that the legal and social structure of England, in its basic principles, was already laid down by the thirteenth century is shown in many passages, only a few of which we can cite here.

We are told that 'at the end of Henry III's reign our Common Law of inheritance was rapidly assuming its final form. Its main outlines were those which are still familiar to us'. By the death of Henry II

---

[20] *Ibid.*, III, 615, 626, 619.   [21] Petit Dutaillis and Lefebvre, *Studies*, v.
[22] Hay, *Annalists*, 169.
[23] Cam, quoting and agreeing with Powicke in Maitland *Selected Essays*, xxix. The reference to 'Mount Maitland' and Maitalnd's pre-eminence is in Mcfarlane, 'Mount Maitland'

(1272), 'English law is modern in its uniformity, its simplicity, its certainty'. Lawyers from the fourteenth century onwards believed that 'the great outlines of criminal law and private law seem to have been regarded as fixed for all time. In the twentieth century students of law will still for practical purposes be compelled to know a good deal about the statutes of Edward I'. This continuity, he believed, had been of great advantage to English historians, setting them off from those of continental nations where it had not occurred.

So continuous has been our English legal life during the last six centuries, that the law of the later middle ages has never been forgotten among us. It has never passed utterly outside the cognizance of our courts and our practising lawyers. We have never had to disinter and reconstruct it in that laborious and tentative manner in which German historians of the present day have disinterred and reconstructed the law of medieval Germany.

This continuity is shown in the treatment of particular subjects. For instance, when analysing the forms of action at common law, Maitland took the period 1307–1833 as one period. He admitted that this was 'enormously long', yet wrote that 'I do not know that for our present purpose it could be well broken up into sub-periods'.[24]

The most important area of all, as Marx would have agreed, was the property law which governed relations of production. Here were the deepest continuities. This 'most salient trait', the 'calculus of estates which even in our own day, is perhaps the most distinctive feature of English private law', Maitland thought very old. It had been a characteristic for six centuries, having taken a 'definite shape' in the second half of the thirteenth century, drawing on much older customs. This continuity was not merely to be found in the common law, even if it was 'one of the toughest things ever made'. In his *Constitutional History of England*, which covered the period from Anglo-Saxon England up to the 1880s, Maitland made no substantial modifications to Stubbs's general vision of continuity. For instance, he wrote 'take any institution that exists at the end of the Middle Ages, any that exists in 1800 – be it parliament, or privy council, or any of the courts of law – we can trace it back through a series of

---

[24] Pollock and Maitland, *English Law*, II, 210; I, 225; Maitland, *Selected Essays*, 123; Pollock and Maitland, *English Law*, I, civ; Maitland, *Forms*, 43.

definite changes as far as Edward's reign'.[25] It was because English constitutional and legal principles had been laid down so early that the history of English law which he largely wrote could amazingly end in 1272.

Maitland pointed to many respects in which thirteenth-century England was like that of the nineteenth century. There was in both an absence of patriarchal power, *patria potestas*, that subjection of children and women to the absolute power of the oldest male; there was an absence of clans or other corporate kin groups; there was no concept of familial property, of joint and communal ownership. Individual possession was characteristic from very early on. The thirteenth century was already dominated by contract and not status, to use Maine's distinction; as Stubbs had also noted, there were no hereditary ranks based on blood and law, no 'castes'. There was equality before the law and all had legal rights, including women, children and villeins.[26]

We may wonder whether this 'legend' of continuity, so powerfully undermining of revolutions, has been destroyed by subsequent research on those documents, many of which Maitland himself first brought to light. In the reprinting of the *History of English Law* in 1968, Milsom describes it as a 'still living authority'. Nowhere in his lengthy introduction does Milsom challenge Maitland's view of the thirteenth century. Indeed, Milsom concludes that 'there can be no doubt that by the end of the period covered by the book, the world was as Maitland saw it'. Maitland, writes Milsom, 'would probably wish his work to be superseded. There is little sign that this will happen soon'. The world Maitland saw was 'essentially a flat world inhabited by equal neighbours. Lordship is little more than a servitude over the land of another'.[27]

If Maitland rejects a revolutionary interpretation of English history, how does he visualize the process of time as changing? It is certainly not in a crude evolutionary pattern, through a series of organic 'stages', as advocated by a number of the evolutionary anthropologists and sociologists of the later nineteenth century. This evolutionary

---

[25] Pollock and Maitland, *English Law*, II, 10–11; Maitland, *Selected Essays*, 127; Maitland, *History*, 20.

[26] Pollock and Maitland, *English Law*, II, 438, 242ff, 13, 19, 27, 233, 402.

[27] Pollock and Maitland, *English Law*, I, xxiii, xlvii, lxxiii, xlvii.

framework, which influenced Marx through the works of Morgan, has had a considerable influence on twentieth-century historiography. Yet in a memorable passage, Maitland calmly shatters such necessary, single-path, evolutionism.[28] What alternative, then, can he offer? Maitland does not usually address the problem directly, but often indicates obliquely how one might use an organic growth model, yet without any *necessity* for things to have occurred in a certain way. An illustration of this approach is shown in his treatment of one of the central and enduring features of English history, the system of local government. Maitland writes that

Certainly to any one who has an eye for historic greatness it is a very marvellous institution, this Commission of the Peace, growing so steadily, elaborating itself into ever new forms, providing for ever new wants, expressing ever new ideas, and yet never losing its identity . . . we shall hardly find any other political entity which has had so eventful and yet so perfectly continuous a life.[29]

Maitland describes here, in a delicate balance, both 'newness' and 'identity' over time, an institution whose history is both 'eventful' and yet 'continuous'. Such an approach allows us the flexibility to admit that by a strange paradox things can both remain the same and also change.

Such a model of change is more subtle and less crude than a revolutionary one, at least when applied to English history. No doubt it will be unattractive to those historians who agree with Butterfield that 'the chief aim of the historian is the elucidation of the unlikeness between past and present . . . It is not for him to stress and magnify the similarities between one age and another'.[30] If we are dedicated to hunt for dissimilarities, then 'revolutions' before which things were very different are what we shall hope to find, and we can safely dismiss Stubbs and Maitland as poor historians. In that case, all that has been put forward in this essay, even if true, is of no interest. It is a species of that 'so what' history to which my former teacher, Lady Rosalind Clay, used to allude. On the other hand, if we are concerned to find out how things have come to be as they are, we may well find that for certain societies the 'continuity with change' paradox is the most flexible way of looking at the past. This approach can best be stated as a contradiction, as the

[28] Maitland, *Domesday Book*, 344–6. [29] Maitland, *Collected Papers*, I, 471.
[30] Butterfield, *Whig Interpretation*, 17.

'Changing Same' (as the jazz singer Leroy James called a song). This changing same is another way of speaking of the parable of the philosopher's shoe, whose various parts were replaced bit by bit. At the end, was it the same shoe or another one? In another form, it is the metaphor used by the great historian of the common law, Sir Matthew Hale, when he likened the changing law to the Ship of the Argonauts. 'The ship went so long a voyage that eventually every part of it decayed and was replaced; yet (says the paradox of identity in spite of change) it remained in a meaningful sense the same ship'.[31] For English history, we would need to modify these metaphors, for the new heel, or the new planks, were of a different shape and length to the ones they replaced. It was still a ship or a shoe, but the overall measurements had shifted very considerably. Put in another metaphor, an organic one, the tree had not changed from being a small oak into a large beech, hence it was still an oak. But a small oak is very different in many respects from a large one.

What I am trying to express has been put eloquently by George Orwell, who could hardly be accused of either sentimentality or 'Little Englander' views. At the end of his essay on 'England, your England', he wrote that 'it needs some very great disaster, such as prolonged subjugation by a foreign enemy, to destroy a national culture'. Thus while the 'Stock Exchange will be pulled down, the horse plough will give way to the tractor, the country houses will be turned into children's holiday camps, the Eton and Harrow match will be forgotten'; yet, even with such changes, 'England will still be England, an everlasting animal stretching into the future and the past, and like all living things, having the power to change out of recognition and yet remain the same'.[32]

One could express this idea in a more modern idiom. In trying to account for the way in which behaviour is generated in a North African society, the anthropologist Pierre Bourdieu has developed the notion of *habitus*, that is the idea of a system of invisible, general, but powerful rules which guide everyday behaviour.[33] This is curiously similar to what is meant by that central English idea of 'custom', as when Bracton wrote of the *Laws and Customs of England* in the early thirteenth century. These are an assemblage of the 'way things are

[31] Gray in the preface to Hale, *Common Law*, xxxi.   [32] Orwell, *Whale*, 90.
[33] Bourdieu, *Outline*.

done', the fundamental and guiding principles, the rules of the game. If we turn Bourdieu's idea from a static one into a changing model over time, we could argue that the *habitus* of the English was very early established. How it expressed itself would vary and change, but the expressions would be in conformity to fairly basic rules which are not easily changed. One might liken these to the tides, which are unaltering. The storms and stillnesses on the surface, the individual waves, are just as important for the sailor as are the tides. Yet ultimately, the ebb and flow remains within various bounds constrained by deeper laws. No one would argue that 'revolutions' never occur, and historians should, of course, describe them when they do. Yet to assume that they occur in every nation's history, and that they do so frequently, cuts short the historian's ability to respond to what the evidence tells us. It debases, by over-use, the historical coinage, and it warps the historian's observations of the past.

Two final questions may be raised, though not satisfactorily answered in such a brief space. The first concerns the degree to which the apparently non-revolutionary nature of the English past is representative or exceptional when compared to the rest of western Europe. England was, in many respects, merely an extreme version of a general west-European socioeconomic pattern, and the inquiring oriental would have been almost as surprised if he had visited Italy, France or Spain, and particularly if he had travelled in Holland or Denmark. On the other hand, as many travellers and observers noted, there was also something special about England. A particularly perceptive account of these differences in economy, society and culture when England was compared to nineteenth century France is that by Hippolyte Taine in his *Notes on England*; but there are many others. One manifestation of this difference seems to be that while there is no evidence of a real revolutionary break in England in any specific century, there are indeed grounds for describing what happened in much of continental Europe in the century after 1789 as a real revolution. The legal, political, social, economic and ideological systems do seem to have undergone a rapid, interrelated and profound transformation. A particularly graphic account of what happened at all levels of economy, society and culture in nineteenth-century France is given by Eugene Weber,[34] but again examples could be multiplied from Italy, Germany,

[34] Weber, *Peasants.*

Spain and elsewhere. Of course, even in these countries, there were continuities, but there are much stronger grounds for speaking of revolution. There is a certain paradox here. While England, with industrialization, urbanization and rapid population growth went through the most rapid physical, technological and material change, its deeper relations of production and ideology were only gradually altered. In many other parts of Europe the material world altered more slowly, but the *Ancien Regime* structures were toppled and a new world was born. Ironically, that 'new' world was partly based on the ancient systems developed in England and exported to her colonies, returning by way of America and the influence of British imperialism.

If it is true that a misleading paradigm of the English past has partially established itself in certain quarters during the first two-thirds of the twentieth century, we are left with an intriguing historiographical question. Why should certain historians have begun to reinterpret the English past in these revolutionary terms? Of course, there are reasons at many levels. Some of these have been hinted at already. There is the need to make the past very different in order to make it interesting, there is the influence of European sociologists, particularly Marx and Weber, there is the self-questioning induced by comparative studies and a growing awareness of the peculiarity of the world in which we now live. Other reasons could be explored, including the obvious use of the past to help predict the future. Writing history cannot be value free, it is bound to have political implications and political incentives. For instance, if all that exists now is the result of a recent 'revolution', then it is easier to consider changing present institutions. What exists now is an artificial, almost accidental, creation of the recent past. If the family system, or the capitalist ethic, is only a few hundred years old, it is easy to feel that it may not last long either. The vision of numerous revolutions in recent history is essentially an optimistic, utopian vision. On the other hand, the premise of continuity can conversely be attractive to those who wish to stress enduring values, who dislike profound change.

Thus the fluctuations in historical interpretation, in this and other cases, tell us a great deal about the changes in political ideology in this century. What appear to be recent errors by a number of historians are not the result of a lack of talent or skill, even if it is difficult to point to historians of the stature of Stubbs and Maitland working today. As historians are well aware, theories of change, for instance the move from cyclical to linear concepts of time, from static to progressive views of history, from evolution to revolution, are deeply linked to changes in the environment within which people live. While it is just about possible to see some of the reasons for shifts in perceptions of change and continuity at the Renaissance, the Enlightenment or in the evolutionary theories of the nineteenth century, it is much more difficult to understand the reasons for the rise and likely decline of what might be called 'Revolutionism'. We are still too close to the phenomenon, some of us having even within our lives switched into and out of 'Revolutionism'. In this essay I have merely tried to show how an inappropriate model of change, no doubt useful in many other situations, distorts English history if it is applied too crudely. I have suggested that other models are available and should not be too lightly discarded.

8
Capitalism

The Cradle of Capitalism – the Case of England

For Marx, Weber and many others it has been evident that capitalism is a peculiar social formation. Its birthplace was in western Europe. Within this region, there was a particular area which was precocious in its development, where the new social formation emerged in its purest and earliest form. Marx noted that in the early dissolution of the preceding 'medieval' property system 'England [was] in this respect the model country for the other continental countries'.[1] It was, as Brenner puts it 'classically in England' that we have 'the rise of the three-tiered relation of landlord/capitalist tenant/free wage labour, around which Marx developed much of his theory of capitalist development in *Capital*'.[2] For Max Weber also, England was 'the home of capitalism'.[3] It was in England above all that the Puritan outlook 'stood at the cradle of the modern economic man'.[4] Since England was the cradle and nursery of capitalism, it is not surprising that later writers have concentrated on that country. For instance, Polanyi takes England's history as the central example of the 'Great Transformation'.[5] It is not unreasonable to suppose that if we could explain why capitalism emerged and developed in England, and specifically what differentiated it from other parts of Europe and allowed this growth, we would have moved some way towards understanding the 'European miracle'.

[1] Marx, *Grundrisse*, 277.   [2] Brenner, 'Capitalist Development', 75.
[3] Weber, *General*, 251.
[4] Weber, *Protestant Ethic*, 174.   [5] Polanyi, *Great Transformation*.

We may look at some of the more outstanding attempts to solve this problem. Marx's treatment of the causes for the emergence of capitalism is intriguing but ultimately unsatisfying. He skilfully shows how the transition may have occurred, and a few of the preconditions. But he totally avoids giving any solution to the questions of why then and why there. He analyses the central features of the supposed transition; the creation of a 'free' labour force through the destruction of a dependent peasantry is the central one. This was linked to the expansion of market forces, money, and production for exchange rather than for immediate consumption. Thus growing trade and commerce is seen as one of the major propelling forces: 'the circulation of commodities is the starting-point of capital ... The modern history of capital dates from the creation in the sixteenth century of a world-embracing commerce and a world-embracing market'.[6] But long-distance trade had been present for centuries and had centred on the Mediterranean. Why should trade suddenly have had this shattering effect, and why should its prime target be north-western Europe? Unsatisfied with the analyses in *Capital*, with its mystic theories of internal contradictions which were bound to lead to inevitable dissolution of the previous social formation, we may look to his other writings.

In *Grundrisse* Marx outlines various combustible elements that would explode into capitalism. There is money, and more specifically, 'mercantile and usurious wealth'. But money, urban craft activity and towns had been present in many civilizations. Why, alone, in western Europe did they lead to the growth of capitalism? Marx does provide some further hints. One central foundation for capitalism was the pre-existence of a rural social structure which allowed the peasantry to be 'set free'. In other words there was something particularly fragile in the pre-existing relations of production. The substratum of feudalism, arising from its origins in the 'Germanic system' was particularly vulnerable to the new urban craft development and accumulation of wealth. The crucial feature of the Germanic system was its form of property. In the ancient and Asiatic civilizations, there was no individual, private property. But in Germanic society something new and odd emerged. In this period no land remained in the possession of the community or group. People had moved

[6] Marx, *Capital*, i, 145.

half-way, according to Marx, from communal property, to half-individualized property based on the household. It would take another thousand years for the second half of the movement to be made. In other words, there is something within feudalism, some hidden spirit, which is special. This is implied in other remarks; for example, that 'the economic structure of capitalist society has grown out of the economic structure of feudal society. The dissolution of the latter set free the elements of the former'.[7] The metaphor of 'setting free' suggests that Marx believed that the spirit of capitalism was already present before the emergence of capitalism.

Weber considered a number of possible explanations for the emergence of capitalism. He rejected the crudely technological and materialistic ones: colonial trade, population growth, the inflow of precious metals. He then isolated some of the necessary but not sufficient 'external conditions', the particular geography of Europe with its cheap transportation by water, the favourable military requirements of the small states, the large luxury demand from an unusually prosperous population. Ultimately, it was not these external factors, but something more mysterious that was important. It was the ethic, the justification of the pursuit of profit. He found the roots of this in a paradox. The new attitudes were waiting to escape. The paradox is summarized by Weber himself. 'The final result is the peculiar fact that the germs of modern capitalism must be sought in a region where officially a theory was dominant which was distinct from that of the east and of classical antiquity and in principle strongly hostile to capitalism'.[8] This region was medieval Christendom.

We may note the use of 'officially' here with its implication of the submerged, unofficial, practice. Judaism was an important background feature in giving to Christianity 'the character of a religion essentially free from magic'.[9] But what was most important was the presence of Protestantism. Protestantism was not the cause of capitalism, but it gave older and deeper tendencies a necessary protection. It was the enabling force. This view of Protestantism as a kind of windbreak which allowed the young plant to grow is well shown in numerous places by Weber. For instance, when writing that the Puritan outlook 'stood at the cradle of the modern economic

---

[7] *Ibid.*, 668.   [8] Weber, *General*, 162.   [9] *Ibid.*, 265.

man', the image is not of a mother giving birth, but of a friend, perhaps a godparent, who gives support and blessing to the new infant. More specifically, Weber wrote that 'we have no intention whatever of maintaining such a foolish and doctrinaire thesis as that the spirit of capitalism . . . could only have arisen as the result of certain effects of the Reformation, or even that capitalism as an economic system is the creation of the Reformation'.[10] Many aspects of capitalism were much older. As Bendix summarizes Weber's position, 'this world historical transformation, then, was not the product of Puritanism; rather, Puritanism was a late development that reinforced tendencies that had distinguished European society for a long time past'.[11]

Weber provides some suggestive clues as to why England should be the cradle of capitalism. There was the peculiar position of the peasantry. In England the peasants were particularly weak and vulnerable because, being an island, they were not needed by the king and nobility as a necessary fighting force; 'hence the policy of peasant protection was unknown in England and it became the classical land of peasant eviction'. In England, he noted

no legal emancipation of the peasants ever took place. The medieval system is still formally in force, except that under Charles II serfdom was abolished . . . In England, the mere fact of the development of a market, as such and alone destroyed the manorial system from within. In accordance with the principle fitting the situation, the peasants were expropriated in favour of the proprietors. The peasants became free but without land.

In France, however, 'the course of events is exactly the opposite . . . France, in contrast with England, became a land of small and medium sized farms'.[12] Not only was this a reflection of the different power of the peasants, the pressures of wealth in England were greater. Because of the rapid development of a particular means of production, the English woollen industry with its division of labour and commerce, the large-scale stock raising, Weber argued, made the tenant weak and redundant. The massive growth of the English cloth

[10] Weber, *Protestant Ethic*, 174, 91.   [11] Bendix, *Max Weber*, 71–2.
[12] Weber, *General*, 129, 85–6.

industry from the fourteenth century onwards meant that a new capitalist class emerged. This was combined with the growth of the 'bourgeoisie', the free dwellers in the peculiar towns and cities of northern Europe.

Having subtly interwoven some of the religious, economic and social factors, Weber does not omit the political and legal dimensions. He argues that 'the State, in the sense of the rational state has existed only in the western world'. He contrasts this western state with the charismatic, patrimonial and other traditional systems of government in China, India and Islam. The state is essential to capitalism; 'very different is the rational state in which alone modern capitalism can flourish'. The basis of the rational state is rational law. Here Weber recognizes another paradox. The most 'rational', that is, the most carefully worked out and logically coherent of legal systems, was that of Roman law. Yet, ironically, capitalism flourished most in the one area of Europe without Roman law, namely England. Weber resolves the contradiction subtly. He distinguishes between the formal side, in modern terms 'procedural' or 'adjectival' law, and its content or 'substantive law'. Thus the 'rational law of the modern occidental state . . . arose on its formal side, though not as to its content, out of Roman law'. Yet, since 'England, the home of capitalism, never accepted the Roman law', it is clear that 'in fact all the characteristic institutions of modern capitalism have other origins than Roman law'. Weber gives a list of these devices. 'The annuity bond . . . came from medieval law, in which Germanic legal ideas played their part. Similarly the stock certificate arose out of medieval and modern law . . . likewise the bill of exchange . . . the commercial company is also a medieval product, so also the mortgage, with the security of registration, and the deed of trust'.[13]

I have dwelt on Marx and Weber at some length because they anticipate almost all the theories that have come later. Though they failed to solve the problem, it is doubtful whether any subsequent writer has reached as close to a solution. A few recent attempts, concentrating specifically on the question of why the miracle occurred in north-western Europe, can be considered. Braudel in his majestic surveys of capitalism and material life has in general

---

[13] *Ibid.*, 249, 250, 251, 252; for a lengthier exposition and criticism of the views of Marx and Weber, see Baechler, *Origins*, chs 1, 2, 3.

accepted the inevitability of the transition, falling back on those material and technological factors which Weber dismissed.[14] The seeds were assumed to be present and we just watch them growing. The sense of marvel and uniqueness which Marx and Weber possessed has gone. A recent voluminous attempt to solve these problems by Anderson does not reach further than the great theorists. The treatment of the central case of England, for instance, is not satisfactory. Anderson admits that the 'feudal monarchy of England was generally far more powerful than that of France', and yet 'the strongest medieval monarchy in the West eventually produced the weakest and shortest Absolutism'. That England should go through an 'Absolutist' phase, seems to be essential for Anderson; it is a precondition of capitalism. Yet he signally fails to show that such a phase occurs. As he admits, most of the more extreme measures of the Tudors were not put into practice and they lacked a standing army. Despite what he believes was an 'inherent tendency' of the Tudor monarchy towards 'absolutism' on the continental model, the Crown was surrounded by a peculiar landowning class which was 'unusually civilian in background, commercial in occupation and commoner in rank'. The result was that this was a state which 'had a small bureaucracy, a limited fiscality, and no permanent army'. Yet a large bureaucracy, heavy taxation and a standing army are the three central criteria of absolutism as defined by Anderson. An England where 'the coercive and bureaucratic machinery of the monarchy remained very slim',[15] hardly seems suited to the Absolutist mantle.[16]

The failure to show that England had either of the two essential prerequisites of the capitalist revolution according to his general model, namely absolutism and Roman law, forces Anderson to fall back on a rehashed version of Marx's theory about the expropriation of the peasants, combined with a certain amount of 'natural tendency' thrown in. Trade and manufacture grew, the peasantry were socially differentiated and weak and were destroyed, both from without and within. We are no further forward.

One of the most interesting developments in the discussion has been in two articles by Brenner. In the first he showed the inadequacy

[14] Braudel, *Capitalism*. [15] Anderson, *Lineages*, 113, 127, 129.
[16] These criticisms, I recently discovered, have also been made by Runciman, 'Comparative Sociology', 169–70.

of demographic explanations of the rise of capitalism, particularly in the work of Ladurie and Postan. By cross-comparative analysis Brenner showed that the same major demographic pressures led to entirely different results in western and eastern Europe. Nor can the explanation lie in trade and commercialization in themselves. The solution lies, as Marx thought, in the relations of production: 'it is the structure of class relations, of class power, which will determine the manner and degree to which particular demographic and commercial changes will affect long-run trends in the distribution of income and economic growth – and not vice versa'.[17] What, then, is his theory? It is that the different trajectories of western and eastern Europe arose out of the fact that in western Europe the peasants were already strong and could not be re-feudalized, as they were in the east. But this general approach leads him into problems with the test case of England.

It has normally been held, as we saw with Weber, that it was the weakness of the English peasantry which led to its destruction. Brenner's thesis leads him into a contradiction. In England the peasantry were both weak and strong. Their strength led them to eliminate themselves. They vanished and conquered at the same time. 'In England, as throughout most of Western Europe, the peasantry was able by the mid-fifteenth century, through flight and resistance, to break definitively feudal controls over its mobility and to win full freedom'. Yet, strangely, in England, they did not win economic security, as they were to do in France. They did not manage to attach themselves to the land and become a strong landholding peasantry: 'it was the emergence of the classical landlord–capitalist tenant–wage labour structure which made possible the transformation of agricultural production in England, and this, in turn, was the key to England's uniquely successful overall economic development'. Brenner is here trying to get the best of both arguments. The peasants were strong and resisted the landlord and did not become serfs again; on the other hand they were weak and were eliminated. 'The contrasting failure in France of agrarian transformations seems to have followed directly from the continuing strength of peasant landholding into the early modern period while it was disintegrating in England'.[18] As well as the inconsistency of this explanation, it is unsatisfying because it does not

[17] Brenner, 'Agrarian', 31.   [18] *Ibid.*, 61, 63, 68.

begin to tackle the reasons for the peculiar nature of the English relations of production. How had this situation emerged and in what, precisely, did the peculiarities lie?

Reactions to this first stimulating essay have pointed out the weaknesses, but failed to go further. Thus a thoughtful response by Croot and Parker agrees that Brenner has pinpointed the significant variable, the differences in social structure, but believes that 'the explanation offered for the emergence or non-emergence of such relations is unconvincing'.[19] Unfortunately, these authors, besides laying stress on one or two factors such as the importance of the small farmer (yeoman) in England, are unable to offer a better solution. Likewise Bois agrees that 'the decisive part in the transition from feudalism to capitalism is played out in the countryside', but provides no more plausible explanation than Brenner. He points to the divergences between English and French 'feudalism', which differed from at least the thirteenth century according to Bois,[20] but this important insight is not followed up.

In a second important article Brenner then demolished another group of theorists, namely the 'Neo-Smithian Marxists': Frank, Sweezy and Wallerstein. He shows that the basic premise of all these accounts is the view that capitalism was already there before it emerged. The profit motive was already present. For instance, we are told that 'Sweezy's mistake was obviously to assume the operation of norms of capitalist rationality, in a situation where capitalist social relations of production did not exist, simply because market exchange was widespread'. Likewise 'the Smithian theory embedded in Sweezy's analysis . . . is made entirely explicitly, and carried to its logical conclusion' in Wallerstein's *Modern World System*.[21] Brenner has much innocent fun showing that these Marxists are at heart followers of Adam Smith. What he fails to point out is that they are also Marxists. As we saw earlier, Marx himself needed to believe that the capitalist profit motive existed, that the germ was present, before the existence of capitalism. Brenner has again cleared the decks, but provided no alternative. His later reply to his critics elaborates the earlier position but takes us no further towards a solution.[22]

---

[19] Croot and Parker, 'Agrarian', 45–6. [20] Bois, 'Against', 62, 65.
[21] Brenner, 'Capitalist Development', 45, 53.
[22] Brenner, 'Roots'.

Two further more recent theories are worth noting. The first is that the development of the west was made possible by the political fragmentation of Europe. Whereas the unified empires of India and China crushed all economic progress, 'the constant expansion of the market . . . was the result of an absence of political order extending over the whole of western Europe'. Thus Baechler's main conclusions are that the 'first condition for the maximization of economic efficiency is the liberation of civil society with respect to the State. This condition is fulfilled when a single cultural area is divided into several sovereign political units', as in Europe.[23] This thesis has been forcefully restated by Hall as the theme of his book. He adds to it the important role played by Christianity which 'kept Europe together . . . the market was possible because people felt themselves part of a single community'.[24] Again these are necessary, if not sufficient, explanations.

We are thus in a position where we have a clearer idea of the problems. These are: why did capitalism emerge and triumph in a part of western Europe in the early modern period? Why this area, and particularly why in England? We also know what not to pursue: towns, population growth, overseas trade, colonialism, the growth of trade and the market, technology were all necessary but not sufficient causes. We know that a particular strand of religion, an integrated and rational state and new kind of law, were all important. The common culture of Christianity holding together several small sovereign political units was also important. Above all, we know that it was not in a single one of these features, but in the way in which economy, politics, law and religion were linked together that the solutions are likely to lie. Furthermore, we have hints that there were some crucial differences here within Europe, and especially as between England and other continental countries. We may now turn to a possible solution to some of these problems.

There is a very widely held belief that the emergence of capitalism was linked to a pre-existing social formation known as 'feudalism'. Two of the most influential proponents of this view were Maine and Marx. For Maine, feudal ties formed the basis for the most momentous of all changes, from relations based on status (kinship) to those based on contract. In feudalism, he wrote, 'the notion of common kinship has been entirely lost. The link between Lord and Vassal produced by

---

[23] Baechler, *Origins*, 73, 113.   [24] Hall, *Powers*, 123, 115.

Commendation is of quite a different kind from that produced by Consanguinity'.[25] He traced the origins of private property of a modern kind to the new feudal ties.[26] Feudalism was connected to what Maine considered to be the central feature of modern society, the idea of indivisible, inheritable, individual property symbolized and enshrined in primogeniture: 'in the ancient world, and in the societies which have not passed through the crucible of feudalism, the Primogeniture which seems to have prevailed never transformed itself into the Primogeniture of the later feudal Europe'.[27] Maitland picked up the implications of Maine's fundamental insight. 'The master who taught us that "the movement of the progressive societies has hitherto been a movement from Status to Contract" was quick to add that feudal society was governed by the law of contract. There is no paradox here'.[28]

Marx, we have seen, also saw that only out of a dissolved feudalism could capitalism emerge. In the feudal system (as opposed to the Asiatic and primitive), the essential divorce which is a precondition of private property of the few had taken place. 'Feudal landed property is already essentially land which had been disposed of, alienated from men.'[29] While Maine and Marx stressed the changes in property concepts, Weber noted other ideological changes. No longer was the kinship sentiment dominant; loyalty to the family based on status was changed to a bond based, ultimately, on contract, the political decision to serve a lord. According to Bendix, Weber argued that 'in western Europe and Japan the specifically feudal combination of loyalty and status honour was made the basic outlook on life that affected all social relationships'.[30] It is on the basis of these views that most of the major theorists of the rise of capitalism – Anderson, Brenner, Barrington-Moore – see feudalism as a vital transitory stage. Yet if this is true, some puzzles remain. Two of these are particularly relevant to this essay. First, why did feudalism have such different consequences in different parts of Europe, and particularly as between England and much of the continent? Secondly, how was it that feudalism dissolved?

[25] Maine, *Lectures*, 86.   [26] *Ibid.*, 115.   [27] Maine, *Ancient Law*, 237.
[28] Pollock and Maitland, *English Laws*, II, 232–3.
[29] Marx, *Writings;* Bloch, *Feudal Society*, II, 445, also noted that feudalism is based on contract, not status.
[30] Bendix, *Max Weber*, 364.

In order to proceed further we need to set up an ideal-typical model of what feudalism is, or was. For Maine, the central feature was the nature of proprietorship. Put very crudely, the economic and the political were not split apart, unlike capitalism, which keeps them in separate spheres. Feudalism 'mixed up or confounded property and sovereignty',[31] for in a certain sense, every lord of a manor was a king as well as a landholder. Political power and economic power were both delegated down the same chain. A second feature, more narrowly economic and legal, was the ability to conceive of different layers of ownership or possession within feudal tenures: 'the leading characteristic of the feudal conception is its recognition of a double proprietorship, the superior ownership of the lord of the fief coexisting with the inferior property or estate of the tenant'.[32]

Marx's characterization of feudalism in his various writings is a fairly conventional and largely economic picture of an immobile, mainly self-subsistent, 'peasant' society, with a hierarchy of owners. There was little division of labour, production was mainly for use, and the serfs were chained to their lords.[33] Perhaps Weber's most important insight was his recognition that feudalism constituted a different political system. His views have been summarized by Gerth and Mills thus:

Feudalism is characterized by Weber in terms of private property of the means of military violence (self-equipped armies) and in the corporate appropriation of the means of administration. The 'ruler' could not monopolize administratiòn and warfare because he had to delegate the implements required for such a monopoly to the several privileged groupings. In time, these latter became 'owners' in their own right.[34]

In other words, there is political and legal decentralization; the centre cannot hold and mere anarchy is loosed upon the world. There is again reference to the fusion of military, political, legal and economic power down a chain of delegation. A feudal society in this sense is a pre-state society; people are not citizens, but vassals of particular lords.

The most influential model of feudalism is that presented by Bloch. Again his stress is mainly on the military, political and legal features of

[31] Maine, *Early Law*, 148.   [32] Maine, *Early Law*, 295.
[33] Marx, *Writings*, 128; Marx, *Capital*, I, 316; Marx, *Pre-Capitalist*, 46.
[34] Gerth and Mills, *Max Weber*, 47.

feudalism, rather than on the economic and property aspects. He summarizes the central features of the model thus: 'a subject peasantry; widespread use of the service tenement (i.e. the fief) instead of a salary; the supremacy of a class of specialized warriors; ties of obedience and protection which bind man to man and, within the warrior class, assume the distinctive form called vassalage; fragmentation of authority, leading inevitably to disorder; and, in the midst of all this, the precarious survival of other forms of association, the family and State'. The fragmentation is well illustrated in his description of the judicial system in Europe in about AD 1000. 'First, we may note the tremendous fragmentation of judicial powers; next, their tangled interconnections; and lastly, their ineffectiveness'. In some ways feudalism is best defined negatively. It was not based on kinship; 'feudal ties proper were developed when those of kinship proved inadequate'. Although modelled on family ties, this was a relation of contract, not status. Nor was feudalism a state system. 'Again, despite the persistence of the idea of a public authority superimposed on the multitude of petty powers, feudalism coincided with a profound weakening of the state, particularly in its protective capacity'.[35] In Bloch's view this strange and unique system was a transition phase, the turbulence of the Germanic invasions led to a fusion of Roman and Germanic that broke the old mould. Ganshof, likewise, stressed political fragmentation. One of his four defining features of feudalism was 'a dispersal of political authority amongst a hierarchy of persons who exercise in their own interest powers normally attributed to the State and which are often, in fact, derived from its break-up'.[36]

We may provide one final description of feudalism. Maitland lamented the difficulty of defining feudalism: 'the impossible task that has been set before the word *feudalism* is that of making a single idea represent a very large piece of the world's history, represent the France, Italy, Germany, England, of every century from the eighth or ninth to the fourteenth or fifteenth'.[37] The result is confusion. Maitland attempted to clarify the situation. The central feature of feudalism, as Maine had stressed, was the strange mixture of ownership, the blending of economic and political. The feud, fief or fee was

[35] Bloch, *Feudal Society*, II , 446, 359, 443. [36] Ganshof, *Feudalism*, xv.
[37] Pollock and Maitland, *English Law*, I, 67.

a gift of land made by the king out of his own estate, the grantee coming under a special obligation to be faithful . . . To express the rights thus created, a set of technical terms was developed: the beneficiary or feudatory holds the land of his lord, the grantor–*A tenet terram de B.* The full ownership (*dominium*) of the land is as it were broken up between A and B; or again, for the feudatory may grant out part of the land to be held of him, it may be broken up between A, B, and C, C holding of B and B of A, and so on, *ad infinitum.*[38]

Maitland believed that 'the most remarkable characteristic of feudalism' was the fact that 'several persons in somewhat different senses, may be said to have and to hold the same piece of land',[39] But there are equally characteristic and essential features. In some mysterious way power and property have been merged. Feudalism is not just a landholding system, but also a system of government. While many have seen 'the introduction of military tenures' as the 'establishment of the feudal system', in fact, when 'compared with seignorial justice, military tenure is a superficial matter, one out of many effects rather than a deep seated cause'.[40] He describes as 'that most essential feature of feudalism, jurisdiction in private hands, the lord's court'.[41] The merging of power and property, of public and private, is well shown elsewhere in Maitland's work. The English lawyer Bracton knew of the distinction of 'private' and 'public', yet 'he makes little use of it'. This was because 'feudalism . . . is a denial of this distinction. Just in so far as the ideal of feudalism is perfectly realized, all that we call public law is merged in private law: jurisdiction is property, office is property, the kingship itself is property; the same word *dominium* has to stand now for *ownership* and now for *lordship*'.[42]

Although we have already quoted extensively from Maitland, it is helpful to summarize his views of the ideal-typical model of feudalism in one further description. This is an elegant synthesis of the essence of feudalism against which particular systems can be measured. It shows the two strands of the economic and political held together. Feudalism is

a state of society in which the main bond is the relation between lord and man, a relation implying on the lord's part protection and defence; on the man's part

---

[38] Maitland, *History*, 152, 153.   [39] Pollock and Maitland, *English Law*, I, 237.
[40] Maitland, *Domesday Book*, 258.   [41] Pollock and Maitland, *English Law*, I, 68.
[42] *Ibid.*, I, 230.

protection, service and reverence, the service including service in arms. This personal relation is inseparably involved in a proprietary relation, the tenure of land — the man holds lands of the lord, the man's service is a burden on the land, the lord has important rights in the land, and (we may say) the full ownership of the land is split up between man and lord. The lord has jurisdiction over his men, holds courts for them, to which they owe suit. Jurisdiction is regarded as property, as a private right which the lord has over his land. The national organization is a system of these relationships: at the head there stands the king as lord of all, below him are his immediate vassals, or tenants in chief, who again are lords of tenants, who again may be lords of tenants, and so on, down to the lowest possessor of land. Lastly, as every other court consists of the lord's tenants, so the king's court consists of his tenants in chief, and so far as there is any constitutional control over the king it is exercised by the body of these tenants.[43]

This completes our attempts to sort out in ideal-typical terms the social formation out of which capitalism was born.

Various things are now clear. The emergence of capitalism required not only a particular geographical, religious and technological complex, but, above all, a particular politico-economic system. This was provided by feudalism. Yet there remain many puzzles. One lies in a general paradox. In many ways feudalism as described in the Bloch/Maitland model seems a very unpropitious ground for capitalism. First, it rests on that very fusion of economic and political which has to be broken if capitalism is to triumph. Of course, the modern market has to rest on a particular political framework; but for capitalism to flourish the economy must be granted a great deal of autonomy. It must be set free. If economic relations are merely a sub-aspect of devolved power, capitalism cannot emerge. Secondly, the political system must be integrated and centralized. The modern 'state' is a necessary concomitant to capitalism; to this extent Anderson's stress on the necessity of absolutism is correct. Yet the overriding and defining feature of feudalism is the dissolution of the state, the loss of power at the

---

[43] Maitland, *History*, 143–4. Among more recent studies of the meaning of feudalism, with attempted definitions, are Ganshof, *Feudalism*, xv; Herlihy, *History of Feudalism*, xviii–xix, xxiii, 207; Brown, *Origins of Feudalism*, 19, 20, 23; Duby, *Early Growth*, 162. Though adding subtlety and depth, they do not seem to me to advance beyond the insights of Maine, Bloch and Maitland.

centre. These puzzles are linked to a more specific one. Feudalism is widely held to be a phenomenon which covered most of western Europe. Why was it then that in England it first dissolved into capitalism? Fortunately, the answers to all these puzzles seem to lie in the same direction.

Many observers past and present have assumed that all of Europe, and particularly most of north-western Europe, went through a similar 'feudal' phase. David Hume, after giving a sketch of feudal anarchy consistent with the 'dissolved state' description, pointed to 'the great similarity among the feudal governments of Europe'.[44] De Tocqueville described how 'I have had occasion to study the political institutions of the Middle Ages in France, in England, and in Germany, and the greater progress I made in this work, the more was I filled with astonishment at the prodigious similarity that I found between all these systems of law'. Having elaborated the similarities he concluded that 'I think it may be maintained that in the fourteenth century the social, political, administrative, judicial, economic, and literary institutions of Europe had more resemblance to each other than they have perhaps even in our own days'.[45] Marx broadly accepted this view, arguing that England was a truly feudal society, indeed it was the most feudal: 'the feudalism introduced into England was formally more complete than the feudalism which had naturally grown up in France'.[46] If this view is correct, then the puzzles remain. But there are reasons for doubting it.

Weber seems to have realized that the English feudal system was in some way different. Having distinguished between two major forms of government in traditional societies, patrimonialism and feudalism, Weber recognized that England did not fall exactly into either. We are told that 'he took England as a borderline case in which patrimonial and feudal elements were inextricably mixed'.[47] England had a powerful, decentralizing force in the old baronial families, through whom the Crown governed, but the Normans had also imposed a powerful central force – the king's ministers and judges.

The suspicion that England had a peculiar form of feudalism is made stronger by Bloch's work. Read superficially, Bloch could be

[44] Hume, *History*, 20. [45] De Tocqueville, *L'Ancien Regime*, 18–19.
[46] Marx, *Pre-Capitalist*, 88.
[47] Bendix, *Max Weber*, 358.

taken to argue that England was an ordinary 'feudal' state in the early middle ages. Writing of vassalage, Bloch noted that England was 'already feudalized on the continental model'. He states that it was one of the countries with 'an exceptionally close feudal structure . . .', 'in certain respects . . . no state was more completely feudal'.[48] Yet if we look more closely at the context of these remarks, we can see that Bloch was aware of the peculiar nature of English feudalism.

Bloch noticed the centralization and uniformity of the English political and social system. This was totally opposed to his major feature of feudalism, devolution, disintegration and the dissolution of the state. The contrasts come out when he compares England and France.

In England there was the Great Charter; in France, in 1314–15, the Charters granted to the Normans, to the people of Languedoc, to the Bretons, to the Burgundians, to the Picards, to the people of Champagne, to Auvergne, of the Basses Marches of the West, of Berry, and of Nevers. In England there was Parliament; in France, the provincial Estates, always much more frequently convoked and on the whole more active than the States-General. In England there was the common law, almost untouched by regional exceptions; in France the vast medley of regional 'customs'.[49]

Thus England was uniform and centralized, France varied and regionalized. Because 'the public office was not completely identified with the fief', Bloch argued, 'England was a truly unified state much earlier than any continental kingdom'. Furthermore, the English parliamentary system had a 'peculiar quality which distinguished it so sharply from the continental system of 'Estates'. This was linked to that 'collaboration of the well-to-do classes in power, so characteristic of the English political structure'.[50]

Bloch noted other central differences. The 'distinction between high and low justice always remained foreign to the English system'.[51] The allodial estates common on the continent, which prevented the final penetration of feudal tenures to the bottom of society, were totally extinguished in England, where all land was ultimately held of the king and not held in full ownership by any subject. England was exceptional

[48] Bloch, *Feudal Society*, I, 232; II, 383, 430. [49] *Ibid.*, II, 425–6.
[50] *Ibid.*, II, 430, 371.
[51] *Ibid.*, II, 370.

in not having private feuding sanctioned after the Conquest; it therefore avoided that disintegrated anarchy which was characteristic of France.[52] Indeed, English feudalism, we are told 'has something of the value of an object-lesson in social organization', not because it was typical of feudal society but because it shows 'how in the midst of what was in many respects a homogeneous civilization certain creative ideas, taking shape under the influence of a given environment, could result in the creation of a completely original legal system.[53] It is this 'completely original legal system' which provides the key to the emergence of capitalism. But what is the secret of this system? For the solution to this puzzle, it is necessary both to understand perfectly the nature of feudalism and to have a deep knowledge of how the English system worked. It needed Maitland to state the essential paradox of English feudalism and to resolve it.

Maitland commented that 'we have learnt to see vast differences as well as striking resemblances, to distinguish countries and to distinguish times' when we discuss feudalism. Thus 'if we now speak of the feudal system, it should be with a full understanding that the feudalism of France differs radically from the feudalism of England, that the feudalism of the thirteenth is very different from that of the eleventh century'. For England 'it is quite possible to maintain that of all countries England was the most, or for the matter of that the least, feudalized'.[54] The paradox is resolved when we remember that there are two central criteria whereby we measure feudalism. In terms of land law, England was the most perfectly feudalized of societies, as Bloch also noted. All tenures were feudal. Maitland wrote, 'in so far as feudalism is mere property law, England is of all countries the most perfectly feudalized'. Thus 'owing to the Norman Conquest one part of the theory was carried out in this country with consistent and unexampled rigour; every square inch of land was brought within the theory of tenure: English real property law becomes a law of feudal tenures. In France, in Germany, allodial owners might be found: not one in England'. For instance the 'absolute and uncompromising form of primogeniture which prevails in England belongs not to

[52] *Ibid.*, I, 128.
[53] *Ibid.*, I, 274; for a subsequent recognition of some of the peculiarities of English feudalism, see Ganshof, *Feudalism*, 67, 164–6.
[54] Maitland, *History*, 143.

feudalism in general, but to a highly centralized feudalism in which the King has not much to fear from the power of his mightiest vassals'.[55] Thus, in terms of tenure, England was the most feudal of societies and Marx was right.

On the other hand, in the even more important sphere of public and private law and political power, that is, in terms of government, England went in a peculiar direction, towards centralization of power, rather than the dissolution of the state. Maitland points out that 'our public law does not become feudal; in every direction the force of feudalism is limited and checked by other ideas; the public rights, the public duties of the Englishman are not conceived and cannot be conceived as the mere outcome of feudal compacts between man and lord'. Maitland outlines the major features of this limitation of public feudalism. 'First and foremost, it never becomes law that there is no political bond between men save the bond of tenure . . . whenever homage or fealty was done to any mesne lord, the tenant expressly saved the faith that he owed to his lord the king'.[56] Thus a man who fights for his lord against the king is not doing his feudal duty; he is committing treason. Over-mighty subjects could not draw on justification from this system. This point is so important that Maitland elaborates it in various ways.

'English law never recognizes that any man is bound to fight for his lord . . . Private war never becomes legal – it is a crime and a breach of the peace'. A man can hardly 'go against' anyone at his lord's command without being guilty of 'felony'. As Maitland wrote, 'Common law, royal and national law, has, as it were, occupied the very citadel of feudalism'. To bring out the full peculiarity of this, Maitland tells us, 'you should look at the history of France; there it was definitely regarded as law that in a just quarrel the vassal must follow his immediate lord, even against the king'. In England, 'military service is due to none but the king; this it is which makes English feudalism a very different thing from French feudalism'.[57]

There are a number of other differences which make this central feature possible and flow from it. There is an alternative army for the

[55] Pollock and Maitland, *English Law*, I, 235; Maitland, *History*, 163–4; Pollock and Maitland, *English Law*, II, 265.
[56] Maitland, *History*, 164, 161.
[57] *Ibid.*, 161; Pollock and Maitland, *English Law*, I, 303; Maitland, *History*, 162, 32.

king, which helps to protect him against an over-dependence on his feudal tenants.

Though the military tenures supply the king with an army, it never becomes law that those who are not bound by tenure need not fight. The old national force, officered by the sheriffs, does not cease to exist . . . In this organization of the common folk under royal officers, there is all along a counterpoise to the military system of feudalism, and it serves the king well.

Another source of strength for the centre is the fact that 'taxation is not feudalized'. Maitland tells us that 'the king for a while is strong enough to tax the nation, to tax the sub-tenants, to get straight at the mass of the people, their lands and their goods, without the intervention of their lords'.[58] Thus he is not entirely dependent on powerful lords for soldiers or money.

Nor is he entirely dependent on them for advice. We are told that 'the *Curia Regis*, which is to become the *commune concilium regni*, never takes very definitely a feudal shape . . . It is much in the king's power to summon whom he will. The tradition of a council of witan is not lost'. Finally, the king is not forced to delegate judicial power to the barons. 'The administration of justice is never completely feudalized. The old local courts are kept alive, and are not feudal assemblies'. As a result of this 'the jurisdiction of the feudal courts is strictly limited; criminal jurisdiction they have none save by express royal grant, and the kings are on the whole chary of making such grants. Seldom, indeed, can any lord exercise more than what on the continent would have been considered justice of a very low degree'. Starting with considerable power, the king 'rapidly extends the sphere of his own justice: before the middle of the thirteenth century his courts have practically become courts of first instance for the whole realm'.[59]

The contradiction is thus resolved. By taking one aspect of the feudal tie, the idea that each person is linked to the person above him both in terms of tenure and power, to its logical limits, the English system developed into something peculiar. By the standards of Bloch's French model of feudalism, England was both the most and the least feudal of countries. Looked at another way, England was the ideal-typical feudal society, with an apex of both landholding and

[58] Maitland, *History*, 162.   [59] *Ibid.*, 163, 162–3.

justice and power in the chief lord, and it was other feudal systems which, through the devolution of too much power, were defective. Both are tenable views. Despite some minor modifications, Maitland's vision is still acceptable, certainly there 'can be no doubt that by the end of the period covered by his book', in other words the end of the thirteenth century, 'the world was as Maitland saw it'.[60]

The argument very briefly stated and summarized is as follows. No single factor explains why capitalism emerged. We do know some of the necessary causes, as outlined by Maine, Marx and Weber. All of them are important. But to proceed further we need to concentrate on hints from all these writers, as well as Brenner and others, that as well as geography, technology and Christianity, a particular form of political and economic system was needed. This was broadly provided by 'feudalism'. But the variant of feudalism which finally allowed the 'miracle' to occur was a rather unusual one. It already contained an implicit separation between economic and political power, between the market and government. While it was not absolutism in Anderson's sense, it was a firm and central-focused system which provided the security and uniformity upon which trade and industry could be based. If we accept the view attributed to Adam Smith by Dugald Stewart that 'little else is required to carry a state to the highest degree of opulence from the lowest barbarism, but peace, easy taxes, and a tolerable administration of justice; all the rest being brought about by the natural order of things',[61] then the English political system provided such a basis. It guaranteed peace through the control of feuding, taxes were light and justice was uniform and firmly administered from the thirteenth to eighteenth centuries. This offered the framework within which there developed that competitive individualism whose later history I have tried to analyse elsewhere.[62]

Yet it would clearly be foolish to over-stress any evolutionary necessity in this process. It could at any time have been reversed; the victory of the Spanish Armada, for instance, might well have changed the direction. Nor is it sensible to over-stress the uniqueness of

---

[60] Milsom in Pollock and Maitland, *English Law*, I, xlvii. Later writers have noted the major differences. Baechler, *Origins*, 80, also notes the peculiarity of English feudalism, as does Pocock, *Ancient*, 119; Ganshof several times recognizes that there were striking contrasts and peculiarities in English feudalism, *Feudalism*, 67, 164–6.
[61] Quoted in Hall, *Powers*, 141.   [62] Macfarlane, *Individualism*.

England. There was clearly much that overlapped with northern France, the Netherlands and Scandinavia. Yet Marx, Weber and others were not wrong to see England as the cradle of capitalism. If Protestantism was one of those who stood at the cradle, an unusual politico-economic system which Bloch and Maitland have so clearly described for us, is another guest at the baptism. Indeed it may even be that it was this guest who lay in the cradle. Who brought it there, and when, is of course another story.

Postscript

Individualism Reconsidered, or the Craft of the Historian

THE ESSAYS in this book have restated, elaborated and attempted to confirm the central argument of *The Origins of English Individualism*. We may wonder, however, to what extent the theories in that book have survived the critical scrutiny of the community of historians. For while most reviewers are agreed that if I was broadly right, then fundamental changes would have to be made to our view of the English past, many have argued strenuously that the thesis is either unproven, or erroneous. That thesis, namely that there was never a conventional peasant society in England and that the supposed revolution from peasant to individualist, or feudal to capitalist, did not occur in the way that many sociologists and historians have suggested, has been restated here in chapter 1, and in passing in many of the other chapters in this book. I will not repeat it here but will look at some of the objections which have been brought against the argument.

More than 50 reviewers have dissected the book in over 160 pages of published reviews.[1] I am grateful to them for many constructive criticisms. If my reply sounds somewhat defensive, this is because I have chosen to concentrate on the strongest criticisms and queries.[2] I am here concerned to answer criticism. What then remains of the central thesis and what modifications need to be made in the light of

[1] The major reviewers, including all those to whom reference is made in this Postscript, are listed at the end of the Bibliography (p. 240).
[2] Not all the reviewers were negative. The reader who would like to see more favourable accounts should also look at those by Ryan, Laslett, Mount and Keates.

comments? It is a humbling exercise to re-examine a work that has been chewed over so carefully, and the tone of certain critics has not made the task easier. But readers may be interested to know what is left of the ship after the gales have blown and the counter-blasts fired.

The heart of the argument of *Individualism* concerned the growth of the concept of private, individual property. The work was an attempt to refute Marx and those who follow him in believing that only through a legal revolution sometime after the end of the fifteenth century was the 'modern' concept of private, individual property introduced. Marx had argued that 'the legal view . . . that the landowner can do with the land what every owner of commodities can do with his commodities . . . arises . . . in the modern world only with the development of capitalist production'. Capitalism as a system 'transforms' the 'feudal landed property, clan property, small-peasant property' into modern, individualistic ownership.[3] Through an examination of the work of legal historians such as Maitland, through an analysis of early law books, and through a re-examination of the arguments of medievalists like Homans, who appeared to have distorted the court roll evidence, I attempted to show that property was highly individualized by the end of the thirteenth century, if not much earlier. It was held by individuals and not by larger groups; it could be bought and sold; children did not have automatic rights in land; there is no evidence of strong family attachment to a particular plot of land. Thus the core of the argument of the book was, as can be seen in a mild form in chapter 1 above, of a legal and technical kind. It is on this argument that the book's thesis ultimately stands or falls. The reactions of critics to this argument are revealing.

G. C. Homans's review does not attempt to refute my criticisms of his work. He admitted that 'the Common Law did indeed make the transfer of land between living persons relatively easy . . . and by the end of the thirteenth century there was an active market in land, even land held in villeinage', even though 'in theory, transfers of such land required the consent of the lord of the manor'. He merely reasserts, referring back to *English Villagers*, 'especially in the common-field areas of England', in practice villagers 'tended to leave their standard holdings intact to their heirs, usually their eldest sons' and to give their daughters dowries and to support other children who were

---

[3] Marx, *Capital*, III, 616, quoted in Macfarlane, *Individualism*, 39.

unprepared to leave the holding. This is, in fact, far less than what
was argued in Homans's book. It is a weakened assertion which is
much easier to accept. It is significant that Professor Homans should
not have attempted to defend or comment on my detailed criticisms of
his use of, and inferences from, medieval court roll materials.

Only two of the other critics of the book even begin to tackle this
most central argument. By their silence, one has to presume that
many of the rest either tacitly accept the argument, or feel
incompetent to argue on the matter. Their failure to discuss the most
central technical issue, let alone reject it, is the clearest indication that
the central thesis of the book, its most important argument around
which all the other arguments are ranged, has withstood the test of
criticism. It is in the light of this tacit acceptance that criticisms
directed at less essential arguments should be evaluated. The critics
can hardly have been unaware of the centrality of this discussion. The
two middle chapters of the book were devoted to 'Ownership' from
1350 to 1750, and from 1200 to 1750, and comprise some 50 pages,
or one quarter of the book. What are the arguments of the two
reviewers who have attempted to challenge parts of this thesis?

Dr Rosamond Faith agrees, in essence, with my argument that
property was held by individuals and not by wider groups in medieval
England. Indeed she suggests a more radical theory, namely that this
feature may be present much earlier, in a pre-Conquest England. She
accepts that there was no restraint on alienation of property imposed
by the lineage, that 'the common law in the middle ages certainly
exemplified a much more individualistic attitude to land than existed
on the continent'. Her major criticism is that medievalists, and
probably even Marx, knew this all along. I have created a straw man
which I then attack. If I have done so, I can only regret that certain
writers did not make their views more explicit. Certainly a number of
historians and sociologists, and not only myself, have been confused
into thinking that they believed that there was some kind of group,
family-based, peasant property system up to the fifteenth century,
which was then radically transformed by a new capitalistic and
individualistic framework.

One of my arguments was that where land is fully alienable and
often bought and sold, it is unlikely that there will be that
characteristic sentimental attachment to specific 'family' plots found
in many peasantries. There will not be a strong feeling that 'the name

should be kept on the land'; that is, the family name on specific
inherited lands. Dr Faith shows more ambivalence on this question.
On the one hand she agrees that there was little attachment to specific
pieces of land. But she is reluctant to give up the idea of a generalized
high sentimental valuation of land. Thus while she agrees that land
was bought and sold freely and frequently for much of the period
after 1300 and probably before, she argues that since land was
'virtually the only source of subsistence' for the major part of the
population, it could not be described as a 'commodity'. Land, she
believes, must have been emotionally important to medieval people,
because it was so crucial in the economy.

Obviously no one would deny that land was of enormous economic
importance, even if it is also necessary to remember the many other
sources of income from manufacture and trade in medieval England.
But this is true of England up to the later eighteenth century and it is
still true in farming regions today. Yet most historians would concede
that in the later seventeenth and eighteenth centuries there was little
sentimental attachment of a 'peasant' kind. What this shows is that to
say that something is economically important, in itself, tells us little
about its social or symbolic importance. The other reviewer who has
commented in any depth on this central argument is Professor
Hilton, manifesting in a classic way that ('we knew it all already, but it
is all wrong anyway') ambivalence to which Elton drew attention.
Hilton alleges that I am 'bemused' by my discovery '(well known to
others)' of the *ante mortem* alienability of freehold tenures. While
'surprised' would be a better adjective, the important fact is that
Hilton agrees that in relation to freehold, I appear to be right. But this
admission is then undermined in a curious way, namely by obliquely
attacking F. W. Maitland.

Hilton alleges that my discussion of medieval property is based
'almost entirely on F. W. Maitland'. Although I did rely heavily on
Maitland, readers of the book will see that this is a considerable
exaggeration. Maitland is essential, but he is supported by many other
cited sources. Having tied me to Maitland, Hilton is then in a position
to undermine me by undermining Maitland. First, it is implied that
Maitland is somehow discredited for the period on which I was
writing, namely from 1300 onwards. I am accused of ignoring S. C.
Milsom's 'gentle warning that Maitland "sometimes places highly
abstract notions of property too early" '. One might answer that

Milsom's views are as liable to be wrong as are Maitland's. But there is a better answer. Hilton must have read two sentences further on in Milsom's preface that 'if Maitland's picture was not true to start with – and here the heretic is most disturbed by his own heresy – it came true'. What is meant is made clearer in the same introduction by Milsom when he writes, 'there can be no doubt that by the end of the period covered by his book, the world was as Maitland saw it'.[4] Now the end of Maitland's period is 1307, the start of my period is 1300. To suggest on Milsom's authority that Maitland cannot be trusted for the early thirteenth century onwards is, to put it mildly, somewhat misleading. But this is not the end of the attempt to undermine Maitland as an authority.

Professor Hilton suggests that Maitland is 'in any case mainly talking about freehold among the upper classes, such as military tenures'. A non-medievalist reading the review, never having read Maitland, might accept this *obiter dicta* from a leading medievalist. If I have really depended 'almost entirely' on this authority, and he is hardly concerned with other than freehold tenures, I must surely be on very weak and unsupported ground. But it is in fact a considerable distortion, as will be evident even from a glance at the table of contents, which shows that 'Pollock and Maitland' devotes a number of sections and chapters to each of the different kinds of tenure. For instance, volume 1, pages 356–83 is specifically devoted to 'unfree tenure'. To suggest that Maitland's writing is not directly relevant to all groups in medieval society is surely indefensible.

Having severed me from my one apparent authority, I am then open to destruction by the expert. Professor Hilton argues that I have misunderstood the nature of villein (that is, servile) tenure, 'attempting to assimilate it to freehold as though it were equivalent to sixteenth-century copyhold'. Hilton does not seek to defend the position that there was group or family ownership. But he argues that villeins were 'severely restricted' in their rights 'by the control exercised by lords'. There was a concentration of power into the hands of nobility, gentry and clergy, and hence it was ridiculous of me to talk about rights, individualism, and so on at this level of society in the medieval period. The same point is made by Lawrence Stone, who wrote that 'it is symptomatic of Mr Macfarlane's myopia that he

---

[4] Pollock and Maitland, *English Law*, lxxiii, xlvii.

totally ignores the close communal control, through the manorial court, of almost every aspect of the use of property. Such courts could tell people when, where, and what to sow or reap'.

There is a half-truth in this argument. No one would deny that from a very early period lasting up to at least the middle of the eighteenth century, there was a considerable concentration of property which put considerable pressure on 'the small man'. I have examined the restrictions imposed by manor courts in Earls Colne from 1380, and in the more conservative north of England from the sixteenth century. Of course tenants were circumscribed and had to work within the rules. But my argument is in fact rather different. I argued two points. First, that the *de jure* position, as shown by an examination of the legal sources, was that property, the right to alienate, was not held by the family but vested in individuals. This was present from very early on and is, cross-comparatively, very unusual. This is not challenged by Hilton, Homans, Faith or any other reviewer. Secondly, I argued that the *de facto* position as shown by recent work on court rolls and other documents seems to have been that people exercised this right very widely. Land sales to non-kin were very frequent, even by those 'villeins' whom historians for long thought were incapable of such activities. This fact also is not challenged. Having studied manorial courts in the fifteenth and sixteenth centuries and seen how they combined control and direction on the one hand, with a perfect ability to allow people to buy and sell land on the other, I see no particular incompatibility. How this was done needs to be documented in detail. What does not seem to have been shown is that in the central argument I was mistaken.

Since it might be thought that my pleading is partial, perhaps I may bring forward a relatively impartial authority. Dr Paul Hyams is a medievalist specializing in these very subjects; namely, the legal position of villeins and the nature of early medieval law. Any inappropriateness of my use of Maitland, any mis-use of medieval legal concepts, any distortions concerning discussions of property would have been revealed by Dr Hyams, who reviewed the book. In particular, any defects in my extended attempt to show where G. C. Homans's work had been misleading, a fairly technical subject, would have been pointed out. Dr Hyams is aware of the seriousness of my challenge. He writes that Homans's views of the medieval peasant community have, for 40 years 'never faced real challenge. Now Alan

Macfarlane offers that challenge'. While Dr Hyams has some criticisms concerning my model of peasantry and notes some sins of omission, to which I will return, there is significantly no defence of Homans, no criticism of the use of Maitland, no fundamental disagreement with the central thrust of the argument concerning the very early development of individualized concepts of property. He concludes by urging that 'specialist indignation of the righteous kind ought not to obscure the book's genuine achievement'.

Although this advice has not been heeded very much, it is difficult to see that the central thesis of the book has been seriously challenged, let alone refuted, by counter-arguments. Until a serious and convincing challenge is mounted, I see no reason to alter the argument. Marx, Weber and those who have followed them were wrong. There was no revolutionary change from one, pre-capitalist, economic formation, to another, capitalist one, in England in the fourteenth, fifteenth, sixteenth or seventeenth centuries.

While the central argument appears to me to stand, critics have rightly pointed to a number of possible weaknesses in the deductions made from this argument, and in the ways in which it was presented. One cluster of criticisms we might label as 'sins of omission'. Many critics would have liked to see the book investigating many other topics. The longest single list of omissions is provided by another medievalist, Dr John Hatcher. He points out that 'rent, conditions of tenure and lordship are scarcely mentioned . . . the odd passing reference to such matters as villeinage, competitive tenures, estate management, farming methods, occupational structure, standards of life, consumption patterns, land–labour ratios, productivity, towns, trade, industry, technology, communications, finance and so on, would not have been superfluous'. In fact, there are passing references to many of these, and Dr Hatcher has overdone the irony. But he has a good point when showing that in a short book many of these topics were hardly developed in any detail. Other topics which reviews have suggested that I should have devoted some, or more, space to include the following: external relations and world markets, the struggles of classes, the labouring classes and social class variations, violence and suffering, the state and state regulation, the role of the bourgeoisie, the historical preconditions of the common law, custom, the role of the Church and religion, the Black Death, enclosures, the open-field system, the traditional village and the

manor, serfdom, law in relation to government and politics. Finally,
several reviewers, for instance the anthropologist Dr Rheubottom,
drew attention to the omission of any extended treatment of
'individualism as a cultural system'. It is suggested that while I seem
aware that 'individualism is more obviously connected with morals,
politics and general culture than with land-holding', as Dr Harding
writes, I tend to ignore these dimensions on the whole.

Several points can be made concerning these formidable omissions. The first is that others have also committed these sins of
omission. Thus Richard Smith (1) suggests that while I am in error 'in
failing to consider the lordship and its relationship to the operational
process of customary law', my 'guilt must be shared' by my 'critics
and legal historians'. The second is that those who drew up the lists
do not suggest that if I had considered all, or some, of these topics it
would have either undermined or even weakened my argument.
Rather, they believe it would have added further weight to it. Thus,
for instance, Barbara Donagan writes that the absence of a discussion
of the moral and sentimental dimensions 'leaves us with only half a
picture of these rediscovered English individualists'. More harshly,
Dr Baker points out that I 'foolishly' ignore 'the role of cities, of
industry and of commerce in medieval England which would have
lent support' to my 'main thesis'. Thus the argument I put forward in
the book, and which has been greeted as unproven and controversial,
could be very greatly strengthened.

The critics are, of course, right. A full treatment of the origins of
English individualism would include all those topics listed above, and
many others which I could add, such as the role and nature of
political power, the legal and administrative structure, language,
literature, art, ideology and so on. My difficulty was that I wanted to
write an interpretative essay, putting forward a simple hypothesis as
clearly and succinctly as possible. I could have waited 20 years and
assembled huge quantities of material into a set of volumes which
could scarcely have been less weighty than Braudel's massive
three-volume history of 'Civilization and Capitalism'. I hoped that by
going to the heart of the argument, the relations of production, I
would then be able to lay a renewed framework on which I and others
could build. In particular, in relation to the moral order, I wrote in
justification in the postscript that the difficulties of using much more
literary evidence, 'combined with the desire to keep the argument

relatively simple in a first presentation', led me to reserve the treatment of the moral order, sentiment, and so on to a later occasion. The essays in this present book are a partial fulfilment of that promise, dealing with selected small parts of the political, moral and sentimental order. In these essays and subsequent research I have tried to answer some of the very sensible criticisms, and in particular that of Donagan and others, that one cannot understand the free-floating individualism described in the book without seeing how individuals were linked to the society and state. What would seem a fair assessment is that by Dr Hyams. He points out that the argument needs refinements and finer gradations and further evidence. 'Macfarlane recognizes the need. His scale and level of generality perhaps absolve him from the duty to satisfy it'. It seemed to me worth the risk.

The inclusion of wider discussions of moral and ideological questions in these essays may also partly answer the criticisms put forward by Goldie and reflected by Smith (2) that I am ultimately an economic determinist. While accepting with Weber that there is likely to be an 'elective affinity' between the material, social, moral and intellectual worlds, I would reject the view that, as Smith puts it, 'the ideological superstructure *follows* the pattern of the economic substructure' (my italics).

The sins of omission are also linked to another perceived weakness, namely that I ultimately failed to explain the origins of the supposed individualism of the English. A number of reviewers were disappointed that my conclusion was so enigmatic: an oblique reference to Montesquieu and the German forests. Having apparently destroyed alternative solutions to the problems of the origins of modern society, they hoped that I would provide something fully worked out and convincing to replace them with. Frankly, so did I. But the task is a very large one, not to be undertaken by one individual or in a few years. I decided to drop a hint, and then to think further about this and encourage others to speculate on these themes, particularly those more expert in the period before the twelfth century.

In the intervening years since *Individualism* I have indeed tried to push the argument further and attempted to provide at least a partial answer to the problems posed. My two main lines of thought are represented in the last chapter of my recent book on marriage and in chapter 8 of this collection. In that chapter, I have taken up a remark which I made at the end of *Individualism* where I mentioned that I seriously doubted that English feudalism was like other feudalism. I have undertaken a preliminary examination of this, and of the related questions of lordship, which Hyams and others have rightly commented on.

Another set of criticisms concerns my treatment of historical change. According to some of the reviewers, I denied the existence of change. Three examples, out of half a dozen along these lines, may be given. Barbara Harris states that ultimately my book 'is a historical work that denies the existence of fundamental historical change for a period of over five centuries. Such a claim boggles the imagination'. She then lists 11 major changes that occurred during this period. It does indeed sound boggling. Or again, Dr Hatcher finds my supposed hypothesis of 'half a millenium of social stability culminating in the Industrial Revolution' very weak, arguing that this is a book 'which seeks to persuade us that in essence society and economy did not change in the 500 years prior to industrialization'. Perhaps the most extreme statement of this criticism is by Professor Stone, who writes that I 'seem to claim' that because there was not a revolution in property relations, this 'indicates that any idea of significant progress – or even significant change – from the thirteenth to the eighteenth century is a mirage'. It is strongly implied that since I do not formally affirm my belief in the Renaissance, Reformation, agricultural revolution, commercial revolution, growth of London, spread of literacy and the invention of the printing press, the development of political theory, and other changes Stone lists, I do not believe they occurred, or if they did, that they had much effect.

It would appear from such reviews that I must be eccentric, if not insane. What was I doing during all those years at school and university studying English history if I managed to avoid noticing all these changes? The answer is that by exaggerating my position, these reviewers have managed to make it ridiculous. It is a well-known demolition technique. The fact that I do not mention or stress something, for instance the growth of London, or the invention of printing, cannot be taken to mean that I do not believe it occurred, or do not know of its existence. If an author had to list every event that occurred during his period of study or be accused of being ignorant of it, books would become very long indeed, and exceedingly boring. Of course there were fundamental and important changes of all sorts and kinds. My thesis is, I hope, slightly less foolish than this; namely, that the speed, nature and depth of change in England is remarkable.

In essence, I am arguing that there was no *revolutionary* change in this period from one order of society, which one could label 'peasant', 'medieval', 'feudal', 'pre-capitalist', or whatever one likes, to another, which is the total antithesis of this. I deny a sudden, dramatic and all-encompassing revolution located in a few decades, whether in the sixteenth, seventeenth or eighteenth centuries. This does not mean that there were not deep changes of many kinds and it would clearly be ridiculous to argue that nothing changed. As Professor Elton wrote, 'one argument already being employed against Macfarlane misjudges him: he never denies that even large changes occurred in the six centuries before 1800, only that change was linked to major upheavals in the social substructure'. The fact that some critics have drawn this conclusion and that Professor Elton feels he needs to come to my defence, does suggest that further discussion of the historian's problem of combining continuity with change is needed. Chapter 7 of this collection is a more extended treatment of this problem where I try to show what I mean by revolutionary change and how it is possible to believe in both continuity and change. I hope that this discussion will go some way to answering those critics who attack me from one flank as an old-fashioned Whig (Goldie, Pocock), on the other as a latter-day idealist (Blok), and from a third as a nineteenth-century materialist (Goldie).

Another group of criticisms concern the nature of the historical evidence I have used and the way I have analysed it. The late Philip Abrams argued that I have brought the wrong sort of evidence forward to try to solve the question of whether there was, or was not, a traditional peasant society in medieval England. As he rightly points out, this is essentially an 'analytical and qualitative', rather than an 'empiricist and quantitative' problem. To find out how many people were or were not 'peasant' is not helpful, 'the head count is simply not the relevant test'. What we are interested in is structures and relationships. With this I entirely agree. Obviously the argument was not as clearly expressed as it should have been if Abrams thought that I was mainly interested in quantities, that my main evidence was 'demographic', or that it was 'essentially empiricist and quantitative', as he claims. My position clearly needs clarification.

Of course there was a good deal of discussion in the book of quantitative matters: the number of sales of land, the size of landholdings, the rates of geographical mobility, and the proportions of land owned by various groups. In a discussion of peasantry, it seems difficult to avoid such matters. But the argument was meant, ultimately, to be analytical. This was indicated by setting out a theoretical model at the start which included many non-quantitative elements in it, such as attitudes towards land. The most detailed part of the discussion in the medieval sections has nothing to do with empirical facts or numbers, but is concerned with legal concepts. F. W. Maitland was not a noted empirical quantifier, nor are the authorities I quoted in the chapter on 'England in Perspective' at all concerned with statistical or empirical facts. Indeed other reviewers have castigated me for not being sufficiently interested in such things, Rosamond Faith writing that my approach is 'by and large . . . polemical and analytical', and Dr Hatcher complaining that it is not sufficiently quantitative. Any misleading impression that I think that the questions of capitalism, individualism and peasantry are ulti- mately quantitative and empirical will, I hope, have been settled by the essays in this volume. Even the sharpest critic will find it difficult to accuse me of undue quantification or disinterest in analytic approaches in discussing such matters as violence, evil, nature, love or revolution.

A second, related criticism is put more harshly. The medievalist Professor Herlihy believed that the book was 'founded on faulty method' and propounds 'a preposterous thesis'. One way in which the method was faulty was in using the wrong documents. Herlihy claims that most of the records I used 'reflect the interests of landlords and princes. Both landlords and princes wished to assign responsibility for rents and taxes to single, easily identified, readily found individuals'. They could not tax larger units. Thus the 'individualism' that I found 'tells us little about the interior life of the family, its values and its spirit'. I am dismissed as having discovered 'the individualism of the rent gatherer and tax collector', but I have not 'gained access to the inner reaches of the peasant household'.

There is, of course, a half-truth in this suggestion. It is indeed very difficult to go beyond the formal records for ordinary villagers before the sixteenth century. My own strategy was to do three things in order to probe behind the records. The first was to use such records as we do have as carefully as possible, usually for purposes for which they were not originally designed. As Marc Bloch put it, we have to interrogate the records: 'from the moment we decide to force them to speak, even against their will, cross-examination becomes more necessary than ever. Indeed it is the prime necessity of well-conducted historical research'.[5]

Secondly, we can place such formal records alongside other records in a period when these other sources do appear in quantity. This is one of the reasons why I worked backwards from the seventeenth and sixteenth centuries. During those centuries we can compare the impression from taxation and manorial records with other, more qualitative records, particularly disputes in courts of law, wills, diaries and other sources. When we do this, as soon as the documentation is present, it is clear that similar taxation and manorial records to those for the medieval period do not merely reflect the individualism of rent and tax gatherers. They fit perfectly with the general mentality and the inner recesses of the family. This does not, of course, prove anything about the period before 1500, but it is suggestive.

The third strategy is to work carefully back using the same procedure where we can. There are sources before 1500 which allow one to probe behind stark lay subsidies or rentals. Ordinary records of the court leet and transfers in the court baron, ecclesiastical and civil court records, literary sources, textbooks of the time on law and morality, these can enrich our analysis. Combining all three approaches, I came to the conclusion that the 'individualism' is not merely a surface phenomenon. Professor Herlihy seems convinced otherwise. He asserts, presumably as a matter of faith, or perhaps on the basis of some English medieval records of which I am not aware, that we know that there really was another world, those 'inner reaches of the peasant household'.

While this may well be true of the areas with which Professor Herlihy is familiar from his own research, namely southern France and northern Italy, where the opposition between the needs of the state and landlords on the one hand, and the inner dynamics of peasant households on the other may have been pronounced, it does not convince me as a helpful approach to the English evidence. The most that

[5] Bloch, *Historian's Craft*, 64.

Professor Herlihy could logically maintain from such'an argument is that my case is not proven. What he strongly implies is that I am patently wrong, 'propounding a preposterous thesis'. It is significant that even the fiercest of the reviewers who had worked on English medieval documents do not make a similar kind of criticism. Having worked extensively with English sources they are presumably aware that it is possible to go beyond a mere landlord's view of the world. If Professor Herlihy had analysed English documents and compared them with his north Italian ones he might perhaps have come to a rather different conclusion.

For those who have worked in southern Europe where medieval records are either very fragmentary, or are clearly entirely the work of those who were trying to extract money from a hostile peasantry, it is difficult to imagine that the English records are good enough to be able to test as complex a theory as whether the ordinary population were 'individualist' or 'familist'. It would be equally impossible, for instance, to make such deductions in medieval India or China. Indeed, it is one of the characteristics of peasant society that the gap between the mainly oral and enclosed world of the peasantry, and the external world of state and landlords is so great that it is almost impossible to do much more than observe from outside and above. In such a situation, records cannot be trusted, they do indeed reflect the mentality of outsiders. Having spent some time working with a team which has been investigating the history of Portuguese social structure I have seen this at first hand. It is not surprising, therefore, that the only other critic to make a similar point, in a much more sophisticated way, has also worked on the records of southern Europe, and particularly Portugal.

Robert Rowland concedes that the English may well have been individualists, but points out that there is a danger that using a 'Weberian/individualistic strategy for recovering the intrinsic meaning of social action (the meaning it has to the actor)', is only legitimate provided I have independent grounds for considering the society to be individualistic. I can proceed on the assumption that the society has such characteristics, but if I proceed in this way I should be careful not to argue in a circle and believe that I have proved what I originally had to assume. The way of escaping the circularity, Rowland suggests, is to consider alternative assumptions, of a non-individualistic, holistic nature. If such an analysis confirmed a basic individualism in the English past, this would validate my argument. A wider range of sources would allow me to sketch out an analysis based on such alternative assumptions. I have only partly answered this objection. I have used a wider range of sources in this book which allow me to look at the political, legal and moral dimensions which are largely missing from the earlier book. Using more qualitative sources, one would not have to impute intrinsic meanings to observed actions. The essays in this book have followed this suggestion. Most of them are concerned with qualitative matters where there are many contemporary statements, a sufficient amount of qualitative and independent evidence, which seem to confirm what was only a hypothesis in *Individualism*. Even on the basis of *Individualism* and my work on violence (see Chapter 3), Rowland felt that if one stripped away all the suspect imputations 'enough remains ... to suggest that English society ... was peculiar, and that this peculiarity appears to derive from the fact that the social system institutes the *individual* (and not the group or quasi-group) as the locus of production of the meaning of social action'. In these essays I hope that I have begun to move towards that 'greater solidity' which Rowland requests, and which allows me to argue that I had 'independent (i.e. not methodologically individualist) grounds for arguing that England was an individualistic society and, assuming this to be the case, for attempting to describe the motivations and orientations of actors'.

Another type of criticism concerns typicality and generalization from specific cases. While one historian, Dr Hyams, has rightly pointed to the need for further refinement of my argument by looking at a wider range of examples to counter the 'geographical sameness', the main criticisms do not come from the historians, but from social scientists who are less familiar with the original materials. Dr Pryor notes that if I am correct in my argument 'then much of what we have learned about English economic history must be given up', but he wonders 'how typical were the cases he cites?', rightly pointing out that 'social and land tenure arrangements differed almost from hamlet to hamlet'. The second, Philip Corrigan, does not merely raise a query, but is more confident as to the answer. He describes the two parishes which are the central examples, Earls Colne in Essex, and Kirkby Lonsdale in Westmorland, as 'extremely non-typical'. They are non-typical because neither is in the large, open-field area of central England, and because they are both 'heavily dominated by particular landowners and specific production markets from an early point in their development'. There is a useful point here. Although I cite work from all over England, it is true that my own detailed work only takes examples from one area of the highland and one of the lowland region. It would be good also to have done a study in equal depth of the open-field areas and not to have had to rely on the extensive studies by W. G. Hoskins and his pupils. Yet the point cannot be pushed too far. It is rather curious to have to argue that East Anglia and the whole of the highland region, of which these two parishes do not seem untypical, are 'exceptional'. It is also interesting that none of the historians who have critically reviewed the book, some of whom have worked in open-field areas, have tried to argue that the sample villages are 'extremely non-typical'. Of course there were very important regional differences, but no one has yet suggested, let alone demonstrated, that evidence from Essex, Norfolk or Cambridgeshire is flatly at variance with that from the midlands.

We can now turn to the other central question of methodology, the one which drew by far the most criticism and which raises some interesting historiographical problems – the use of comparative models in general, and my use of a specific model of peasantry in particular. What I tried to do was as follows. As an anthropologist looking at English history, I thought it would be useful to bring out some of the essential features of that history over the centuries by using a comparative approach. I decided that it would both be most honest and most helpful if I made the comparison explicit, rather than implicit. The comparison I would make would be between English characteristics as revealed in the records and a model of the central characteristics of 'peasant' society, along the lines of the analysis in chapter 1 above. I pointed out that it

> is clear that attempting to compress the major characteristics of a society into part of a chapter, when whole books have been devoted to the subject, will not only mean leaving out a great deal, particularly concerning the religious and ideological level, but will lead to the creation of a very simplified 'ideal-type' model in Weber's sense. It is likely that no particular society will fit exactly, at any time, all the features to be enumerated.[6]

[6] Macfarlane, *Individualism*, 16.

At the end of the detailed analysis of the features of peasant society, I repeated this statement. 'It should again be stressed that the description above is a model, a simplified abstraction from reality. As a result it would be absurd to expect any particular society to fit all the features exactly; nor would we expect any specific feature to be entirely "pure". There are always some who marry late, there is almost always some marketing, some cash, some wage labour, some geographical mobility'. Nevertheless, I still believed that 'it is useful to have a strong model of the basic socio-economic nature of peasantry with which to confront a particular historical reality.'[7] When model and historical data are compared, we need not abandon the whole model if some of the features are absent. But if almost all of the characteristics are missing, then it becomes difficult to go on labelling the historical society as 'peasant'.

The necessity for historians to create explicit ideal-types of this kind is well known, but it is worth repeating Weber's advice on this. 'Hundreds of words in the historian's vocabulary are ambiguous constructs created to meet the unconsciously felt need for adequate expression and the meaning of which is only concretely felt but not clearly thought out.' Such words would include Christianity, capitalism, peasantry, individualism, patriarchalism and so on. If we do not provide explicit definitions of these terms, we will be imprisoned by our unanalysed implicit assumptions. 'If the historian . . . rejects an attempt to construct such ideal types as a "theoretical construction", i.e., as useless or dispensable for his concrete heuristic purposes, the inevitable consequence is either that he consciously or unconsciously uses other similar concepts, without formulating them verbally and elaborating them logically or that he remains stuck in the realm of the vaguely "felt" '.[8] It was partly for this reason that I attempted to define 'peasantry' so carefully.

The nature of an 'ideal-type' in Weber's sense and in mine can also be formally stated.

An ideal type is formed by the one-sided *accentuation* of one or more points of view and by the synthesis of a great many diffuse, discrete, more or less present and occasionally absent *concrete individual* phenomena, which are arranged according to those one-sidedly emphasized viewpoints into a

[7] Ibid., 32.   [8] Weber, *Methodology*, 92–3, 94.

unified *analytical* construct (*Gedankenbild*). In its conceptual purity, this mental construct (*Gedankenbild*) cannot be found empirically anywhere in reality. It is a *utopia*. Historical research faces the task of determining in each individual case, the extent to which this ideal-typical construct approximates to or diverges from reality, to what extent for example, the economic structure of a certain city is to be classified as a 'city-economy'.[9]

Such was the ideal-type that I was trying to construct as an heuristic device in relation to understanding England.

In specifying how one should construct such ideal-types Weber pointed to various difficulties. The principal one was in the confusions that occur when using real materials to give substance and clothing to models. Since this is an area where I have come under particular attack and may indeed have failed to escape entirely from the difficulty it is worth elaborating more fully what Weber meant. A comparison of the ideal-type and the 'facts' is a procedure which 'gives rise to no methodological doubts so long as we clearly keep in mind that ideal-typical developmental *constructs* and *history* are to be sharply distinguished from each other. But this is not easy.

The maintenance of this distinction in all its rigour often becomes uncommonly difficult in practice due to a certain circumstance. In the interest of the concrete demonstration of an ideal type or an ideal-typical developmental sequence, one seeks to *make it clear* by the use of concrete illustrative material drawn from empirical-historical reality. The danger of this procedure which in itself is entirely legitimate lies in the fact that historical knowledge here appears as a *servant* of theory instead of the opposing role. It is a great temptation for the theorist to regard this relationship either as the normal one or, far worse, to mix theory with history and indeed to confuse them with each other.[10]

The example Weber cites of such a confusion is in Marxism, where ideal-types of Marxian theory are sometimes used to manipulate evidence.

With such an ideal-type in mind I constructed a model of peasantry. I first pointed out that 'peasant' has two meanings, one common sense and another precise and technical, as described in chapter 1 above. Often historians use the word in the common-sense way, and we

[9] Ibid., 90.   [10] Ibid., 102–3.

cannot object to this. What I was interested in was to alert readers to the fact that certain analysts were either consciously, or unconsciously, assuming that the English had once been peasants in the stronger, more technical sense.

I then surveyed a good deal of the general literature on peasantry. The classic analyses and surveys of authorities like Redfield, Wolf, Thorner, Nash, Sahlins, Shanin, Galeski and others were used to bring out some of the essential features of peasantry. I explained that the model I was creating was based on these general accounts and on reading I had undertaken on peasantries in the Mediterranean (eight studies were cited), Asia (12 books were cited) and northern Europe (three studies were cited). At this point I could have stopped in the creation of my model. Indeed, in my first formulations of the argument, for instance in chapter 1 above, I did stop here, and the analysis was not slanted towards any specific peasantry. The general argument would not have been altered by doing so and, in view of the inordinate amount of criticism that has been levelled at my next step, it might have been wise to do so.

As it was, it seemed to me that I should clothe the model in some specific detail, rather than leaving it very bare and abstract. In order to bring out some of the consequences of being a 'peasant' society, I felt it would be helpful to see how such societies worked in one particular area of the world, rather than leaving a broad general description of the lowest common denominator of peasantry throughout the world. This was not done in order to characterize peasantry. That had already been done. It was to give readers, most of whom would not have a strong feeling of what a 'real' peasant society was like, a solid alternative picture to place alongside the English evidence. To create such alternative possible worlds by the use of comparative models seems a useful procedure on occasions; without it one is trapped into believing that what did happen is all the could have happened.

I decided to take eastern Europe as the illustrative area for comparative purposes. I gave four reasons for this. First, the earliest classic studies of peasant society and economy had been undertaken there from the 1920s onwards. Secondly, some of the very best studies had been undertaken in this region, models of their kind. Thirdly, I felt that in order to provide a sufficiently strong sense of 'otherness' it would be helpful to move outside western Europe. I did not want to go too far away as it would be easy to ridicule attempts to compare

England with India or China, for instance. Finally, it seemed useful to look at this area because it began to emerge that implicit analogies with east European peasantries had already strongly influenced many of those who had written on medieval England; namely Kosminsky, Vinogradoff, Homans, Postan, Titow and others. By making the comparisons more explicit, it would be possible to see how far such analogies were helpful.

I then tried to draw out the central features of east European peasantry based on the works of Galeski, of Thomas and Znaniecki, on Poland, of Shanin on Russia, and others such as Czap and Hammel. During this discussion, I also made constant comparisons with peasantries in other parts of the world – India, China, Mexico, Turkey and so on – in the work of Nash, Redfield, Wolf, Hajnal, Marriott, Stirling and others. From this it seemed to me that although eastern Europe, as described by the authorities I relied on, was an extreme case, there were many features which could be found in other agrarian civilizations which comparative analysts termed 'peasant'. At the end of the discussion I briefly compared this to western Europe and pointed out that the peasantries of western Europe were probably very different from what I called this 'classical' peasantry. In terms of the 'presence of cash and markets, land sales, rural specialization, age at marriage and all the other features, ethnographic accounts suggest that west European peasantries had moved a long way from the "classical" peasantry described above'.[11] I showed that this was true also in relation to the concept of ownership and its overlap with the family.

I then proceeded to look to see to what extent sociologists, anthropologists and historians had believed that England had once been 'peasant' in the technical and 'classical' sense. In a chapter on this subject, I showed that there was a widely held view that England had moved from a situation approaching a classical peasantry, to an individualistic and capitalist society, through a great transformation or revolution which occurred in the sixteenth to eighteenth centuries. Often the authorities were using the word 'peasant' in the common-sense way, as in the title of a book by Dr Thirsk, *English Peasant Farming*. But often they really believed that there had been a different socio-economic formation before the sixteenth century

[11] Macfarlane, *Individualism*, 33.

along the lines suggested by Marx and Weber. The major rupture was supposed to have occurred in the sixteenth or seventeenth centuries.

Roughly up to the sixteenth century there were 'peasants' throughout Europe. After that they disappeared in England, while elsewhere in Europe they lingered on in a muted form, disappearing in France, for instance, only in the second half of the nineteenth and early twentieth centuries.[12] The rest of the book set out to test this general theory, using the model I had created as a benchmark, a set of indices, against which to judge the historical evidence starting in the seventeenth century and gradually working back to the thirteenth.

It may sound strange, but when I began research on this, having set up a preliminary model and being curious as to when the peasants had 'disappeared', I genuinely believed that I would find real peasants up to about the fifteenth century. I believed this on the basis of reading accounts of the great transformation by certain medieval and early modern historians. But when I looked at their accounts more closely, and incorporated my own work on documents with the results of recent research, particularly by Dr Richard Smith, it began to dawn on me that this was a huge myth. The explosion in my mind, surprise and amazement that the data did not fit the predictions of a model which I had unconsciously accepted over the years, is what is captured in the book. The method may be rather a curious one, but in my own case, and for a number of others, it has forced a rethinking of stereotypes. Since the method led to the conclusion that one of the central orthodoxies of modern historical and sociological thought was wrong, and hence directly challenged the work of Marx, Weber and many recent historians, it not unnaturally attracted considerable critical attention. We may briefly look at some of the objections that have been brought.

One set of criticisms focused on the procedure; that is, on the choice of models, what was included in them, how they were constructed. A first argument was that the model of peasantry was based on too few instances. Dr Harris alleged that it was 'constructed from three works on peasants in Poland and Russia', and Faith, Hilton, Dyer, Hyams and Herlihy also stated that the model was basically Slavonic, or east European. As I hope to have shown in the summary above, this is a distortion. The model was based on several civilizations and on many

---

[12] Weber, *Peasants*.

of the leading accounts of the basic nature of peasantry throughout the world. It is only a part of the model that is based on the concrete east European case. I do not believe that the model can be dismissed in this easy way. In fact, none of the reviewers, with the exception of Hirst and Tribe, challenged the wider work of Wolf, Sahlins, Dalton, Redfield, Nash, Thorner and the rest, which is just as important to my argument as the books on eastern Europe.

Having asserted that my model was based on only three cases, Harris goes on to ask whether any meaningful model can be made from so few cases, and whether 'abstracting an ideal type from a particular context (in this case eastern Europe) and using it to create a general category of thought (i.e. the peasantry)' is a valid method. It is probably not valid, but it is equally not what I did, as chapter 1 above shows. Rather curiously, the same author then suggests that my comparison is undermined because while my material on classical peasantry is 'constructed from three works of the most general and synthetic sort', my English material is based on specific studies of particular villages, manors and so on, and hence I am not comparing like with like. In answer to this, we might note that this does not seem to be a correct characterization of the work by Thomas and Znaniecki. More importantly, however, my model, as I make clear, is also based on several dozen field monographs, anthropological studies of particular villages and communities.

Harris's next criticism is one which is also made by Faith, Herlihy and Rowland. It is basically that rather than using eastern Europe as my central concrete comparison, I should have used a model based on western Europe, perhaps located in France, Italy or elsewhere. This is a reasonable point. I have given my reasons for not doing so, but these critics, and Dr Baker, may have a point that by taking a very pure concrete case, I have pushed the argument to its extremes. It would have been safer to have chosen somewhere nearer to England, and this would indeed have brought out some of the subtler similarities and differences within western Europe. But I am not sure that as a first effort it would have revealed as much. Like Jack Goody and John Hajnal[13] I find it refreshing to look from outside western Europe in order to see some of the peculiarities. The work of making the finer discriminations within Europe I saw as a second

---

[13] Goody, *Family;* Hajnal, 'European Marriage'.

stage. It was begun in the last two chapters of the book, where I compared England to other parts of Europe, using some of the insights gained from this wider perspective. Yet there is no doubt that Robert Rowland has a strong argument when he points out that I need to show why England, France and Italy all 'differed in *different ways* from the ideal type'.

Philip Corrigan seemed to find my use of models confusing in two ways. First, he finds that taking definitions of peasantry 'developed since 1945 to describe peasants defined within a capitalist world market' and applying such definitions to thirteenth to seventeenth-century England, not finding such peasants there, and then arguing that there was no peasantry at all, an odd procedure. I would agree that there are dangers in using modern categories and foisting them on the past. In some ways this was my very point. What I was arguing was that this was exactly what some historians were implicitly doing. They were taking unexamined assumptions of what 'peasants' are like from their experience of modern societies, and then making medieval man look like them. Perhaps it would clear up this misunderstanding if I stated that basically I am not interested in whether medieval or modern English people were or were not 'peasants'. My interest was in whether the numerous features that nowadays we associate with peasantry – that is, the absence of individual rights in property, constraints on the extensive penetration of money and markets down to the village level, low geographical mobility, a symbolic attachment to the land, a certain type of household formation, and other features – were present in England in past centuries or not. I do not really see that the capitalist world market of 1945 is really relevant to these ultimately empirical questions.

A second criticism by the same reviewer is that in some places, apparently, I see that I am checking one 'representation' (or model) against another, in other places I suggest that I am 'comparing two comparable realities'. No specific instances are cited, and without these I find it difficult to answer this criticism. In principle and generally, both seem to be valid procedures. At times I would like to compare observers' models of classical peasantries against historians' models of medieval England. At other times, I would like to compare what I consider to be the 'reality' of peasant societies in the present against the 'models' of certain historians. At other times it is present 'reality' against past 'reality', or past 'reality' against past 'model'. As long as I am clear in the book as to which of these things I am doing, it seems to me legitimate to do them all, always acknowledging that the relationship between 'reality' and 'representation' is a much more complex one than is implied in the brief preceding remarks. It may be that I was not always sufficiently clear about what I was doing, however, since one perceptive critic, Robert Rowland, suggests that I 'appear to confuse the ideal type with a simplified empirical model of a [any] peasant society'.

Dr Anton Blok, an anthropologist, has some other methodological criticisms. He sees my model as 'at once ideal-type, stereotype, and description of "real" peasantries'. He does not object to this in itself, but finds that the model I have created is too simple. He does not like the way it lumps together the peasants of Russia, India and the Mediterranean, ironing out very important differences in the process. In general, this is a fair criticism. As I acknowledge, the model is very simple and reality is very complicated. I had to rely on generalizations made by the leading experts, against whom, presumably, the same criticisms would be levelled when they wrote books or articles on 'peasants' at a global level.

Dr Blok then goes on to pursue a particular argument which I find less helpful. He states that I prefer 'to sacrifice cultural diversity on the altar of sterile nominalism', and that I apparently feel 'uneasy about concepts which do not have sharp boundaries'. These are harsh words, and I can only leave readers to judge whether they are true. I would say, however, that to believe that for heuristic and analytic purposes it is better to have a clear, unambiguous and simple, if oversimplified model, than to have a more realistic, but probably highly qualified and complex model, does not necessarily mean that I feel 'uneasy' in general about concepts without sharp boundaries. I just happen, on this occasion, to have found them less useful.

My 'misunderstanding', Blok writes, is 'closely connected with the belief that the only aim of the comparative method is to look for similarities'. Unless I have misunderstood Blok's meaning, this is rubbish. While it may be true that I ironed out certain differences as between peasantries elsewhere, the two central themes of my book are precisely concentrated on differences and not similarities. My use of the comparative method was precisely to show the differences between medieval England and classical peasantries, and to show the differences between England and much of the continent. Indeed, it has been for stressing these differences that I have been roundly condemned. It is not helpful to be admonished, particularly with an allusion to Marc Bloch, for only being interested in similarities. Bloch, Blok and I are in agreement that the purpose of the comparative method, of which this book was meant to be a prime example, is to look for both similarities and differences.

Another criticism is that the model is incomplete in certain ways. Dr Faith argues that I have created a model of 'a peasantry' rather than of a 'total society in which the peasantry is a subordinate class'. The evidence for this charge is that 'the landlord hardly makes an appearance in this book'. In England, in Poland, Russia and so on, peasants were not autonomous but were 'subordinate to a ruling class'. Apart from the anachronistic and loaded use of the phrase 'ruling class', Dr Faith has a point here. Although my model did in fact incorporate quite strongly the relations between lord and peasant, this was an area to which, as I acknowledged earlier, I should have given more attention when dealing with medieval England. It does not undermine either model or treatment, but it is one of the threads which would have strengthened the argument still further.

Dr Faith's second criticism is that the model 'does not contribute very much to our understanding of peasant production as an economic system'. This is not surprising, she says, because it is 'primarily the creation of anthropologists and sociologists, whose interests lay elsewhere'. Dr Faith is not convinced that I am very familiar with what peasants actually do. By this she appears to mean ox-team cultivation, open-field agriculture, and other features of agricultural techniques and organization. Now it is true that I do not devote much of the book to these matters, but it is a slur on people like Wolf, Thorner, Sahlins, Nash and others to say that they ignored such matters because their 'interests lay elsewhere'. It is also the case that having lived for 15 months in what might be described as a "peasant" village and written a book which analyses the production methods of this society in extreme detail, I do have some familiarity with these subjects.[14] It is a field which I ought, of course, to know more about, but I have read many of the classic accounts of agricultural production methods. I did not deal with these topics in more detail in the brief constraints of the book because they did not seem central to my particular argument. I do not happen to

[14] Macfarlane, *Resources*.

believe that open-field agriculture, ploughs, the physical aspects of production, throw much light on whether people are, or are not, peasants. Some may disagree, and argue for some kind of technological determinism where the means of production inevitably lead to certain relations of production. It would be interesting to hear the arguments. My knowledge of agricultural societies throughout the world does not support such a crude association and I do not feel that this is a large gap in the model.

Further evidence that I am not very familiar with what peasants do, according to Dr Faith, is the fact that 'in a rather odd footnote' I write that I decided 'not to include any discussion of peasant production or of Chayanov's contribution to our knowledge of it (p. 15, note 31)'. This seems damning. I seem to have admitted that I will include no discussion of peasant production. In fact, if one turns to the note, there is no mention in it of peasant production at all. What I do say is that a number of Russian scholars have contributed very significantly to the 'general discussion of the domestic economy of the peasantry', a different subject, and I have decided not to go into their work in detail.

The footnote arose from discussions with Professor Shanin, an expert in this field. I had written a certain amount about Chayanov and others in an earlier draft, but he pointed out that this was a very large and complicated field of debate which I should either enter more fully, or not at all. I therefore decided to use Chayanov's important work indirectly, through his well-known and extensive influence on almost all of my main authorities on peasants and the domestic mode of production, including Shanin himself, Sahlins and Wolf. I thought that by writing that 'I have decided to omit any direct reference to their work', joined to the fact that I presumed that most people knew that I was drawing heavily on Chayanov's insights through the wider literature, this would be sufficient. But this footnote had given several reviewers, as well as Faith, the chance to strike a wider blow.

Paul Hirst has raised some interesting theoretical points, claiming that ultimately I cannot avoid the populist versus Marxist arguments in this way. At the widest level he is probably right and I will return to his arguments. But in the context of the book, I still feel that to have spent an extra ten pages or so at the start of the work going over these very specialist debates would have alienated many readers. Professor Herlihy is less helpful. He claims that 'Macfarlane dismisses the work of the foremost theorist of a peasant economy, the Russian scholar

A. V. Chaianov, for fear of "complicating the argument" '. As a stark accusation, this sounds bad. I certainly do not 'dismiss' Chayanov's work; my book is very heavily indebted to it and I respect it greatly. It is merely that it seemed possible to obtain his major insights without getting bogged down in a detailed treatment of those Russian writers of whom he is only one.

Two final criticisms of the general methodology are particularly interesting. Barbara Donagan suggests that the 'careful sociological–anthropological definition of peasantry' is 'in a sense a red herring'. She admits that 'it allows demonstration of the weakness of medievalists' arguments by analogy to other peasant societies when their English evidence fails' and, since this was part of my purpose, has some justification. It is a red herring because my belief in a classical peasantry has a 'theological element', suggesting that I am a 'believer' in something that is merely a matter of faith. Since matters of faith are disputable and unprovable, presumably Dr Donagan feels they should be kept out of the argument.

After the sometimes rancorous responses to this use of the peasant model, I would like to feel that the argument could indeed have been made without any reference to a comparative model of peasantry. Unfortunately, I am not sure how, in practice, I could have done so. If I had listed a set of criteria which I asserted were interlinked, and then merely shown how they were not present in medieval or early modern England, it is likely that many would have replied that they did not exist anywhere, rightly asking me to make explicit and document my comparative model. Furthermore, I am certain that without making it explicit to myself, I would not have been in a position to question much of the growing orthodoxy of the supposed capitalist revolution. I suppose I could have used an explicit model for my own purposes, and then disguised it. This might have been a safer procedure, but I believe it would have been a less honest one. Honesty, an attempt to share one's procedures of thought, may not charm all the critics, but I still believe that historians and others should make their comparative models explicit.

These appear to be the main methodological criticisms of the nature of my comparative model building. Some, we have seen, are possibly right, others absolutely right, others are exaggerations, misrepresentations or based on misunderstanding. In sum, they do not convince me that my procedure was basically flawed in either conception or execution, though of course it could have been done better. I leave others to judge whether I have answered the criticisms.

There is no doubt that I could have improved the contents of the model. Here I come to a second class of criticism, that basically the ingredients of the comparative model are wrong. There are two main criticisms. The first is that peasants are much more diverse, less 'pure' and uniform than my model allows. I had already tried to anticipate this, as my quotations above show. If one considers a model as a kind of ruler or benchmark, then on all the different indices specific societies will be at different positions. I particularly stressed that this was the case in western Europe. Thus it is useful to be reminded by Dr Blok that peasants in southern Italy are not always 'familistic', that they are often market-orientated, selling and buying land, and sometimes geographically mobile, even in non-European peasantries. This is, of course, true. But I do not see that it invalidates the discussion; it merely adds nuances to that very difficult problem of creating a lifelike model.

The severest criticism, however, was reserved for my treatment of east European peasantries. We have seen that certain reviewers convinced themselves that my whole model of peasantry was based on eastern Europe, and that my whole account of eastern Europe was based on three synthetic accounts. The next stage was to show that these three accounts were inaccurate. I was pushed out onto the gangplank, step by step and then given the final push to the sharks. I have refused to accept the first two steps in the argument; the book, as chapter 1 above shows, could easily have been written without mention of eastern Europe. But supposing I was now at the end of the plank and the question was put, 'Has he based his whole model on faulty reporting?', what would be the answer?

The first thing to say is that there has been little direct challenge to the authority of Galeski on Poland, of Thomas and Znaniecki's massive work, or of Shanin on Russia. The approach is usually more indirect. Dr Faith argues that there is doubt as to whether the model is accurate; Kula's work on Polish feudalism 'would certainly cast doubt on this rigid conception of a "natural" economy by showing that both seigneurial and peasant economies were alike both monetized *and* "natural"', and that from very early on peasants in Poland were anxious for access to the market. Likewise, Chayanov's work would not support the view that there was no land market and a virtual absence of wage-labour. I expect Dr Faith is right. As I wrote, in practice no situation is pure; indeed peasant society is bound to have some of these elements since the very definition of peasantry makes it a 'part-society', a part in relation to a greater whole which includes a state, a market, towns and so on. If there were none of these, it would not be peasant, but something else.

The same point is made in another form by Professor Hilton. On the cited evidence of R. E. F. Smith's work, we are told that medieval Russian peasants were much more mobile, lived in nuclear families, did not have a sentimental attachment to a particular piece of land, bought and sold land and so on. Quite so. I was not trying to paint a picture of a fossilized east European 'peasantry' that had been unchanging since time began. It does not discomfort me to hear that medieval Russian peasants also do not fit the stereotypes of certain English medievalists. But I do not see that this has a great bearing on the model. Are Galeski, Shanin, Thomas, Znaniecki wrong about the time and groups they were describing? If so, this should be shown, rather than implied by innuendoes such as 'Macfarlane has been badly let down by his advisers'.

Two reviewers constructively discuss this matter. Keith Tribe alleges that Shanin's *Awkward Class* 'relies on a combination of development sociology and Slavophilism to present an image of the Russian peasantry as a cohesive and natural order'. Tribe then proceeds to make several other criticisms of Shanin's work. I am not competent to go far in this debate, but the most that is alleged is that Shanin, one of my three major authorities on eastern peasantry, has made the Russian peasantry of the early twentieth century more communal-minded, more stable and family based than they really were. If this criticism is correct, then my model needs some adjustment. Shanin's peasants may not have been as close to one end of the bench as I had thought.

Paul Hirst makes some interesting comments on this problem. He rightly points out that the theoretical literature I draw on is 'strongly influenced by the work of . . . Chayanov, notably Shanin, Thorner and Sahlins'. He then reminds us that 'this model of peasant economy is by no means uncontroversial'. He writes that I cannot avoid this controversy between the populists and Marxists. Hirst claims that my model of peasantry is so extreme that it may not fit the Russian case; in other words, Shanin is possibly wrong. What is his support for this claim? 'It is arguable that Russia (certainly after 1861)' was characterized 'by individualistic and highly monetised agricultural producers, family members having few rights in relation to the head, the communal or clan regulation of landholding playing a marginal role, moneylending, sale and rent of land, wage labour, etc. playing by contrast a prominent role'. He then proceeds with further detailed points which suggest that, if he is right, my picture of Russia is too simple.

If it turns out that the model I have created of east European peasantry is too extreme, or even that it is a model in the minds of Shanin, Galeski and the rest, and not a very accurate representation of even the period they were studying, this would not be a crippling blow to my book. As we have seen in the discussion of Weberian models, this is precisely what models are for. Indeed, it would be somewhat refreshing if it were the case that while I had thought my work would have its main implications for English history, in a boomerang way it made people question peasant stereotypes for eastern Europe. Naturally it would be more convenient if the debate were resolved in a way that showed that model and reality in eastern Europe matched in the way that I had assumed. But my main interest was in the use of a model, a thought-experiment, to expose three things: first, what goes on in the minds of historians and sociologists when they try to study the development of English history; secondly, some interesting questions we could ask of the historical evidence; thirdly, as a kind of predictive system.

When treating historical materials, and particularly when analysing periods like the thirteenth and fourteenth centuries when the documents are often scanty, it is necessary to have a hunch about what would be interesting questions; in other words, to have a thesis to test. The creation of a simplified model of peasantry gave me an interlocking set of predictions about how the society might have been. I was not trying merely to show 'at some length' that English villagers 'seem always to have differed from the inhabitants of nineteenth-century Poland and Russia, or twentieth-century Turkey or Mexico' as John Hatcher facetiously put it. If this had been so, it would clearly have been a ridiculous activity. What I was trying to show was that there is a strong, and recently heightened, tendency to lump the histories of all societies together. It is easy to slip into thinking that all societies progress through a uniform 'peasant' stage into the 'modern' world. It is tempting then to conclude that the only difference in the case of England was that it did so earlier than anywhere else (with the possible exceptions of Holland and Denmark). My use of an abstract model was to help myself, and hopefully others, in their escape from such a narrowing approach.

We may ask what is left of the arguments put forward in *Individualism.* Have they survived, or have they been destroyed? Here I have to leave the decision to others. Certainly it was recognized that I was sailing for large prizes. As Lawrence Stone wrote, 'it is not often that a book appears which challenges the whole corpus of conventional wisdom about the evolution of the modern world'. If I should happen to be right in my facts and deductions from them, then he agrees that I would be saying 'something very important'. Indeed, it is so important that if I am roughly correct, then I could well be, Stone suggests 'the Einstein of history'.

Certainly others have sailed along the same route and have found a land which was until very recently denied to exist. One flotilla is described in chapter 6 above, where it will be noticed that most of the books published up to 1978 argued strongly in one direction, while those published in the wake of *Individualism* took an entirely different view. A great deal of subsequent historical research, very ably summarized by Dr Clark, has now been published which basically supports the thesis of continuity.[15] But whether the account I have given of the battles that have been fought, or the further evidence presented in this volume, will convince others that I have succeeded in destroying, in Stone's words 'the grand theories about England propounded by all those foreigners, Marx, Weber, Durkheim, Tocqueville, Rostow, and the rest', is up to the reader. Stone argues that 'this . . . is an unlikely consequence of an implausible hypothesis based on a far-fetched connection with one still unproven fact of limited general significance', and one could not be more damning than that. Others are more encouraging.

Personally I would accept that the argument is faulty in several respects and I would no doubt modify it a little if writing the book now. In particular, I would make more explicit some of the remarks which, in a naive way, I had thought would be treated charitably and sensibly, rather than being ripped out of context and held up to ridicule in order to discredit the book. Furthermore, in the light of the almost universal

---

[15] Clark, *Society* and *Revolution*.

statement of the medievalist reviewers that they never believed in real peasants, family property and so on, I would not now present their findings in quite the same way. It appears that we agree more than I thought. Yet the ambivalence of the reactions, often fiercely trying, by some fairly piratical means, to sink the book, while loudly proclaiming that they were really friends and why had I ever thought otherwise, does suggest that there was something in what I wrote.

Appendix

A Note on the Nature of Capitalism

THE WORD 'capitalism' is used frequently throughout this book and I should specify what I take it to mean. It is simplest to do so in relation to the classic formulation of the set of interrelated features by Marx and Weber. Capitalism is one among many types of social formation. In Marxian analysis a social formation consists of an infrastructure or 'mode of production', and a superstructure. Marx, as is well known, was particularly concerned with the 'mode of production' of capitalism; that is, with the historically specific infrastructure which he believed had arisen in western Europe sometime between the fifteenth and eighteenth centuries. What were its central characteristics?

Of crucial importance were the relations of production, how people are related in the productive process. In capitalism, there is a full development of individual, private property. No longer is property communal, owned by the state, community or family, or even by the lords, as in earlier social formations, but it is fully owned by the individual. This applies not only to real estate but to the ultimate 'property' of an individual, his labour power. In capitalism, all becomes alienable, everything is a commodity to be traded on the market, people can buy and sell objects, and their own and each other's labour. All is apparently set 'free' and given a monetary value. Thus the emergence of individual private property and of widespread wage-labour are central characteristics of capitalism. These features allow the emergence of classes; the owners and the owned; the landlords, farmers and labourers; the capitalists and the workers.

Alongside this change in the relations of production, there is a change in the means of production. The tools and the physical environment change. Mankind begins to live more and more in an artificial and man-made world. Machinery replaces human labour. Although the connection between relations and means of production is not automatic and unidirectional, there is likely to be some link, as is shown in the famous remark that the water mill is the basis of feudalism and the steam engine the basis of capitalism. As the tools of man change, so do his relations to other men. This includes changes in the organization of production. There is a massive shift from a world where there is little specialization and division of labour, to one with increasing differentiation. The only specialization before capitalism is between the major orders in society: the priests, educators, warriors and rulers on the one hand, and the mass of agricultural workers on the other. There are pockets of craft skills, but the towns and markets are small and peripheral and artisans are few. In capitalism all this changes and the rise of factory production entails ever-increasing division into minute tasks.

There are associated changes noted by Marx which tie in with these central features. There is a change from a largely non-monetized to an almost completely money-dominated system of exchange, from barter to a money standard. Agricultural and other goods which had hitherto been primarily produced to be immediately consumed or, sometimes, bartered, are now mainly produced for sale. There is a growth in geographical and social mobility. People are no longer tied to a lord or to the land. The mobility of labour needed for the capitalistic mode of production emerges in the shape of a largely propertyless proletariat.

Marx concentrated on these infrastructural features and paid less attention to the juridico-political and ideological dimensions of capitalism, except in some throwaway comments. For instance he states that when aristocracy is dominant the concepts of honour and loyalty will be stressed, but 'during the dominance of the bourgeoisie, the concepts of freedom, equality etc' will be dominant.[1] In order to broaden the definition to include superstructure we can turn to Max Weber.

Several of Weber's characterizations of capitalism naturally overlap with those of Marx. The presence of a 'free' labour force, freed from the constraints of those fetters such as serfdom, slavery or kinship, is

[1] Marx and Engels, *German Ideology*, 65.

of great importance for Weber. Likewise, there is increasing division of labour, though here Weber elaborates a new distinction: 'the separation of business from the household, which completely dominates modern economic life' is of central importance. This is not necessarily a physical separation as between place of work and household, it is 'our legal separation of corporate from personal property'.[2] It is the realization that a person may act in one way as a businessman, and another as a family member, it includes the devices of limited liability, of companies, of corporations. This separation of the economic unit of production from the social unit of reproduction lies behind the destruction of the hitherto widespread 'domestic mode of production' which blended the two. The distinction is behind the growing separation of public and private domains in politics, economics and elsewhere. It is also related to the new development of 'rational accounting'.

When contrasting feudal and capitalist systems, Weber argued that the large demesne farming of medieval Europe was not 'capitalist'. It would only have been so 'if it were oriented to capital accounting, particularly to an estimate, beforehand, in money of the chances of profit from a transaction'.[3] Weber expands this view very clearly elsewhere.

We will define a capitalistic economic action as one which rests on the expectation of profit by the utilization of opportunites for exchange, that is on (formally) peaceful chances of profit ... The important fact is always that a calculation of capital in terms of money is made, whether by modern book-keeping methods or in any other way, however primitive and crude. Everything is done in terms of balances: at the beginning of the enterprise and initial balance, before every individual decision a calculation to ascertain its probable profitableness, and at the end a final balance to ascertain how much profit has been made.[4]

Thus the central feature is not in the actual method of accounting, double-entry book-keeping or whatever, but in the mental attitudes, the desire to work out the likelihood of profit on a transaction.

Thus Weber is already talking about attitudes and ideology and it is in his insights into the ethos of capitalism that he made his most

[2] Weber, *Protestant Ethic*, 21–2. [3] Weber, *Theory*, 267.
[4] Weber, *Protestants Ethic*, 17–18.

important contributions. Ultimately the uniqueness of capitalism lies
in its attitudes towards such things as money, time, effort, accumulation and so on. Weber believed that what happened under
capitalism was that accumulation, saving, and profit-seeking had
become ethically and emotionally attractive, whereas before they had
been unacceptable. The ethic of endless accumulation, as an end and
not as a means, is the central peculiarity of capitalism.

> Man is dominated by the making of money, by acquisition as the ultimate
> purpose of his life. Economic acquisition is no longer subordinated to man
> as the means for the satisfacton of his material needs. This reversal of what
> we should call the natural relationship . . . is evidently as definitely a leading
> principle of capitalism as it is foreign to all peoples not under capitalistic
> influence.[5]

This ethic or spirit could flourish in the backwoods or be absent in
great markets in ancient civilizations. For what Weber saw was that it
is not money in itself, it is not markets by themselves, it is not even
particular accounting systems that are significant, it is the use and
purposes to which these are put. It is not money which is the root of
capitalism, but the love of money.

Weber is an elusive and often contradictory thinker, yet occasionally he drew up checklists of what he thought were the necessary,
if not sufficient, preconditions of capitalism. One such list is in his
General Economic History. He enumerates six such features. The first,
'rational capital accounting', the second, 'freedom of the market' (in
other words, the absence of class or other constraints on trading), and
the fifth, 'free labour', we have already encountered. The other three
need to be added to the definition of capitalism. His third
precondition is a 'rational technology', 'that is, one reduced to
calculation to the largest possible degree, which implies mechani-
zation'. Here he overlaps with the point we have already encountered
with Marx, that capitalism is likely to be linked to a certain set of
tools, and particularly with machines which give man control over his
environment. Weber's last two additions take one again into the
borderland between superstructure and infrastructure, that artificial
distinction out of which Weber breaks. His fourth point is the

[5] Ibid., 53.

necessity for 'calculable law'. As he puts it, the 'capitalistic form of industrial organization, if it is to operate rationally, must be able to depend upon calculable adjudication and administration'. This was not present in the Greek city-state, the patrimonial state of Asia, nor, Weber believes 'in western countries down to the Stuarts'. But without political and legal certainty, rational decisions cannot be taken. The final feature is also related to law, but in another way. It is the 'commercialization of economic life', by which he means 'the general use of commercial instruments to represent share rights in enterprise, and also in property ownership'.[6]

Of course one could add further features of capitalism, the psychological alienation which Marx drew attention to, the individualistic family system documented by Engels, the new attitude towards nature in Weber's famous 'disenchantment of the world'. But we have enough already to gain a good picture of many of the deeper characteristics of that historically specific phenomenon whose origins and development is one of the themes of this book.

[6] Weber, *General*, 208–9.

Bibliography

Note: all books are published in Britain, unless otherwise specified.

Adler, *Auto da Fé*. Adler, Elkan N., *Auto da Fé and Jew*, 1908.
Ady, *Candle*. Ady, Thomas, *A Candle in the Dark*, 1656.
Anderson, *Approaches*. Anderson, Michael, *Approaches to the History of the Western Family, 1500–1914*, 1980.
Anderson, *Lineages*. Anderson, Perry, *Lineages of the Absolutist State*, 1974.
Anglicus. *Properties*. Anglicus, Bartholomaeus, *On the Properties of Things*, 2 vols, translated by John Trevisa, 1975.
Appleby, *Famine*. Appleby, Andrew B., *Famine in Tudor and Stuart England*, 1978.
Arensberg, *Irish Countryman*. Arensberg, Conrad, *The Irish Countryman: an Anthropological Study*, reprinted 1959.
Ariès, *Centuries*. Ariès, Philippe, *Centuries of Childhood*, 1962.
Atkinson, 'Trial at York'. Atkinson, C. M. 'Trial at York for Counterfeiting', *Thoresby Society*, IX, 1899.
Bacon, *Essayes*. Bacon, Francis, *The Essayes or Counsels Civill and Morall of Francis Bacon, Lord Verulam*, Everyman Library, 1910.
Baechler, *Origins*. Baechler, Jean, *The Origins of Capitalism*, translated by Barry Cooper, 1975.
Bagot, 'Manorial Customs'. Bagot, A., 'Mr Gilpin and Manorial Customs', *Transactions of the Cumberland and Westmorland Antiquarian and Archaeological Society*, new series, 1961.
Baker, *Introduction*. Baker, J. H., *An Introduction to English Legal History*, 1971.
Baroja, *World*. Baroja, Julio Caro, *World of the Witches*, 1964.
Beattie, *Crime*. Beattie, J. M., *Crime and the Courts in England, 1660–1800*, 1986.

Becon, *Works*. Becon Thomas, *Works of Thomas Becon*, edited for the Parker Society by Rev. John Ayre, 1845.

Bellamy, *Crime*. Bellamy, John, *Crime and Public Order in England in the Late Middle Ages*, 1973.

Bendix, *Max Weber*. Bendix, Reinhard, *Max Weber: an Intellectual Portrait*, University Paperback ed., 1955.

Bennassar, *L'Inquisition*. Bennassar, B., *L'Inquisition Espagnole XVe-XIXe Siècle*, Paris, 1979.

Blackstone, *Commentaries*. Blackstone, Sir W., *Commentaries on the Laws of England*, 18th ed., 1829.

Blanchard, 'Review'. Blanchard, I., 'Review of R. H. Hilton, *The English Peasantry in the Later Middle Ages'*, *Social History*, 1977.

Bloch, *Feudal Society*. Bloch, Marc, *Feudal Society*, 2 vols, translated by L. A. Manyon, 2nd ed., 1962.

Bloch, *Historian's Craft*. Bloch, Marc, *The Historian's Craft*, 1954.

Blok, *Mafia*. Blok, Anton, *The Mafia of a Sicilian Village*, 1974.

Boas, *Primitive Man*. Boas, Franz, *The Mind of Primitive Man*, New York, rev. ed., 1938.

Bois, 'Against'. Bois, Guy, 'Against the Neo-Malthusian Orthodoxy', *Past and Present*, 79, 1978.

Boserup, *Agricultural Growth*. Boserup, Ester. *Conditions of Agricultural Growth*, 1965.

Boserup, *Woman's Role*. Boserup, Ester, *Woman's Role in Economic Development*, 1970.

Bouch and Jones, *Lake Counties*. Bouch, C. M. L. and Jones, G. P. *The Lake Counties, 1500–1830: a Social and Economic History*, 1961.

Bourdieu, *Outline*. Bourdieu, Pierre, *Outline of a Theory of Practice*, 1977.

Brain, *Friends*. Brain, Robert, *Friends and Lovers*, 1977.

Braudel, *Capitalism*. Braudel, Fernand, *Capitalism and Material Life*, 1973.

Braudel, *Mediterranean*. Braudel, Fernand, *The Mediterranean and the Mediterranean World in the Age of Philip II*, Fontana ed. vol. I, 1976.

Brenner, 'Agrarian'. Brenner, Robert, 'Agrarian Class Structure and Economic Development in Pre-Industrial Europe', *Past and Present*, 70, 1976.

Brenner, 'Capitalist Development'. Brenner, Robert, 'The Origins of Capitalist Development: a Critique of Neo-Smithian Marxism', *New Left Review*, 104, 1977.

Brenner, 'Roots'. Brenner, Robert, 'The Agrarian Roots of European Capitalism', *Past and Present*, 97, 1982.

Briggs, *Hecate's Team*. Briggs, K. M., *Pale Hecate's Team*, 1962.

Britton, 'Peasant'. Britton, E., 'The Peasant Family in Fourteenth-Century England', *Peasant Studies*, V, 1976.

230 *Bibliography*

230 *Bibliography*
History, Pelican ed., 1973.
Campbell, *Honour*. Campbell, J. K. *Honour, Family and Patronage*, 1964.
Campbell, *English Yeoman*. Campbell, Mildred, *The English Yeoman under Elizabeth and the Early Stuarts*, Yale, 1942.
Chamberlayne, *Present State*. Chamberlayne, E., *The Present State of England*, 19th impression, 1700.
Churchill, *Poems*. Churchill, Charles, *Poems of Charles Churchill*, edited by James Laver, 1970.
Clark, *Society*. Clark, J. C. D. *English Society, 1688–1832: Ideology, Social Structure and Political Practice During the Ancien Regime*, 1985.
Clark, *Revolution*. Clark, J. C. D., *Revolution and Rebellion: State and Society in the Seventeenth and Eighteenth Centuries*, 1986.
Cockburn, *Crime*. Cockburn, J. S. (ed.) *Crime in England, 1550–1800*, 1977.
Cohn, *Inner Demons*. Cohn, Norman, *Europe's Inner Demons*, New York, 1975.
Comenius, *Orbis*. Comenius, Joannes Amos, *Orbis Sensualium Pictus*, facsimile of 3rd ed., 1672.
Cowper, *Hawkshead*. Cowper, Henry S., *Hawkshead: its History, Archaeology, Industries*, 1899.
Croot and Parker, 'Agrarian'. Croot, Patricia and Parker, David, 'Agrarian Class Structure and Economic Development', *Past and Present*, 78, 1978.
Dalton, 'Peasantries'. Dalton, G., 'Peasantries in Anthropology and History' *Current Anthropology*, 13, 1972.
Davis, 'Institutional Patterns'. Davis, Kingsley, 'Institutional Patterns Favouring High Fertility in Underdeveloped Areas', *Eugenics Quarterly*, 2, 1955.
Dawson, *Lay Judges*. Dawson, John P., *A History of Lay Judges*, Cambridge, Mass., 1960.
De Beer, *Diary*. De Beer, E. S. (ed.), *Diary of John Evelyn*, 1955.
De Mause, *Childhood*. De Mause, Lloyd (ed.), *The History of Childhood*, 1976.
De Rougemont, *Passion*. De Rougemont, Denis, *Passion and Society*, 1940.
De Tocqueville, *Democracy*. De Tocqueville, *Democracy in America*, abridged ed., edited by Richard D. Heffner, 1956.
De Tocqueville, *L'Ancien Regime*. De Tocqueville, *L'Ancien Regime*, translated by M. W. Paterson, 1957.
Defoe, *Journal*.Defoe, Daniel, *A Journal of the Plague Year*, Everyman ed., 1963.

Defoe, *Tour*. Defoe, *A Tour through the Whole Island of Great Britain*, edited by Pat Rogers, 1971.
Douglas, 'Population Control'. Douglas, M., 'Population Control in Primitive Groups', *British Journal of Sociology*, 17 : 3, 1966.
Dronke, *Love Lyric*. Dronke, Peter, *Medieval Latin and the Rise of the European Love Lyric*, 2 vols, 1965–6.
Duby, *Early Growth*. Duby, Georges, *The Early Growth of the European Economy*, 1974.
Duby, *Knight*. Duby, Georges, *The Knight, the Lady and the Priest*, 1984.
Engels, *Origin*. Engels, Frederick, *The Origin of the Family, Private Property and the State*, Chicago, 1902.
Fisher, *Essays*. Fisher, F. J. (ed.), *Essays in the Economic and Social History of Tudor and Stuart England*, 1961.
Flandrin, *Families*. Flandrin, J. L., *Families in Former Times*, 1979.
Fleming, *Description*. Fleming, Sir Daniel, 'Description of the County of Westmorland' edited by Sir G. F. Duckett (Cumberland and Westmorland Antiquarian and Archaeological Society) Publ. Tract Series, no. 1, 1882.
Fletcher, *Civil War*. Fletcher, A. *The Outbreak of the English Civil War*, 1981.
Fortescue, *Learned Commendation*. Fortescue, John, *A Learned Commendation of the Politique Laws of England*, facsimile reprint of 1567 ed., 1969.
Foster, 'Peasant Society'. Foster, G., 'Peasant Society and the Image of Limited Good', *American Anthropology*, 67, 1965.
Fox, *Kinship*. Fox, Robin, *Kinship and Marriage*, 1967.
France, 'Register'. France, R. S. 'A High Constable's Register, 1681', *Transactions of the Historic Society of Lancashire and Cheshire*, CVII, 1956.
Freedman, 'Human Fertility'. Freedman, R., 'The Sociology of Human Fertility', *Current Sociology*, 10/11, 1961–2.
Freeman, *Essays*. Freeman, E. A., *Historical Essays*, fourth series, 1892.
Fussell, *English Countrywoman*,Fussell, G. E. and K. R. *The English Countrywoman*, 1981.
Gairdner, *Paston Letters*. Gairdner, James (ed.), *The Paston Letters 1422–1509*, 1901.
Galeski, *Basic Concepts*. Galeski, B., *Basic Concepts of Rural Sociology*, 1972.
Ganshof, *Feudalism*. Ganshof, F. L., *Feudalism*, 3rd English ed., translated by P. Grierson, 1964.
Gellner and Waterbury, *Patrons*. Gellner, Ernest and Waterbury, John, *Patrons and Clients*, 1977.
Gerth and Mills, *Max Weber*. Gerth, H. H. and Mills, C. Wright, *From Max Weber: Essays in Sociology*, 1948.
Ginzburg, *Cheese*. Ginzburg, Carlo, *The Cheese and the Worms* 1980.
Given, *Homicide*. Given, James B., *Society and Homicide in Thirteenth-Century England*, Stanford, 1977.

Gluckman, *Custom*, Gluckman, Max, *Custom and Conflict in Africa*, 1963.
Gluckman, *Politics*, Gluckman, Max, *Politics, Law and Ritual in Tribal Society*, 1965.
Goode, 'Love'. Goode, W. J., 'The Theoretical Importance of Love', *American Sociological Review*, 24, 1959.
Goode, *World Revolution*. Goode, W. J., *World Revolution and Family Patterns*, 1963.
Goode, *Family*. Goode, W. J., *The Family*, New York, 1964
Goody and Tambiah, *Bridewealth*. Goody, J. and Tambiah, S. J., *Bridewealth and Dowry*, 1973.
Goody, *Inheritance*. Goody, J., Thirsk, J. and Thompson, E. P. (eds), *Family and Inheritance*, 1976.
Goody, *Production*. Goody, Jack, *Production and Reproduction*, 1976.
Goody, *Domestication*. Goody, Jack, *Domestication of the Savage Mind*, 1980.
Goody, *Family*. Goody, Jack, *The Development of the Family and Marriage in Europe*, 1983.
Gough, *Myddle*. Gough, Richard, *Antiquities and Memoirs of the Parish of Myddle, Salop*, n.d.
Hajnal, 'European Marriage'. Hajnal, J., 'European Marriage Patterns in Perspective', in Glass, D. V. and Eversley, D. E. C. (eds), *Population in History*, 1965.
Hale, *Common Law*. Hale, Sir Matthew, *The History of the Common Law of England*, Chicago University Reprint, 1971.
Hall, *Powers*. Hall, John, *Powers and Liberties: the Causes and Consequences of the Rise of the West*, 1985.
Hanham, *Cely Letters*. Hanham, Alison (ed.), *The Cely Letters 1472–1488*, 1975.
Harrison, *Description*. Harrison, William, *The Description of England*, edited by Georges Edelen, New York, 1968.
Hay, *Annalists*. Hay, Denys, *Annalists and Historians: Western Historiography from the VIIIth to XVIIIth Century*, 1977.
Hay, *Albion's Tree*. Hay, Douglas, et al. *Albion's Fatal Tree: Crime and Society in Eighteenth-Century England*, 1975.
Henningsen, *Witches' Advocate*. Henningsen, Gustav, *The Witches' Advocate, Basque Witchcraft and the Spanish Inquisition, 1609–1614*, Nevada 1980.
Herlihy, *History of Feudalism*. Herlihy, David (ed.), *The History of Feudalism,: Selected Documents*, 1970.
Hey, *Myddle*. Hey, D. G., *An English Rural Community: Myddle under the Tudors and Stuarts*, 1974.
Hill, *Revolution*. Hill, Christopher, *The Century of Revolution, 1603–1714*, 1961.
Hill, *Reformation*. Hill, Christopher, *Reformation to Industrial Revolution*, 1967.

Hilton, 'Medieval Peasants'. Hilton, R., 'Medieval Peasants – Any Lessons?', *Journal of Peasant Studies*, 1, 1974.
Hilton, *English Peasantry*. Hilton, R., *The English Peasantry in the Later Middle Ages*, 1975.
Hilton, *Peasants*. Hilton, R. (ed.), *Peasants, Knights and Heretics: Studies in Medieval English Social History*, 1976.
Hirschman, *Passions*. Hirschman, Albert O., *The Passions and the Interests*, New Jersey, 1977.
Hobsbawm, *Bandits*. Hobsbawm, E. J., *Bandits*, 1972.
Hoebel, *Primitive*. Hoebel, E. Adamson, *Man in the Primitive World*, 1958.
Homans, *Villagers*. Homans, G. C., *English Villagers of the 13th Century*, New York, 1941.
Horsfall Turner, *Autobiography*. Horsfall Turner, J. (ed.), *Autobiography, Diaries, etc. of Rev. Oliver Heywood, 1630–1702*, 1822.
Horsfall Turner, *History*. Horsfall Turner, J., *The History of Brighouse, Rastrick and Hipperholme*, 1893.
Hoskins, *Midland Peasant*. Hoskins, W. G., *The Midland Peasant: the Economic and Social History of a Leicestershire Village*, 1957.
Houlbrooke, *English Family*. Houlbrooke, Ralph, *The English Family 1450–1700*, 1984.
Hufton, 'Languedoc'. Hufton, Olwen, 'Attitudes Towards Authority in Eighteenth-Century Languedoc', *Social History*, III : 3, 1978.
Hume, *History*. Hume, David, *The History of England from the Invasion of Julius Caesar to the Revolution in 1688* (1754–1761), abridged edn, Rodney W. Kilcup, 1975.
Humphreys and King, *Mortality*. Humphreys, S. C. and King, Helen (eds), *Mortality and Immortality*, 1981.
Hunt, *Love*, Hunt, Morton M., *Love*, 1960.
Ibn Khaldûn, *Muqaddimah*.Ibn Khaldûn, *An Introduction to History: the Muqaddimah*, various editions.
James, *Family*. James, Mervyn, *Family, Lineage and Civil Society*, 1974.
Kantner and McCaffrey, *Population*. Kantner, J. F. and McCaffrey, L., *Population and Development in Southwest Asia*, Lexington, Mass., 1975.
Kaplan, *Human Fertility*. Kaplan, Bernice A., *Anthropological Studies of Human Fertility*, Detroit, 1976.
Kerry, 'Leonard Wheatcroft'. Kerry, Rev. C., 'Leonard Wheatcroft of Ashover', and 'The Autobiography of Leonard Wheatcroft', *Journal of the Derbyshire Archaeological and Natural History Society*, XVIII, 1896 and XXI, 1899.
Kroeber, *Anthropology*. Kroeber, A. L., *Anthropology*, New York, 1948.
Kuhn, *Structure*. Kuhn, Thomas S., *The Structure of Scientific Revolutions*, Chicago, 1970.

Langbein, *Prosecuting Crime.* Langbein, John H., *Prosecuting Crime in the Renaissance: England, Germany, France,* Cambridge, Mass., 1974.

Larner, *Enemies.* Larner, Christina, *Enemies of God: the Witch-hunt in Scotland,* 1981.

Larner, *Witchcraft.* Larner, Christina, *Witchcraft and Religion: the Politics of Popular Belief,* 1984.

Lasch, *Haven.* Lasch, Christopher, *Haven in a Heartless World,* New York, 1977.

Laslett, *Lost World.* Laslett, Peter, *The World We have Lost,* 2nd ed., 1971.

Laslett, *Household.* Laslett, Peter (ed.), *Household and Family in Past Time,* 1972.

Laslett, *Family Life.* Laslett, Peter, *Family Life and Illicit Love in Earlier Generations,* 1977.

Laslett and Harrison, 'Clayworth'. Laslett, P. and Harrison, J. H., 'Clayworth and Cogenhoe', in Bell, H. E. and Ollard, R. L. (eds), *Historical Essays, 1600–1750, Presented to David Ogg,* 1963.

Latham and Matthews, *Diary.* Latham, Robert and Matthews, William (eds), *The Diary of Samuel Pepys,* 1970–83.

Le Goff and Sutherland, 'Brittany'. Le Goff, T. J. A. and Sutherland, D. M. G., 'The Revolution and the Rural Community in Eighteenth-Century Brittany', *Past and Present,* 62, 1974.

Le Roy Ladurie, *Peasants.* Le Roy Ladurie, E., *The Peasants of Languedoc,*, 1974.

Leach, *Political.* Leach, Edmund, *Political Systems of Highland Burma,* 1954.

Lévi-Strauss, *Elementary Structures.* Lévi-Strauss, C., *The Elementary Structures of Kinship,* 1969.

Lewis, *Allegory.* Lewis, C. S., *The Allegory of Love,* 1959.

Llorente, *Inquisition.* Llorente, D. Juan Antonio, *The History of the Inquisition of Spain,* 2nd ed., 1827.

Lorimer, *Culture.* Lorimer, F. (ed.), *Culture and Human Fertility,* 1954.

Lowie, *Social Organization.* Lowie, R. H. *Social Organization,* 1950.

Macfarlane, *Family Life.* Macfarlane, Alan, *The Family Life of Ralph Josselin,* 1970.

Macfarlane, *Witchcraft.* Macfarlane, Alan, *Witchraft in Tudor and Stuart England,* 1970.

Macfarlane, *Ralph Josselin.* Macfarlane, Alan, *The Diary of Ralph Josselin (1616–1683),* 1976.

Macfarlane, *Resources.* Macfarlane, Alan, *Resources and Population: a Study of the Gurungs of Nepal,* 1976.

Macfarlane, *Reconstructing.* Macfarlane, Alan et al., *Reconstructing Historical Communities,* 1977.

Macfarlane, 'History'. Macfarlane, Alan, 'History, Anthropology and the Study of Communities, *Social History,* 5, 1977.

Macfarlane, *Individualism.* Macfarlane, Alan, *The Origins of English Individualism,* 1978.

Macfarlane, 'Review'. Macfarlane, Alan, 'Review of Lawrence Stone, *The Family, Sex and Marriage in England 1500–1800*', *History and Theory*, XVIII; 1, 1979.

Macfarlane, *Justice*, Macfarlane, Alan, in collaboration with Sarah Harrison *The Justice and the Mare's Ale*, 1981.

Macfarlane, *Guide*. Macfarlane, Alan, *A Guide to English Historical Records*, 1983.

Macfarlane, *Marriage*. Macfarlane, Alan, *Marriage and Love in England 1300–1840*, 1986.

McFarlane, 'Mount Maitland'. McFarlane, K. B., 'Mount Maitland', *New Statesman*, 4 June 1965.

McKeown, *Modern Rise*. McKeown, Thomas, *The Modern Rise of Population*, 1976.

Machell, *Antiquary*. Machell, Rev. Thomas, *Antiquary on Horseback*, edited by Jane Ewbank, 1963.

Maine, *Lectures*. Maine, Sir Henry, *Lectures on the Early History of Institutions*, 1875.

Maine, *Early Law*. Maine, Sir Henry, *Dissertations on Early Law and Custom*, 1883.

Maine, *Ancient Law*. Maine, Sir Henry, *Ancient Law*, 13th ed., 1890.

Mair, *Witchcraft*. Mair, Lucy, *Witchcraft*, 1969.

Maitland, *Collected Papers*. Maitland, F. W., *Collected Papers*, edited by H. A. L. Fisher, 1911.

Maitland, *History*. Maitland, F. W., *The Constitutional History of England*, 1919.

Maitland, *Domesday Book*. Maitland, F. W., *Domesday Book and Beyond*, 1921.

Maitland, *Selected Essays*. Maitland, F. W., *Selected Historical Essays*, introduced by Helen Cam, 1957.

Maitland, *Forms*. Maitland, F. W., *The Forms of Action at Common Law*, 1968.

Malthus, *Population*. Malthus, T. R., *An Essay on Population*, 'Everyman' ed., n.d.

Mamdani, *Myth*. Mamdani, Mahmood, *The Myth of Population Control: Family, Caste and Class in an Indian Village*, 1972.

Mandeville, *Fable*. Mandeville, Bernard, *The Fable of the Bees*, edited by Philip Harth, 1970.

Mann, *Urban Sociology*. Mann, Peter M., *An Approach to Urban Sociology*, 1965.

Marshall and Polgar, *Culture*. Marshall, John F. and Polgar, Steven (eds), *Culture, Natality and Family Planning*, 1976.

Marx, *Writings*. Marx, Karl, *Selected Writings in Sociology and Social Philosophy*, edited by T. B. Bottomore and M. Rubel, 1963.

Marx, *Pre-Capitalist*. Marx, Karl, *Pre-Capitalist Economic Formations*, translated by Jack Cohen, 1964.

Marx, *Grundrisse*. Marx, Karl, *Grundrisse*, translated by Martin Nicolaus, 1973.

Marx, *Capital*. Marx, Karl, *Capital*, 3 vols, Lawrence and Wishart ed., 1954.

Marx and Engels, *German Ideology*. Marx, Karl and Engels, Frederick, *The German Ideology*, edited by C. J. Arthur, 1974.

Millican, *History*. Millican, Percy, *A History of Horstead and Stanninghall, Norfolk*, privately printed, 1937.

Mitterauer and Sieder, *European Family*. Mitterauer, Michael and Sieder, Reinhard, *The European Family*, 1982.

Moore, *Social Origins*. Moore, Barrington, Jr, *Social Origins of Dictatorship and Democracy*, 1966.

More, *Utopia*. More, Thomas, *Utopia*, translated by Paul Turner, 1965.

Morrill, *Britain*. Morrill, J. S. *Seventeenth-Century Britain, 1603–1714*, 1980.

Morris, *Celia Fiennes*. Morris, Christopher (ed.), *The Journal of Celia Fiennes*, 1947.

Moryson, *Itinerary*. Moryson, Fynes, *An Itinerary*, 4 vols, 1908 reprint of 1617 ed.

Mount, *Subversive Family*. Mount, Ferdinand, *The Subversive Family*, 1982.

Myrdal, *Asian Drama*. Myrdal, Gunnar, *Asian Drama*, Penguin, 2 vols, 1968.

Nag, *Human Fertility*. Nag, Moni, *Factors Affecting Human Fertility in Non-industrial Societies*, New Haven, 1962.

Notestein, 'Economic Problems'. Notestein, Frank W., 'Economic Problems of Population Change', in *Proceedings of the Eighth International Conference of Agricultural Economists*, 1953.

Order, *Court Leet*. *The Order of Keeping a Court Leet and Court Baron*, 1650.

Orwell, *Whale*. Orwell, George, *Inside the Whale and Other Essays*, 1962.

Osborn, *Thomas Wythorne*. Osborn, James M. (ed) *The Autobiography of Thomas Wythorne*, 1962.

Outhwaite, *Marriage*. Outhwaite, R. B. (ed.), *Marriage and Society*, 1981.

Oxford, *Dictionary*. *The Oxford Dictionary of English Proverbs*, 2nd ed., revised by Sir Paul Harvey, 1952.

Parkin, *Evil*. Parkin, David (ed.), *The Anthropology of Evil*, 1985.

Parsons, *Essays*. Parsons, Talcott, *Essays in Sociological Theory*, New York, 1964.

Pascal, *Pensées*. Pascal, Blaise, *Pensées*, edited by P. Faugère, Paris, 1844.

Pearson, *Elizabethans*. Pearson, Lu Emily, *Elizabethans at Home*, Stanford, 1957.

Petit-Dutaillis and Lefebvre, *Studies*. Petit-Dutaillis, C. and Lefebvre, Georges, *Studies and Notes Supplementary to Stubbs' Constitutional History*, 1930.

Plucknett, *Common Law*. Plucknett, T., *A Concise History of the Common Law*, 5th ed., 1956.

Pocock, *Ancient.* Pocock, J. G. A., *The Ancient Constitution and the Feudal Law*, 1957.

Polanyi, *Great Transformation.* Polanyi, Karl, *The Great Transformation*, 1944.

Pollock, *Forgotten Children.* Pollock, Linda A., *Forgotten Children*, 1983.

Pollock and Maitland, *English Law.* Pollock Sir F. and Maitland, F. W., *The History of the English Law Before the Time of Edward I*, 2nd ed., 1968.

Postan, *Medieval Economy.* Postan, M. M., *The Medieval Economy and Society*, 1972.

Radcliffe-Brown, *African Kinship.* Radcliffe-Brown, A. R. and Forde, Daryll (eds), *African Systems of Kinship and Marriage*, 1950.

Raistrick, *Yorkshire.* Raistrick, Arthur, *Old Yorkshire Dales*, 1967.

Redfield, *Peasant Society.* Redfield, R., *Peasant Society and Culture*, Chicago, 1960.

Redfield, *Human Nature.* Redfield, R., *Human Nature and the Study of Society: Papers of Robert Redfield, Vol. 1*, edited by Margaret Redfield, Chicago, 1962.

Rennell, *Valley.* Rennell of Rodd, Lord, *Valley on the March: a History of a Group of Manors on the Herefordshire March of Wales*, 1958.

Rich, 'Population'. Rich, E. E., 'The Population of Elizabethan England', *Economic History Review*, 2nd series, 2, 1950.

Robertson Smith, *Lectures.* Robertson Smith, William, *Lectures on the Religion of the Semites*, 1899.

Rosen, *Witchcraft.* Rosen, Barbara (ed.), *Witchcraft*, New York, 1969.

Rowland, 'Fantasticall'. Rowland, Robert, 'Fantasticall and Develiche Persons: European Witch Beliefs in Comparative Perspective', in Ankerloo, B. and Henningsen, G. (eds), *Early Modern European Witchcraft*, 1987.

Runciman, 'Comparative Sociology'. Runciman, W. G., 'Comparative Sociology or Narrative History?', *Archives of European Sociology*, XXI, 1980.

Russell, *Parliaments.* Russell, C., *Parliaments and English Politics 1621–1629*, 1979.

Sachse, *Roger Lowe.* Sachse, William L. (ed.), *The Diary of Roger Lowe of Ashton-in-Makerfield, Lancashire, 1663–74*, 1938.

Sahlins, *Stone Age.* Sahlins, M., *Stone Age Economics*, 1974.

Salzman, *English Life.* Salzman, L. F., *English Life in the Middle Ages*, 1926.

Sarsby, *Romantic Love.* Sarsby, Jacqueline, *Romantic Love and Society*, 1983.

Schapera, 'Population Growth'. Schapera, I., 'An Anthropologist's Approach to Population Growth', in Cragg, J. B. and Pine, N. W. (eds), *Numbers of Men and Animals*, 1955.

Shanin, *Peasants.* Shanin, Teodor (ed.), *Peasants and Peasant Societies*, 1971.

Shanin, *Awkward Class.* Shanin, Teodor, *The Awkward Class*, 1972.

Shorter, *Modern Family.* Shorter, Edward, *The Making of the Modern Family*, 1975.

Simmel, *Sociology*. Simmel, Georg, *The Sociology of Georg Simmel*, edited by Kurt H. Wolff, Glencoe, Ill, 1950.

Simons and Dyson, 'Comments'. Simons, John and Dyson, Tim, 'Comments on Macfarlane's paper on Modes of Reproduction', *Journal of Development Studies*, 16 : 1, 1979.

Simpson, *Land Law*. Simpson, A. W. B., *An Introduction to the History of the Land Law*, 1961.

Sjoberg, *Preindustrial City*. Sjoberg, Gideon, *The Preindustrial City, Past and Present*, 1960.

Smith, *Wealth*. Smith, Adam, *The Wealth of Nations*, edited by Edwin Cannan, Chicago, 1976.

Smith, 'Nuclear Family'. Smith, Richard M. 'The Nuclear Family and Low Fertility: A Spurious Correlation?', IUSSP Seminar on 'Family Types and Fertility in Less Developed Countries', August, 1981.

Smith, *Land*. Smith, Richard M. (ed.), *Land, Kinship and Life Cycle*, 1984.

Southall, *Social Change*. Southall, A. (ed.), *Social Change in Modern Africa*, 1961.

Spence, *Woman Wang*. Spence, Jonathan D., *The Death of Woman Wang*, 1978.

Spufford, *Contrasting Communities*. Spufford, M., *Contrasting Communities: English Villagers in the Sixteenth and Seventeenth Centuries*, 1974.

Spufford, *Books*. Spufford, M., *Small Books and Pleasant Histories: Popular Fiction and its Readership in Seventeenth-Century England*, 1981.

Stirling, *Turkish Village*. Stirling, Paul, *Turkish Village*, New York, 1965.

Stone, *Family*. Stone, Lawrence, *The Family, Sex and Marriage in England 1500–1800*, 1977.

Stubbs, *Constitutional History*. Stubbs, William, *The Constitutional History of England in its Origin and Development*, 5th ed., 1874.

Swinburne, *Last Wills*. Swinburne, H., *A Treatise of Testaments and Last Wills*, 5th ed., 1728.

Taine, *Notes*. Taine, Hippolyte, *Notes on England*, 1957.

Tawney, *Agrarian Problem*. Tawney, R. H., *The Agrarian Problem in the Sixteenth Century*, 1912.

Tawney, *Religion*. Tawney, R. H., *Religion and the Rise of Capitalism*, 1926.

Thirsk, *Peasant Farming*. Thirsk, J.,. *English Peasant Farming*, 1957.

Thomas, 'History'. Thomas, Keith, 'History and Anthropology', *Past and Present*, 24, 1963.

Thomas, *Religion*. Thomas, Keith, *Religion and the Decline of Magic*, 1971.

Thomas, *Natural World*. Thomas, Keith, *Man and the Natural World*, 1983.

Thomas and Znanieki, *Polish Peasant*. Thomas, W. I. and Znaniecki, F., *The Polish Peasant in Europe and North America*, New York, 1958.

Thompson, Peculiarities. Thompson, E. P., 'The Peculiarities of the English', *The Socialist Register*, eds R. Miliband and John Saville, 1965.

Trevelyan, *Social History*. Trevelyan, G. M., *English Social History*. 1948.
Turnbull, *Mountain People*. Turnbull, Colin, *The Mountain People*, 1974.
Verney, *Memoirs*. Verney, Frances P., *Memoirs of the Verney Family During the Civil War*, 1970.
Walker, *Crime*. Walker, J. C. M., *Crime and Capital Punishment in Elizabethan Essex*, BA Thesis in Essex Record Office, 1964.
Watt, *Novel*. Watt, Ian, *The Rise of the Novel*, 1983.
Weber, *Peasants*. Weber, Eugene, *Peasants into Frenchmen: the Modernisation of Rural France, 1870–1914*, 1977.
Weber, *Methodology*. Weber, Max, *The Methodology of the Social Sciences*, translated and edited by E. A. Shils and Henry A. Finch, New York, 1949.
Weber, *General*. Weber, Max, *General Economic History*, translated by Frank H. Knight, New York, 1961.
Weber, *Theory*. Weber, Max, *The Theory of Social and Economic Organization*, New York, 1964.
Weber, *Protestant Ethic*. Weber, Max, *The Protestant Ethic and the Spirit of Capitalism*, Unwin University Books ed., 1970.
West, *Wrangle*. West, F., *The Social and Economic History of the East Fen Village of Wrangle, 1603–1657*, PhD Thesis, University of Leicester, 1966.
Westermarck, *Marriage*. Westermarck, Edward, *The History of Human Marriage*, 3 vols, 5th ed., 1921.
Williams, *Country and City*. Williams, Raymond, *The Country and the City*, 1973.
Wolf, *Peasants*. Wolf, E., *Peasants*, New Jersey, 1966.
Wrightson, *English Society*. Wrightson, Keith, *English Society, 1580–1680*, 1982.
Wrightson and Levine, *Terling*. Wrightson, Keith and Levine, David, *Poverty and Piety in an English Village: Terling 1525–1700*, 1979.
Wrigley, 'Family Limitation'. Wrigley, E. A., 'Family Limitation in Pre-industrial England', *Economic History Review*, 2nd series, 19 : 1, 1966.
Wrigley, *Population*. Wrigley, E. A., *Population and History*, 1969.
Wrigley and Schofield, 'English Population'. Wrigley, E. A. and Schofield, R. S., 'English Population History from Family Reconstruction: Summary Results 1600–1799', *Population Studies*, 37, 1983.
Zubrow, *Anthropology*. Zubrow, Ezra B. W., *Demographic Anthropology: Quantitative Approaches*, Albuquerque, 1976.

LIST OF MAJOR REVIEWS OF *THE ORIGINS OF ENGLISH INDIVIDUALISM*

This list includes 39 of the 52 reviews known to me. All reviewers mentioned in the Postscript and the Appendix are included. A few short or very general reviews have been omitted.

Abrams. Philip Abrams, in *Historial Sociology* (1982), 322–6.

Blok. Anton Blok, 'In Search of the English Peasantry', *Theoretische Geschiedenis* (Sept. 1980).

Charlesworth. A. Charlesworth, in *Environment and Planning: A*, 13 : 2 (1981), 254.

Corrigan. Philip Corrigan, in *Sociological Review* 28 (May 1980), 465–70.

Delbos. Genevieve Delbos, in *L'Homme*, xx : 3 (1980), 162–5.

Donagan. Barbara Donagan, in *Ethics* 91 (Oct. 1980), 168–70.

Dyer. Christopher Dyer, in *Economic History Review* 32 (Nov. 1979), 600–1.

Elton. Geoffrey Elton, in *Times Literary Supplement* 23 (Nov. 1979), 27.

Faith. Rosamond Faith, in *Journal of Peasant Studies* 7 (April 1980), 384–9.

Goldie. Mark Goldie, 'Old Whiggery, New Bottle: Macfarlane's English Individualism', *Cambridge Review*, CI : 2255, (1978) 111–4.

Harding. Alan Harding, in *British Book News* (March 1979), 250.

Harris. Barbara J. Harris, in *Journal of Social History*, 14 : 1, 1980, 169–172.

Hatcher. John Hatcher, in *The Historical Journal*, 22 : 3 (1979), 765–8.

Herlihy. David Herlihy, in *Journal of Family History*, 5, (Summer 1980), 235–6.

Hilton. Rodney Hilton, 'Individualism and the English Peasantry', *New Left Review*, 120 (March–April 1980), 109–11.

Hirst. Paul Hirst, in *Cambridge Anthropology*, 5 : 1, (Jan. 1979).

Homans. George C. Homans, in *Contemporary Sociology: A Journal of Reviews*, 9 : 2 (March 1980), 262–3.

Hyams. Paul R. Hyams, in *English Historical Review* 96 (July 1981), 605–7.

Keates. Jonathan Keates, 'In the Woods', *New Statesman* (5 Jan. 1979) 21.

Kurtz. Lester R. Kurtz, in *American Journal of Sociology*, 86 (1980) 430–7.

Laslett. Peter Laslett, 'Always Individualist', *New Society*, (14 Dec. 1978), 649–50.

Levine. David Levine, in *Journal of Interdisciplinary History*, XI : 4 (Spring 1981), 669–76.

Mount. Ferdinand Mount, 'Goodbye to the Peasants', *Spectator*, (17 Feb. 1979), 4.

McCloskey. Donald N. McCloskey, in *Journal of Political Economy*, 89 : 4 (August 1981), 839–40.

Pocock. J. G. A. Pocock, in *History and Theory*, XIX : 1 (1980), 100–5.

Pryor. Frederic L. Pryor, in *Journal of Economic Literature*, XVIII (March 1980), 133–5.

Raftis. J. A. Raftis, in *Journal of European Economic History*, 11 : 1 (1982), 242–4.

Rheubottom. D. B. Rheubottom, in *Man*, 15 : 3 (September 1980), 574–5.

Rogers. Alan Rogers, in *The Local Historian* (May 1980), 105–6.

Rowland. Robert Rowland, 'Robinson por computador, Alan Macfarlane e as origens do individualismo inglês', *Ler Historia*, 5 (1985), 83–104.

Ryan. Alan Ryan, 'Yeomen, not peasants', *The Listener*, (14 Dec. 1978), 790–1.

Smith (1). Richard Smith, 'Some Thoughts on "Hereditary" and "Proprietary" Rights in Land under Customary Law in Thirteenth and Early Fourteenth-Century England', *Law and History Review*, 1 (1983).

Smith (2). Richard Smith, ' "Modernization" and the Corporate Medieval Village Community in England: Some Sceptical Reflections', in A. R. H. Baker and D. Gregory (eds), *Explorations in Historical Geography* (1986).

Stone. Lawrence Stone, 'Goodbye to Nearly All That', *New York Review of Books* (19 April 1979), 40–1.

Timm. Lenora A. Timm, in *American Anthropologist*, 82 : 3 (Sept. 1980), 679–80.

Todd. Emmanuel Todd, 'Hypothese revolutionnaire d'un Britannique', *Le Monde* (9 November 1979).

Tribe. Keith Tribe, in *Social History*, 4 : 3 (October 1979), 520–2.

Trumbach. Randolph Trumbach, 'Kinship and Marriage in Early Modern France and England: Four Books', *Annals of Scholarship*, 2 : 4 (1981), 113–28.

Waugh. Scott L. Waugh, in *Journal of Economic History*, 39 (Sept. 1979), 770–2.

Worsley. Peter Worsley, in *Journal of Development Studies*, 16 (January 1980), 263–4.

Wrightson. Keith Wrightson, in *History*, 65 (February 1980), 87.

Index

Index

violence in 17th century, 54, 55, 63,
68, 70, 72, 74
Chippenham (Cambridgeshire), 22–3
choice and marriage, 153–4
see also love
Christianity *see* religion
Churchill, C., 117
Clark, J. C. D., 221
class
emergence of, 21, 22
lack of, 21
relations and rise of capitalism, 176
violence, no evidence of, 63
see also castes; middling groups;
peasants; ruling
Clay, Lady R., 165
Cobbett, W., 83
Cockburn, J. S., 57n, 71n
cognatic descent, 7, 29, 36, 139, 151
cohabiting outside marriage, 38, 44–6,
139
Cohn, N., 100, 101n, 108n, 110, 111n
coin-clipping *see* counterfeiting
Comenius, J. A., 84–85
common law, 144, 149, 153, 162, 163,
192
'community' bonds, 7, 8
see also geographical mobility
companionate love and marriage, 123,
132, 141, 154
Confucianism 100
consent and marriage, 153–4
constitutional peculiarities of England,
see political
'continuity with change' paradox,
165–6
'controlled' fertility model of
population, 31–2, 35–6, 50–2,
156–7
in England, 37–50
copyhold land, 15–16, 17–18
Corrigan, P., 205, 213
counterfeiting and coin-clipping, 60,
61, 62, 71
countryside *see* nature
courts *see* law
'couverture', 14
Cowper, H. S., 56
crafts, 13, 224
crime *see* violence

'crises', 31–2, 64–5
lack of, 93, 146, 155
Croot, P., 177
Crown
and feudalism, 188
and Parliament, 145, 149
cruelty to animals, campaigns against,
80, 85–6
Culpepper, Sir T., 41, 49
culture
meaning of, xv–xvi
and capitalism *see* England
Cumbria, 64
see also Kirky Lonsdale
'custom' concept, 166–7
'cyclical mobility', 6, 21

Dalton, G., 1n, 2, 4, 212
Darby, H. C., 92
Darwin, C., 79
Davies, K., 133, 134
Dawson, J. P., 73n
De Beer, E. S., 113n
De Rougemont, D., 136
De Tocqueville, A., 144, 184, 221
death
sentences 59; reprieves, 71
see also homicide; infanticide;
mortality
defensive fortifications, lack of, 65–6,
92–3
Defoe, D., 85, 88
Democritus, 83
'Demographic Transition Theory', 27
demography
insecurity *see* mortality
pressure and rise of capitalism, 176
and revolution, 155–7
see also children, numbers of;
fertility; mortality; population
descent *see* inheritance
Devil, 105–6, 109, 110, 112, 115–7
diaries and autobiographies
evil not mentioned, 111–13
farmers in England, 8–13, 18, 55
fertility, 50
violence not mentioned, 55
see also Josselin
disease, 93
see also 'crises'

Index

Index by Ann Hall

Printed and bound by CPI Group (UK) Ltd, Croydon, CR0 4YY